Himalayan Architecture

Ronald M. Bernier

With a Foreword by His Holiness the Dalai Lama

Madison • Teaneck
Fairleigh Dickinson University Press
London: Associated University Presses

Associated University Presses
440 Forsgate Drive
Cranbury, NJ 08512

Associated University Presses
16 Barter Street
London WC1A 2AH, England

Associated University Presses
P.O. Box 338, Port Credit
Mississauga, Ontario
Canada L5G 4L8

The paper used in this publication meets the requirements of the American National Standard for Permanence of Paper for Printed Library Materials Z39.48-1984.

Library of Congress Cataloging-in-Publication Data

Bernier, Ronald M.
Himalayan architecture / Ronald M. Bernier.
p. cm.
Includes bibliographical references and index.
ISBN 0-8386-3602-0 (alk. paper)
1. Architecture—Himalaya Mountains Region. 2. Vernacular architecture—Himalaya Mountains Region. I. Title.
NA1510.8.H56B47 1997
720.′.95496—dc20 95-35280
CIP

PRINTED IN THE UNITED STATES OF AMERICA

For Dianne

We were experiencing the most sublime dawn of our lives. Everest, in all her isolated grandeur, came first, and next the chameleon-like and fascinating Kanchenjunga, lacking only a few hundred feet of Everest's height. Yonder was Makalu, three hundred feet below Kanchenjunga, but all soaring into the sky over five miles. We stood at Phalut, twelve thousand feet, approaching the height of the Matterhorn, and yet to see the proud heads of these snowy monarchs we must from that height look up four miles above us to the heavens. As we stood on this sacred spot we were awed into the silent realization that we were beholding the three highest points of earth, in which God had chisled in ice the word "eternity."

—Welthy Honsinger Fisher,
The Top of the World

Contents

Foreword
by His Holiness the Dalai Lama

We live in an era of rapid change. Improving standards of living, broadening education, raising levels of health, and easing means of transport are all of utmost importance. However, as we progress from one way of living to another there is a risk of throwing out what is tried and tested, what appears to be old, merely to have something modern instead. In the process we may lose our sense of values.

Because of the difficulties its terrain places on transport, the Himalayan region as a whole has been much slower to change than other places. The people who live there are much more governed by the seasons than elsewhere. They place a much lower premium on time than the inhabitants of our teeming modern cities. During the long winters, for example, travel, farming, and outdoor activities are restricted. Skilled artisans have the time and leisure to carve wood, to paint, to weave, and to create ornamental metalwork and stone sculpture without pressure or haste.

This patient, unhurried approach is reflected in the architecture throughout the region. Buildings are strong and sturdy, constructed in a practical way from natural materials, often decorated with careful attention to detail. They are also well suited to their environment. This may be why building techniques have changed so little down the centuries. These qualities, to some extent, reflect the character of the people of the region. Although I am mostly acquainted with Tibetans, I have observed that the majority of the Himalayan people are similarly mild-mannered, easily contented, satisfied with whatever conditions are available, and resilient in the face of hardship.

Artistic heritage is an essential and living expression of people's culture. Many of the most significant and striking buildings throughout the region, and therefore those described in this book, are of a religious nature. They represent the aspirations of the communities that built them and serve as an inspiration thenceforward. In Tibet, for example, the Jokhang, the central temple of Lhasa, is the principal focus of nationwide pilgrimage. Besides being intrinsically interesting themselves, these temples, monasteries, and places of worship also contain a wealth of paintings, statutes, and other religious images. Thus, the visual arts serve to express a community's values. And in the Tibetan case these focus largely on the nonviolent teachings of Buddhism with its stress on wisdom and compassion.

In painstakingly describing and illustrating the buildings of the Himalayan region, the author has done a great service, particularly to those readers who are unable to visit them for themselves. Who knows what the future may bring? Already much of the architecture that so magnificently distinguished Tibet barely forty years ago has been destroyed. Records such as this book, by generating awareness of this valuable heritage, contribute to the enjoyment and preservation of these buildings that have been an inspiration for generations.

Introduction

THIS STUDY OF HIMALAYAN ARCHITECTURE WITH extension to the Karakoram range is meant to analyze a cohesive tradition of mountain aesthetic preferences from the foothills of Assam to the Northwest Frontier Province of Pakistan. The monuments treated here are animistic, Buddhist, Hindu, and Islamic, and they have very rarely been brought together to show the important relationships that make them the same, from a wood-chipped doorway in a house of Pakistan's Kalash to the great sophistication of Nepalese palace windows to the trabeate frames of Alchi monastery in Ladakh.

The main focus is upon temples and mosques, although palaces and houses are treated as well. Related arts sometimes require as much attention as the architecture itself, whether they be brass sculptures of Himachal Pradesh or the murals of Sikkim and Bhutan. The reader is invited to stand back from the details of story and dating and technique and design, in order to grasp the larger picture of the unique identity of the mountain arts, not only in Asia but in the world.

A special effort has been made to draw upon early and pioneer accounts of this wondrous region, to keep earliest records current in the reader's thoughts, and to give credit where it is due. The marvels of the mountain arts have long been known even as their interpretation continues to the present day. Terminology can be vexing and some questions will remain unanswered, but the challenge of understanding the mysteries of art that is borrowed and original, simple and complex, earthy and exhalting, is worth the effort.

For the present author the mountains of South Asia have been a magnet for many years of trekking, photography, drawing, and analysis. Much gratitude is due to the authors who are credited in the following pages and to the local scholars who generously shared their unmatched knowledge of their cultures from the inside. Research support also has been very generous through the years. Thus this study moves from the foothills of the eastern mountains to the expanse of the central range at the edge of Tibet and on to the western extremities of little known geography and lesser known architectural monuments. If ever works of art stood for the aspirations as well as the talents of the artists and artisans who made them, this is true of the mountain buildings of the Himalaya and Karakoram ranges. The following pages are meant to express respect and admiration and wonder.

* * *

Line drawings in this volume were made by the author, unless otherwise noted. Unless indicated to the contrary, all photographs were taken by the author.

Himalayan Architecture

1

Himalaya at a Crossroads

In recent times the hill that is crowned by the great *stupa* of Svayambhūnātha in Kathmandu Valley began to crumble because of erosion. The "Self-Existent One," on the hilltop where it represents the birth of the nation of Nepal and marks the spot where a miraculous lotus flower studded with jewels bloomed above primordial waters, was threatened with collapse. Also in recent times, the great fourteenth-century monastery of Thyangboche, a storehouse of sacred arts and sacred truths, caught fire. In its otherworldly setting below the peak of Ama Dablam ("Mother's Charmbox"), the great study and worship center was nearly destroyed. These happenings are warnings that the arts of the Himalaya, like arts anywhere, are fragile and fleeting things that are vulnerable to floods, fires, and the foibles of humankind. Yet vulnerability is far from the first characteristic that one thinks of when first seeing Thyangboche, a human-built mountain among the peaks and foothills that tower over isolated temple sites.

The term Himalaya translates from Sanskrit as "Abode of Snow," and the correct Sanskrit pronunciation puts emphasis on the second syllable and not on the third, as is commonly heard among non-Asians. The east to west range of mountains that joins with the Karakoram range as the greatest heights on the planet is often called a frontier, and it is true that it is a great divide, like the Rocky Mountains in North America. The Himalaya is a natural demarcation between Central Asia (including Tibet) and South Asia with its cultures of India, Pakistan, Nepal, Sikkim, Bhutan, and the foothill civilizations of Assam and Nagaland. The southern part has long been known as Himachal, especially those areas that are snow-covered for at least part of the year. The northern slopes reach the high plateau of Tibet, its name taken from Arabic as a version of the Tibet expression *Toh Po* meaning "Upper Tibet." The Sanskrit term is *Bhota,* perhaps derived from the word *Boda* that is found on some coins of Emperor Kanishka in the second century A.D. *Bhota,* according to A. A. MacDonnell's *A Practical Sanskrit Dictionary,* means Tibet, while *Bhauta* can mean "possessed by evil spirits." The second description may seem justified as this study treats dangerous forces that must be conquered and otherwise dealt with in the early and shamanistic ways of Bön Po as a system of beliefs and magic that preceded Buddhism in the high country. Lamaist priests continue the battle to hold them back even today.

Language and epigraphy will be useful tools as monuments and religious traditions are encountered along with long-term customs of borrowing and invention. Pradyumna P. Karan and William

M. Jenkins, Jr., present the special cases of Bhutan, Sikkim, and Nepal in their *Himalayan Kingdoms,* explaining that those states are "completely landlocked and cut off from the rest of the world by mighty mountains and malarial forests" so that they "remained a sealed book for a long time, territories whose rulers actively discouraged foreign visitors and alien ways." This remains true to some extent of Bhutan even today. For all three countries, "Until 1951 no more than a few hundred Westerners had seen the interior of the three kingdoms, and only a few could locate any of the three on a world map."[1]

And so, the physical location and features of the awesome Himalaya are essential subjects with which to begin this study of architecture, gods, and people. In the *Bhagavad Gītā,* Lord Kṛṣṇa says, "Among mountains, I am the Himalaya." He also says, "Of letters, I am A." Both terms are superlatives. The long history of the mountain range with its many varied features takes these pages back millions of years even though the Himalaya is still "young," still physically growing in height. Karan and Jenkins explain that the area that is now the mountain range was once the shallow Tethys Sea, but that the tertiary period in geological history saw enormous geological forces fold and thrust the marine deposits of that sea upward, as "gigantic earth waves" rose out of the waters. These were eroded by water and ice so that longitudinal valleys were formed along the length of the range, but much more important as a factor pushing the mountains to their abrupt heights, as well as their continued growth, was and is the collision of the two great earth masses of Asia and India, as explained by the concept of plate tectonics and the work of scholars like Malcolm McKenna and Norman Newell of the American Museum of Natural History.

The mass of the mountains follows a shallow southward curve as it extends from Bhutan and Assam in the east, through Sikkim and Nepal in the center, and toward the Indian states of Himachal Pradesh, Ladakh, and Kashmir in the west, with final and dramatic identity in Pakistan with the Karakoram peaks and K-2 as the world's second highest peak. This boomorang-shaped crescent is itself divided into the Great Himalaya in the north and at the edge of Tibet, the middle lands of the Inner Himalaya including Kathmandu Valley and lower Bhutan, and the foothills and plains region from the Siwalik Hills to the Nepalese Terai and to the Daurs plain of southern Bhutan and the lower elevations of Assam. The entire length of the extraordinary Himalayan land mass is more than seven hundred miles and its width from north to south is rarely greater than one hundred miles. Lhasa is tantalizingly close to Kathmandu.

The distances may not seem great at first, but to anyone traveling the length of the great mountain wall with its constant barriers of deep river valleys that must be crossed countless times in order to move between east and west, it is indeed giant. The high Himalaya is the "abode of snow" but not the abode of humankind. Yet its length *was* and *is* traveled, and no part of the Himalaya—the search for Shambala notwithstanding—has ever been completely isolated. Even the Dards come out from under their hivelike underground dwellings on the pass between Kashmir and Ladakh for part of the year. It is a thesis of this study that pan-Himalayan trade was constant since at least the second century B.C. with the founding of the Silk Route across Asia by Han Dynasty Chinese, if not much earlier, and that ideas and artistic styles were exchanged along with goods.

The central part of the highest mountain mass was always the most rugged, with Mount Everest "conquered but defiant" along with Kanchenjunga, Makalu, Dhaulagiri, Gosainthan, and Annapurna. All of these are said to be divine, for "here gods are mountains." If we do not feel awe in their presence, we must be very callous. Romance, not facts alone, keeps the quest alive.

The great Himalaya has many raging rivers that divide the long crescent as if it were sliced along its length. The Indus, Manas, Ganges, Sankosh, Amo, Tista, Kosi, Gandak, Karnali, and Brahmaputra river systems all have headwaters in the Himalaya, and often further north in Tibet. Life is difficult along these waters that are harnessed to limited degree for irrigation, and settlements are small. The Sherpas are perhaps the best known inhabitants of the high Himalaya, with Kumjung at about 17,000 feet in Nepal's Solo Khumbu region often being called the world's highest permanently inhabited village. It is a village with some of the world's highest art in more ways than one, for it is the home of the artist Kumjung Kapa Kalden Sherpa, a painter who has kept alive a charming and traditional kind of landscape painting that shows peaks, yaks, monks, tourists, Thyangboche Monastery, and the Yeti or abominable snowman. This conglomerate crowd is shown together above the clouds. His strongly contrasting colors are like those found inside the monastery itself: intense saturated hues that are in total contrast to the brown and barren earth outside of the artist's studio and chapel. Such art is breathtaking and luxurious. The interior of a Buddhist temple in Kumjung is like the artist's painting becoming an enclosing environment. Yet Kumjung is part of a land where only one crop can be grown each year, protected by stone walls against the constant wind. Potatoes, barley, and wheat are found in this fierce country where iris flowers bravely bloom on two-inch stems.

The second division of the range is the inner Himalaya where forests are often heavy (although deforestation has become one of the greatest threats to mountain civilization) and more than one crop can sometimes be grown annually. Rhododendron are glorious on tree-size bushes in the spring and brief summer. Trekkers who come to see for themselves find that heavy jackets must be removed as one descends into the endless succession of river valleys that offer great depths and great upward climbs. At the end of a full day of trekking, first down and then back up, hikers may arrive at a place that is only one or two air miles from the place where they started.

As Karan and Jenkins point out, fertile valleys that are separated from one another by steep forested ranges are often homes of small kingdoms and former independent states that are still quite isolated from each other. Pakistan's examples of such once self-sufficient kingdoms include Hunza and Gilgit. The only large valleys in all of the rugged land of the Himalaya are Paro and Thimpu in Bhutan, Gangtok in Sikkim, Kathmandu and Pokhara in Nepal, the vale of Kashmir, and Skardu and Gilgit further west in Pakistan. Each of these has a fairly large settlement, with Kathmandu Valley once controlled by the three important kingdoms of Kathmandu, Patan, and Bhaktapur.

If civilization is defined as "the art of living in towns" (an extreme oversimplification to say the least), one might expect little refinement or "civilization" in the Himalaya. But the opposite is true. Invention and technology have been shared along with belief systems and artistic invention. Barriers of topography have been forced to yield to rope bridges, roads passible in jeeps, animal transport (mainly by yaks), and ropeways like the one that used to regularly carry large volumes of goods from Kathmandu all the way down to the Terai and the border of India. That practical custom ended with the completion of the Raj Path highway along the same rugged route for trucks, busses, and other vehicles. Elephants have been driven along this highway for participation in Nepalese coronations and weddings, and the story is still well-remembered of luxury European cars being dismantled and carried to Kathmandu Valley piece by piece from India on the backs of human porters before the highway was built.

The third and southernmost region or belt of the Himalaya belongs to its foothills and adjacent plains. It is most useful to this survey to take note of transition zones between so-called "great traditions" of the Indian subcontinent and of Tibet as change is witnessed in special customs of the Great or Middle Himalaya. Because much of the lower area is swampy and malarial, with elephant grass savannah that grows to heights of fifteen feet to impede human movement, its special geography may be considered to be yet another barrier of the Himalayan region.

Maintaining contact in this dramatic but problematical region, despite the presence of relatively modern and centralized rule, is hindered in many ways so that relative isolation continues to be a political as well as a geographical problem for today's governments. There is great diversity of language and dialects, and often there is desperate and illegal immigration that is difficult to police (as revealed by tensions in recent years for the people of Darjeeling, Gauhati, and Gangtok). But in terms of cultural history, semisecluded growth and production in isolation have provided the world with some of its most unique societies and most unique arts.

Many of the publications that have appeared in recent years may be called pioneer studies, like Michael Aris's *Bhutan—The Early History of a Himalayan Kingdom*. The present writer's *Temples of Nepal* was the first book on architecture of that kingdom. And new information is continually appearing in periodicals like *The Journal of Central Asia* published in Islamabad and *Ancient Nepal* published in Kathmandu. The full significance of the Silk Road as part of the network that brought distant cultures together from China to Rome is just beginning to be fully recognized with the aid of exhibitions like *Nomads of Eurasia* that was mounted by the Natural History Museum of Los Angeles County in association with the Denver Museum of Natural History. Many questions about Asian people and Asian arts remain unanswered, and the wide-reaching impact of the Silk Road remains mysterious. A woodchipped window frame on Hidimba Devi temple in Kulu Valley's Manali town in India is echoed in Central Asian carving of the Uygur people.

This work on Himalayan sacred and royal architecture proceeds from the plain and foothill areas of Assam that are almost entirely Hindu to the still sequestered kingdom of Bhutan which is officially Buddhist. Then it looks at the former kingdom of Sikkim where traditional spirit concerns must contend with new influences from India more than ever before, and to Nepal with its history of Gurkha, Newar, and other ethnic accomplishments. It then proceeds to northwestern India including Himachal Pradesh, Ladakh, and Kashmir before entering the Hindu Kush and the once-forbidden kingdoms of northern Pakistan. This is intended to be a study of the quality of Himalayan art rather than its mere quantity, and questions of aesthetic judgment and cultural conditioning will arise.

Some works in stone, like the Hindu towers of lower Kulu Valley, are best approached as artistic extensions of India's Gangetic plain. Some works in stone and wood, like the Buddhist monasteries of Sikkim and Bhutan, preserve the traditions and tastes of Tibet. Still other monuments—especially those made of wood with lavish carving and with multiple roofs—are analyzed as particularly Himalayan accomplishments. The latter group is of most concern. To treat the arts that the author has visited in all Himalayan states, this text travels to many little-known places. But rather than function as a gazeteer with long lists of facts about one village after another, these pages seek to develop artistic themes that compliment and contrast each other. Such themes lead the reader through the mountains in search of very special sites and to monuments that animate the landscapes around them, buildings that stand as timeless symbols of each culture's world view. With each chapter a different kind of art—sometimes central like wooden "pagoda" structure and sometimes auxiliary like *repoussé* metal applied to roof edges—is documented. In the end, the reader should have gained a sense of individual attractions but also of the wholeness of Himalayan mountain arts.

Himalayan arts are often born of dramatic events, like the westward expansion of Gurkha forces under the leadership of Pṛthvī Narāyāna Śah and other warrior kings, and the Kot Massacre in the heart of Kathmandu that wiped out an entire class of opponents to those in power. The land itself has been a destroyer, with the horrors of the 1934 earthquake that toppled monuments in Kangra, Kathmandu, southern Tibet, and elsewhere still remembered as a time when "mountains fell." In the event of natural disaster or military attack, Himalayan people go for solace and shelter to the temples, where they cling to symbolic and physical protection. In every way, the temple is the Center. Its radiating goodness animates the land. It is the engine of divine life and it stands for constancy amid change. It is little wonder that the *maṇḍala,* as perfect axis and cosmic map, is an ideal pattern that stands for highest aspirations and truth. It is known, used, and reinterpreted throughout Himalayan region from east to west and back again.

Study of the Himalaya has long held fascination for foreign scholars, philosophers, and adventurers. The painting of the European Roerich family that the world knows for intense color and simple, monumental shapes provide an imaginative glimpse into the mystique of the high peaks with their temples and palaces. In the semiabstractions and expressive colors of these European artists who settled at Naggaṛ, high above the Kulu Valley in Himachal Pradesh, there are hints of the wonders of a special world. As this study moves from Assam to Bhutan and on to Sikkim and Nepal before concluding in Himachal Pradesh, Kashmir, Ladakh, and Pakistan, it carries forward many facts. But the romance and mystery of the Himalaya region must also come through or the effort will be incomplete, without a heart. Can the reader possibly empathize with a holy man who sits near-naked and deep in meditation on the ice and snow near an Indian cave called Gomukh, "Cow's Mouth"? Inside the cave is a vertical formation of ice that is honored as the phallic *liṅga* of Śiva, Lord of Destruction. From this honored place Himalayan glaciers melt and create the headwaters of the Ganges River—Mother Gaṅgā—to flow down to the earth through the tangled locks of Lord Śiva's hair and help the human world to survive. Fact and myth are combined absolutely in the realm of the high and splendid peaks.

2

Assam and Nagaland in the Eastern Himalayan Foothills

VISITORS TO ASSAM ARE LIKELY TO FIRST ENCOUNTER temporary "festival arts," items that are carried on the roads, left as offerings in prominent places, or placed in the branches of trees along the Brahmaputra River as it flows past Gauhati, the capital of the state. The great Mothers who are prominent in Hindu settings anywhere are honored here, especially in the form of female spirits who are incarnate in rivers and who, like the River Brahmaputra with its headwaters in the Tibetan plateau, have control over life and death. "Snake stones" are found along with figures of major gods like Śiva and Viṣṇu that are carved in living rock along the river banks, but serpents are less revered here than in the context of "tree and serpent worship" in the western Himalaya. Any of these features is to be expected in the Hindu world of Assam, even as the state is criss-crossed by tribal people who are not Hindus as well as by Muslim and Buddhist immigrants from West Bengal and Nepal.

From Gauhati to Barpeta, from Shillong to Nowgong, from Jorhat to Sibsagar, there is an art tradition that is familiar and surprising at the same time. It is true that Assam and Nagaland are hill states that lead to the Himalaya without being properly part of the high range itself, but it must be recognized that the foothills provide much more than a pathway from India's Varanasi to Nepal's Kathmandu and far beyond. Themes of art and belief are established here and continuous in the mountain range.

The *śikhara* towers of stone or brick that are prominent in Assam owe much to Indian traditions beyond the borders of the state, and their "classical" elements are to be expected in a land where such established architectural guides as the *Śilpasarini* of Orissa, translated by Alice Boner, are in use.[1] The temples can be measured to reveal *prasáda* blueprints of perfectly intersecting circles and squares as proof of the ideal geometry that is a constant feature of architecture in South Asia. They are part of the broad tradition of Indian trabeate architecture with stability dependent on mass and corbel structure. In addition, Assam provides abundant sculptures made of stone, clay, wood, and metal, and they, too, are often closely related to counterparts on the Indian plains. But they also follow their own directions—with powerful statements of aggressive volumes and clearly cut silhouettes—which are born of folk traditions. Durgā slaying the buffalo demon in her guise as Durgā Mahiṣāsuramardinī, found on the outer wall of Assam's Śivadol temple in Sibsagar, can be compared to the same subject as it is represented on the exterior of the Bajaura temple in distant Kulu Valley of the western hills. Both figures swell with *prana* or inner life breath, and they both have twins on the northern plain of India. Thus pan-Indian themes are important clues to the form and meaning of Assamese hill art.

Gupta preferences and artistic accomplishments of ca. 320–650 A.D. relate to the arts of both Assam and faraway Kulu, such as a fine Gupta-related image found at Dah Parbativa in Assam that is examined below. But a more immediate inspiration for Assamese art is Pāla-Sena art of ca. 730–1250 A.D., and Assam shares this dynastic tradition with neighbors in Burma to the southeast and in Nepal to the west. While contrasting indigenous arts to those that are borrowed, it may be helpful to compare an eighteenth-century Durgā from Tinisukha in Lakhimpur District of Assam to refined and delicate arts of much earlier Pāla-Sena origin. The Assamese Durgā seems to reject the soft fluidity that India's *cire-perdue* bronzes so often reveal, as memory of wax models that melt away to be replaced by molten bronze, in favor of frosty solidity. This Durgā is a creature of the hills.

Assam and nearby Nagaland are protected by natural geographic barriers. These foothill regions of North India, with the high Himalaya as their impressive neighbor and the nearby wall of Tibet, are inhabited by colorful tribes who are keepers of India's famed folk art tradition. The arts of the Naga people are still relatively unstudied, although their textiles are widely known, especially the rich black, white, and red cottons that are embroidered with bold white animal patterns having yellow and red accents. These are among South Asia's boldest arts of cloth. Elephants and birds are outlined in typically geometric and expanding shapes while peacocks are flattened to have perfectly round tails that make the birds' bodies look like table tennis paddles. Naga cloth is noted for such refreshing and powerfully direct imagery.

Naga architecture is bold and impressive, with houses having steeply pitched roofs (a hallmark of hill and mountain building) along with projecting rectangular gables that serve as rain-shields over small entryways. Houses of the Ao Naga people, however, are noted for their curved rooflines that exploit the tensile strength of bamboo. The pent-roof meeting houses of the Phom tribe of Yaong village and elsewhere recall Shinto shrines of Japan because of their heavy thatch roofing and projecting bamboo sticks that follow the eye-lifting diagonals of roof planes and edges. But their unique qualities are most memorable, and Assamese domestic buildings cannot be called typical of the Himalayan region as a whole.

The extreme northeastern corner of the Indian subcontinent holds small states that are connected to the rest of the country only by the narrow strip of land that extends between Bangladesh, Bhutan, and Nepal. Political tension here is often high as disparate groups coexist in reportedly uneasy confinement, and it is not always possible for foreigners to visit these hills. The same was often true in ages past, with these areas being among the only parts of the Indian subcontinent that were not absorbed into the empire of Aśoka and other powerful kings of the Mauryan Dynasty (322–185 B.C.). Thus a rich and long-established heritage survives.

The prominent anthropologist Christoph von Fürer-Haimendorf was well aware of the rarity of his official permit to visit Assam in 1944, and he notes that during his work in the Naga hills in 1936 and 1937, "I had often looked with longing at the line of blue mountains and glittering snow peaks which on fine days were clearly visible on the northern horizon."[2] Such yearning for distant horizons is common among Himalaya specialists, and the present author can recall that during twenty years of visits to Nepal he coveted access to the nearby hills of Tibet. When he finally reached Tibet in the late 1980s and early 1990s there was little disappointment, although the loss of most Tibetan religious arts since the second half of this century is always keenly felt. The anthropologist's careful recording of Assamese tribal customs and his or her documentary photographs remain essential research materials today; they are still effective to "acquaint us with populations living in seclusion from the modern world."[3] Ethnographic paths to the history of art are often the most productive here, as in so many parts of the world. Still, the range of tribal arts, although as rich as the figural wood carvings made by Nagaland's Konyak people and the imposing costumes, fine musical instruments, and brilliantly painted houses of the Angami Naga tribe, are largely subjects of studies still to come. Access by researchers is extremely limited, and these are not "mainstream" mountain arts. Nor are they Hindu or Buddhist. Yet the words of Jawaharlal Nehru remain relevant:

> I am confident that the vigour and vitality of the people of Nagaland will not only make a substantial contribution towards the achievement of a fuller and happier life for the people of Nagaland but will further enrich the National development of the Indian Union.
> I am anxious that they should advance, but I am even more anxious that they should not lose their artistry and joy in life and the culture that distinguishes them in many ways.[4]

Earlier history finds the Mughal armies of India's Islamic empire mounting an invasion of Assam under command of Emperor Aurangzeb in 1662. The invasion failed and the Assamese remained fiercely independent. Their insularity was tested, however, by Burmese occupation of Assam in the eighteenth century. In 1825 the Burmese were driven out by the British, who chose to govern Assam along with Manipur and Bengal in an uneasy alliance. The British Crown, and Queen Victoria as empress of India, defined and governed the subcontinent's easternmost state as lying between latitudes of 28°18′ and 24° north and longitudes 90°46′ and 97°46′ east. Under British rule, successful tea plantations were soon thriving in Assam's moist atmosphere and high elevation. The farms were under direct British management, and some of the original plants are still productive today.

In his excellent study, *Archaeology of the Brahmaputra Valley of Assam,* R. D. Choudhury points out that the middle of the state consists of a plateau through which the Brahmaputra River flows from its source in Tibet. It may be useful to note that Cherrapunji in Assam is one of the places that is claimed to be the world's wettest, with annual rainfall of around five hundred inches. The state's topography, like that of Nagaland, is dramatically varied. Flooding is both frequent and very destructive. Yet Anna Manni notes, in *The Himalaya* of 1981, that "vast areas of the Himalayan foot-hills have been stripped of forest" and "the soil itself is washed away" while "the only silver lining is Assam, where the problem is less severe on account of the smaller population and the immensity of the rain forests." And what forests they are! K. C. Sahni states:

> The mingling of species in this region has possibly favoured natural hybridization with subsequent enrichment of the variability of flora. The lower reaches of Arunachal, Bhutan and Sikkim comprising the evergreen rain-forests teem with plant life and have a bewildering number of species and genera. If fact, this region including the old Assam State is perhaps the richest botanical region in the world.[5]

The verdant northeastern hills saw chaos during the Second World War, as Naga hill tribes that were once known for head-hunting joined the allied forces to resist the Japanese invasion that was directed from Burma in 1944. Assam also served as an essential link in the chain of crucial allied flights over the "hump" of northern India and Burma to nationalist China. The two hill districts of present-day Assam are the Karbi-Anglong Hills and the North Cachar Hills. To the north of Assam and of Nagaland, which has its capital at Kohima, the Northeast Frontier Agency was long known and often feared, and at least twenty-five tribes with distinct identities and their own languages have fought to keep their independent value systems intact. This persists in spite of a history of political realignment and change that continues to the present. Modern maps show that Assam's nearest southern neighbors are Meghalaya and Nagaland, with Mizoram, Manipur, and Tripura located further to the south, along with the borders of Bangladesh. Arunachal Pradesh is critically demarcated to Assam's north, where it borders Bhutan and Tibet. Bengal is a western neighbor while Burma lies to the east. The cultures are richly varied, yet the Himalaya itself makes for the clearest border.

Tribal arts are richly varied throughout the entire hill area between Tibet to the north and the mighty Brahmaputra to the south. Most are different from "stationary" arts in brick and stone that are more vulnerable to destruction during strife or natural disasters. The great river, fast-moving and gray, floods almost annually, and temples that were built near its banks have been damaged or destroyed frequently. Still, enough remains to show that northeastern India developed its own styles while honoring its own regional gods and borrowing pan-Indian visual arts, and while worshipping the Hindu family of gods. The omission of the northeast from far too many "surveys" of Indian art history is unfortunate.

In *The Wonder That Was India,* A. L. Basham refers to the valley of Assam as the easternmost outpost of Hindu culture to which the Brahmaputra, "Son of Brahmā," flows from the high plateau of Tibet.[6] The river is written of again and again, and it is so respected that it has been called the "Lord of the Universe" by the Assamese. It is the controller of death and life, and has numerous river shrines dedicated to it. It is the northeastern equivalent of the Ganges; and like the Ganges it is dangerous. Floods raise its waters by as much as forty feet, and Y. K. Murthy estimated in 1981 that average annual flood damage in Assam alone totalled about eighty-six million rupees (more than four million dollars U.S.) while "large sums have to be spent every year on the relief and rehabilitation of flood-affected people."[7] Himalayan catastrophes are anticipated by these words, but what is left behind in this often ravaged land still shows the ideals of Assam.

Once again, the most influential "classical" art traditions to reach the northeast are those of the Gupta and Pāla dynasties, subjects that are thoroughly analyzed by Frederick M. Asher in *The Art of Eastern India, 300–800.* Also concerned with shared traditions is A. L. Basham, who notes that the Gupta king Harṣa (Harṣavardhana) received King Bhaskaravarman of Assam in a meeting on the bank of the Ganges near a place called Kajurgira early in the seventh century. This meeting took place on the regular route from Buddhist Nalanda and Orissa to Kamarupa (Assam) east of the Brahmaputra. It happened in changing times. Earlier kings of Assam had been paying tribute to Gupta rulers since the fourth century. But upon the death of Harṣa in the mid-seventh century, a long history of subservience to Indian kings ended. This happened as China's Tang Dynasty leader, Emperor Tai Tsung, joined with the kings of Nepal and Assam, along with the famous King Srong-tsan Gampo of Tibet, to defeat an "unworthy" usurper who had tried to hold the Gupta throne. The Gupta Dynasty was never reunited. Assam was well located for much more regular contact with the Pāla and Sena dynasties from the eighth through thirteenth centuries, and the shift of prominence and power to those regimes in northeastern India affected Assam.

Much earlier than Gupta and Pāla-Sena times, perhaps in the second century B.C. according to N. D. Choudhury, the oldest land route between India and China was probably drawn through Assam, upper Burma, and Yunan province. Unfortunately, there are no complete architectural records in Assam that predate Ahom presence, which begins in the thirteenth century. But it is known that the almost simultaneous decline of the Pratihāra, Pāla, and Rāṣṭrakūṭa dynasties in India took place as new kingdoms were thriving in the north, such as those of Nepal, Kashmir, and Assam (Kamarupa) itself. We may remember, along with N. D. Choudhury, the controversial observation of R. C. Majumdar that, "One of the gravest defects of Indian culture which defies rational explanation, is the aversion of Indians to writing history." For India, important records and speculation may be said to concern higher matters, especially matters of the soul.

It has been possible, even with only scattered evidence, to partly reconstruct a temple in late Gupta style from fragments found at Dah Parbativa near the town of Tezpur in Assam (illustrated in both N. D. Choudhury, plate 13, fig. 43(b) and R. D. Choudhury, fig. 11). The presence of this temple in the hills is hardly surprising at the time of a dynasty whose influence extended from the Oxus to Ceylon (Sri Lanka), as explained by Percy Brown in his classic architectural studies *Indian Architecture* (2 vols., 5th edition, Bombay, 1965) that remain useful to the present day. With Gupta comparison, it is not surprising that the *garbha gṛha* as inner chamber and sanctum of Assamese temples is square, with a *pradakṣiṇā patha* as passage for clockwise circumambulation around it. Nor is it surprising that the inner room is preceded by one or more *maṇḍapas* as porches of approach, or that a *śikhara* mountain tower was erected in corbel pattern over the inner room. Less expected, though, is a special, compound origin for the plan of the square sanctum that R. M. Nath suggests is made up by the magical Śri *cakra* of the Śakti cult—a kind of "wheel" that is a squared combination of nine triangles with four pointing up and five pointed down, all being oriented to a common center of gravity. Tantric references of late Hindu-Buddhist origin are also important to interpreting mountain arts, and Assam provides some of the earliest such references.[8]

Gauhati is the capital and most prominent city of Assam—more accessible and more "modern" than its former capital at Shillong, with its dominant populace being the matrilineal Khasi tribe who honor megaliths as ancestral symbols. Gauhati is the most practical base for visiting the hills and river valley in search of both sacred arts and folk arts. Located on the river is the important Assam State Museum with holdings that include illustrated manuscripts and refined bronze arts, all of which were generously made available to the present author. Tall stone *śikhara* temples near Gauhati relate to important Pāla monuments, and it is suggested that temple IV of Begunia Group in stone at Barakar in Burdwan District resembles the earliest towers at Bhubaneshwar in Orissa.[9] The more bulbous and squat Hindu temples that are most frequent in Assam are sometimes placed in dramatically elevated positions, but they call for comparison to the architecture of Bengal rather than to the Himalaya. Any of these reveals the expansion of Aryan influences into the northeast, an impulse that legend credits to Lord Kṛṣṇa himself.[10]

Important monuments that may be reached from Gauhati include Kamakhya Temple dedicated to the goddess Kālī on Nilachal Hill, and the sixteenth-century tower that is locally dubbed "Hayagrib Madhab" (Hayagrīva Madhav/Mahādeva), temple of Viṣṇu which is a place of pilgrimage associated in legend with Buddha's attainment of Nirvana. K. N. Dikshit, in *The Archeological Survey of India Annual Report of 1923–24,* notes that, "Midway up the western slope of Kamakhya hill, are to be seen numerous cuttings in the rock. They include temple miniatures of the Orissan *śikhara* type with small Śivaliṅgas enshrined in them."[11]

Both the *śikhara* as mountain tower and the *liṅga* as phallic symbol of Lord Śiva's virile power are found throughout India and Southeast Asia. The Orissa comparison to widespread Hindu features proves to be valid as rippling surfaces of angular wall segments containing niches are seen on the Viṣṇu temple at Jaisagar or as one views the individual framed deities on the outer surface of the Śiva temple at Negretting. Dancing *devī* figures that are part of the ruins at Numalegarh recall both northeastern and northwestern sculptures on the Indian plains, but comparison to Bengal is more rewarding.

To begin, as with any area of the Himalaya, the relation between the land and building art is absolute in Bengal. There are philosophical concerns as the ground is disturbed and the advice of a priest is required, at least if a planned building is to be sacred. Stone is not abundant in Bengal, other than laterite in the southwest and some basalt in the central area. Clay is much more common and much more in favor as it is used for temple construction in brick. Another major feature of Bengali architecture is inspiration from the sophisticated and polished features of Pāla-Sena art, much of which disappeared in its places of origin with the impact of iconoclastic Islam in the thirteenth century and later. Percy Brown explains that the standard proportion of southern Bengali temples is found in heights that are about three and one-half the width of each tower, and that such proportion resembles the pattern of Orissan art at Bhubaneshwar. But Bengal reveals indigenous tastes as well, in curve-roof structures that Brown terms peculiarly expressive as they relate to Bengal's native and cabinlike structures of wood, bamboo, and thatch. George Michell's *The Hindu Temple* treats Bengali temples, mostly dating from the seventeenth century and later. He defines sloping roofs that have curved ridges and pot finials, the so-called "Bengal roof," that might be compared to Assamese tribal architecture. Also noted are Bengal's use of terra cotta tiles that are applied to the outer walls of temples, a feature that is also found at Negretting's Śiva temple in Assam. Both elements are found in Bengal's mid-seventeenth-century Keshta Raya temple in Bishnupur. Other examples of Assamese monuments that may be considered in terms of Orissan and Bengali prototypes include the Śiva temples at Jaisagar, Sibsagar, and Gaurisagar. The double-roofed temple of Ghana-Shyam, built by the Ahom king Rudra Singha at Jaisagar, is the best example of Bengal's curved-roof style found in Assam.

Sibsagar was the capital of the powerful Ahom kings in Assam and it is marked by an underground garrison called the Talatal-Ghar that was built in 1699 by King Rudra Singh. Koreng-Ghar is a seven-storied palace located nine miles from the present town, and Gargaon palace is an earlier monument, also of seven stories, that was built

Śiva Temple at Gaurisagar, Assam (copyright Archaeological Survey of India).

thirteen kilometers to the east in 1540. The earliest datable Assamese monuments, however, are found in Dharaido, the first Ahom capital and located twenty-two kilometers from Sibsagar, where they were established by King Sukhapha in 1229. Sacred monuments in Sibsagar itself are the best preserved.

In the 1924–25 *Annual Report* of the Archaeological Survey of India, R. D. Banerji notes that "Assam is the only province of India, the history of the architecture and sculpture of which is still practically unknown," and he adds, perhaps too simply, that "while the history of Assam begins with the conquest of the lower part of the valley by the Ahoms in the fourteenth century, the history of its architecture begins with the introduction of Bengali masons and architects in the sixteenth." Of Kamakhya he states that, "the temple of the goddess Kali or Kamakhya on the top of the hill was built during the dominance of the Ahoms. Its *śikhara* is in the shape of a bee-hive, which is characteristic of many of the temples in lower Assam." The tower is made of brick while the sanctum is made of stone. Rebuilding was undertaken by King Narananrayana, and the full dates of the monument are from the seventh to eighth centuries to the sixteenth to eighteenth centuries A.D. While it is very important locally, the building does not relate to Himalayan monuments proper in any crucial way, except that it is a transitional design between those of the plains and those of the mountains. It helps show that Assam and its arts are useful as introductory subjects when Himalayan civilization is investigated.

Jorhat in upper Assam is near the monasteries on Majuli in the Brahmaputra, the largest river-island in the world. Two Śiva temples and a dilapidated shrine with a *yoni* as female symbol and focus of worship survive there. Sualkuchi, across the Brahmaputra and fourteen miles from Gauhati, may be mentioned as a very different goal of visitors because it is famous for production of exquisite Assamese silk, with Basham pointing to Assam and Bengal as the earliest centers of silk weaving in India.[12] The tea center of Jorhat is not far from the town of Sibsagar, a place that has already been noted for its sacred art.

Sibsagar holds the imposing eighteenth-century temple complex of Jay Sagar, the term *sagar* referring to a very large tank that looks like a lake, in this case the lake of Śiva. Nearly all of the temples in Sibsagar are Hindu, particularly Śaivite or Śiva-oriented, but Bauddha Vihār of the nineteenth century at Disangpani is considered to be one of Assam's finest Buddhist temples. Surviving Buddhist images are very infrequent here, although some stone and metal images of Tārā, Buddhist goddess of compassion and wisdom, have been found. Only three images of male bodhisattvas are known so far, suggesting that the Buddha-to-be was not a major ideal in this region. Assam as a whole was never a Buddhist state, yet when the famous Chinese pilgrim Hsüan Tsang was touring India in the middle of the seventh century, the king of Assam insisted that the Chinese visit his realm, where the Buddhist scholar was very well received.

Queen Madambika followed the prevailing Hindu tradition of Assam, and she is remembered for building three Hindu temples in 1734. They are described in superlatives: the *greatest* Śiva temple as a monument that attracts crowds of worshippers from all over India each March, the Viṣṇu temple as the *highest* in the country, and the temple of Devī Dol, goddess of the hills, as India's *largest*. Still, the most intriguing artistic site in Assam may be one that appears in no published survey of South Asian architecture. It is a site that is devoted to orthodox Hindu worship at Barpeta, upriver from Gauhati, with an overlay of precious and unique arts. It will be the final illustration of this brief encounter with the arts of Assam.

But first, to look back at the temple of Kamakhya is to study one of many signs and symbols of the divine goddess Kali in Assam and the dominance of Hinduism in local belief systems. Kālī occupies her shrine on the south bank of the Brahmaputra at a site patronized by King Narakasura, a legendary ruler who is traced back to the ancient times of the *Mahābhārata*. The temple is a center of *śakti* worship today, especially during its August festival that draws thousands to the worship of the frightful female power that is Kālī. Three terrifying representations of Cāmuṇḍā, horrific aspect of Durgā, are part of the Kamakhya site, showing that ghastly but necessary female who is known to the mountains and all of India. To be noted later in this study, her beautiful sister image occupies the elevated shrine of Bhīma Kālī in Sarahan, Himachal Pradesh.

Such concern for the frightening but ultimately positive goddess recalls many parts of the Himalayan region, just as does frequent occurrence of *nāga* serpent worship. The great goddess is everywhere, and her Assamese expression is tied to an enormous and forceful family that indeed dwells in Himalayan states from Bhutan in the east to Himachal Pradesh in the west. In Assam most images of Durgā Mahiṣāsuramardinī, the most frequent *śakti* character as balance to male forces, are carved from the living rock, with an important exception being described below. Most of the Durgā Mahiṣāsuramardinī sculptures date from the ninth and tenth centuries A.D. The last major reconstruction of the Kamakhya temple, however, took place in 1565. It is suggested that Śaktism with its glorification of female powers became the dominant religion in Assam during later periods, becoming even more popular than Śiva worship from late medieval times into the eighteenth century. It is even proposed that Assam, or at least its northeastern corner, is the place of origin for both Śaktism and Tantrism. The mix of Tibetan, Mongolian, and Indian values along with animism and other neighboring beliefs was sometimes combustible, and it is said to have created controversial religious directions, so that even the conservative *Oxford History of India*[13] states that, "All the processes by means of which the members of rude animistic tribes become fanatical Hindus, may be illustrated in Assam." No such conclusion has yet been proven, however.

Among many other Hindu temples of note in Assam is the famous temple of Śiva, called Ūmananda, on Peacock Island in the Brahmaputra, a place that comes most alive during the great Śiva Rātri or "birthday" of Śiva festival that is held each year. There is also the brick Navagraha temple with stone symbols of the Nine Planets (Sūrya, Soma, Bhauma, Budha, Guru, Śukra, Śani, Ráhu, and Ketu according to N. D. Choudhury) that is found east of Gauhati on Chitrachala Hill where it was built during the eighteenth-century reign of Rajeśwar Singha. The Janārdan Devālaya temple of Viṣṇu was built in the eighteenth century and is said to incorporate an image of Buddha. The hermitage of the sage Vasiṣṭha that is built at the confluence of the Sandhya, Lalita, and Kanta rivers is also noteworthy. For readers familiar with major Indian themes, these monuments illustrate old stories in new settings and with the touch of new artists.

At Hajo, twenty-two kilometers south of Gauhati, are several monuments that are important to Hindu, Buddhist, and Muslim believers, while the abovementioned Barpeta, located some ninety miles northwest of Gauhati, is the setting for an important Vaishnava monastery that contains a shrine of Śri Madhav Deva and his teacher Śri Śaṅkara Deva, a famous reformer of the paths that are followed by Hindu devotees. The birth and death of both the saint and his disciple are celebrated each year with pious enthusiasm. As mentioned, the remarkable architectural complex that honors them will be further examined below.

It has already been stated that the proportions and scale of Assamese monuments are generally

Viṣṇu Temple at Sibsagar, Assam (copyright Archaeological Survey of India).

not far removed from sacred structures in Orissa and nearby Bengal. As in Bengal, brick is the most favored material. The spires of Assam hill temples are more elongated than in Bengal, but, as in that neighboring state there are niches in the exterior walls that hold statues made of clay or brick in sizes of up to half life-size. Damaged temples like those of Śiva and Viṣṇu at Sibsagar maintain their swelling, volume-filled sanctity whether they are made of brick or stone. The Śiva building is gracefully towering with its repeated vertical indentations and multilevel pinnacles while the Viṣṇu monument appears more earthbound with its cross-hatch of roof ridges in horizontal and vertical balance. A nearby ruin, however, is noticed for something quite different and something that may be a link to the mountains proper.

Gargaon Palace was rebuilt by King Rajeśwar Singha in 1752. It is squared and multi leveled and its elongated step-pyramid form is at least generally like that of multistage temples, if not palaces, in Nepal. If this brick palace recalls Nepalese pagodas—and Brown illustrates gabled and multiple roofs from Malabar, Orissa, south Kanara, Kashmir, Kathiawar, and Nepal—it is less than remarkable. The Śiva temple has a porch that is covered by the kind of dramatically curved roof that derives from Bengal but reappears as far away as Kathmandu Valley. In that important valley, it is rendered in metal as part of the Hanuman Dhoka Palace of brick and wood. Another major building tradition that developed in Assam to affect its neighbors to the north and west is the *śikhara* tower itself. The tradition may have roots to the south of Assam if we follow Percy Brown's statement in *Indian Architecture (Buddhist and Hindu)* that:

> the temples of Orissa provide the most logical beginning for a study of Indo-Aryan style. The main group is concentrated in the town of Bhubaneśwar where there are over thirty examples.[14]

The mixture of Bengali, Orissan, and local traditions of building in the northeast can be confusing, but structural variety is one consistent feature of the mountain arts.

If architecture needs support from allied arts, sculpture may provide more convincing evidence of shared values and expanding styles in Assam and in the higher elevations. It is worth repeating that ruins at Numelgarh include voluptuous females in *tribhaṅga* hip-shot poses that have all of the vitality of North Indian arts in any great tradition of the Hindu Renaissance, even that of the Chandellas. Another expressive female in the tradition of Durgā, this one stone-carved with weapons and crown, is much more localized in her directness, described in part by the sharply cut details of her costume and her pet parrot.

A strong statement of the pan-Himalayan links for Assamese sculpture is found in an image of Durgā slaying the evil buffalo-headed king Mahiṣa that adorns the outside of the eighteenth-century brick temple of Śivadol in Sibsagar. The goddess is very popular in both Assam and Bengal, where the present writer was literally swept off his feet by Calcutta's celebrations of Durgā Pūja in 1966. She is exciting for her appearance as well as for her story as she plunges her spear into the body of the sinful Mahiṣa. Her *vāhana* or vehicle is the lion who fights beside her, and in her sixteen hands she holds weapons of righteous destruction. She is just one feminine form of the god Śiva but one whom the Himalaya adores. This medieval image may be compared to a representation of the same story on the western Himalayan temple of Viṣveśvara Mahādeva at Bajaura in Kulu Valley. Both of the images are energy charged and dramatic. Yet the design of the structures to which they are attached provides little to suggest specifically Himalayan tastes.

Pāla traditions of northeastern India are shown by huge images of Śiva and Viṣṇu carved into boulders that now crumble on riverbanks near Gauhati. They preserve some of the energetic line and intricate detail that characterize both Pāla and Sena dynastic arts between ca. 730 and ca. 1250 A.D. The same is true of medieval bronzes that survive in the Gauhati Museum. Gupta reminders are harder to find and often more fragmented in these hills, but Asher examines a fine example of Gupta-influenced survival and change as he attributes the doorway of the temple at Dah Parbativa near Tezpur to the time of King Bhaskaravarman's reign in ca. 594–650 in Assam. This was a time when Gupta rulers were increasingly brought into the realm of East Indian politics and culture. The doorway in Assam offers remarkably large, breath-filled, and comely images of the river goddesses Gaṅgā and Jamunā whose prominence in the total composition suggests a date no earlier than the seventh century. The center of the lintel is occupied by Lakulīśa—Śiva with club—and smaller images of Surya and Viṣṇu to either side. Lakulīśa is regarded as the twenty-eighth incarnation of Śiva and the creator of the Paśupata doctrine that is important in Nepal and elsewhere in the Hindu world, but Assamese images of this deity are rare.

Comparison to early Bhubaneshwar is called for as Asher examines some essentially two-dimensional designs of this Śiva sculpture that is active and rhythmical, and he finds that the bold, even "stark" modeling of the attendant females' bodies belongs especially to Assam. The images anticipate works from Deopani that are found further east in Sibsagar District. The story of preservation here is much happier than that of the Viṣvanātha temple that was constructed about 51 kilometers from Tezpur in 1685. There the river has eroded the structure to little more than a few stone posts.

While local invention is continuous, the impression may remain that Assamese art is, in many ways, a positive pastiche made up from other traditions. Relationships to Burma, Bengal, Nepal, and India's best-known northern dynasties are frequently evident, and there is more that comes from outside. Yet it is possible to find early works that are special, even in light of constant borrowing that went on. A fine example is an eighteenth-century bronze from Tinisukia in Lakhimpur District that is now in the collection of the Assam State Museum in Gauhati. While being masterfully cast in bronze by the lost-wax method and easily recognized as Durgā, the image is stark and simplified in such a way that the kind of appealing fluidity of form and detail that so often emerges as metal replaces wax is rejected in favor of a "harder" effect. That hardness conveys cold solidity and blunt force with only the slightest touch of cast and incised details to soften the form.

The asymmetrical wave of Durgā's ten arms and the action of her lion who leaps from the left to bite the elbow of the hapless adversary bring the composition to life. The buffalo demon has already lost his head and it lies at the feet of Durgā, so that the battle has possibly reached the point when the inner spirit of the enemy appears to "escape" in human form. Weapons are not necessary; Durgā and her lion do not need them.

Still more direct, even aggressive, is a very simple metal face of Durgā that shines on a circular plaque above the head of the conquered buffalo that replaces her body. She is Durgā Mahiṣāsuramardinī once again, slayer of the buffalo demon and destroyer of wickedness. The effect of the work might be compared to the directness and strength of a stone column with figures from the fourteenth to sixteenth centuries that was found at Naksaparbat in Shillong District. In both examples one is reminded, perhaps, of the forceful simplicity of *devī* or *devata* masks that are carried processionally in the Kulu Valley of the northwestern Himalaya. Finally there is a small "tribal Durgā" made of clay that comes from Burhi-Gosahi, Assam, as a modern/traditional work that continues themes and values of the past. Isn't this what is to be expected from folk art? The images are kept in the Assam State Museum.

While the above images may briefly deflect our concern from sacred buildings, they do serve to underscore both Assamese invention and borrowing. A final sculpture that summarizes this point is a small bronze figure of Indra, the Vedic god of war, that is attributed to the tenth century and also kept in the Assam State Museum. It is a seminal work for later images that have already been seen. It stands twelve inches tall as another *cire-perdue* accomplishment, shining and perfect. It was found at Kalilipara (Odalbakra) in Assam, but it is credited by the Museum to Gauhati manufacture. It recalls the best of Pāla and Sena art because of its shimmering surfaces, supple movement, and precision of lines that are both incised and three-dimensional. Perhaps it reveals a resurgence of Hinduism after the gradual demise of Buddhist ideals in medieval India; in any case it may betaken to stand for the excellence of eastern hill metalwork.

The process can be analyzed in reverse, with the smooth body and the jewel-like three-dimensional details as reminders that the figure was first modeled in fine quality beeswax. "Extra" elements like the lotus flowers on stems that connect two pillars at either side of Indra are there partly to serve as sprues during the most difficult step of the *cire-perdue* process: the pouring of molten alloy of copper and tin into the cavity that was left after the original wax model was melted out of its clay enclosure. Clay must be mentioned because it makes up an enclosing mold that is carefully put over the wax original, first as a painted slip and then as a heavier coating that seals the wax that is to be evaporated or poured off. After the metal-filled mold has cooled slowly and the clay broken away as a used mold, and possibly a clay core pulled out of its base, a rough metal image first appears. It must be smoothed with files and some incised linear details are usually added. Sprues that are not harmonious with the finished artwork are cut away and their tracks are polished down. Thereby the idealized form of Indra and his elephant is fully captured in precious material.

This version of the god does not seem to portray the powerful Indra who was the great conquerer in Vedic literature and who is shown crushing opponents with his elephant at Bhaja cave as early as the second century B.C. Instead, it shows the lover of intoxicating *soma* and the admirer of adoring females who is portrayed in later Hindu writing. Indra still rides his elephant, but because he became so well-known for his love affairs in later stories—even after he wed the beautiful Indrani who is his female counterpart—we cannot be sure whether the lovely, lotus-borne women who attend him on either side include Ahalya, wife of Indra's teacher, or other female ideals. A worshipper, also female, kneels down at his right. Perhaps, as at Changu Nārāyaṇa temple in Nepal, she represents a donor or patron of the art. Indra himself is benign, gentle, peaceful, and thoroughly a high country ideal. More effectively than any of the above images, this sculpture stands for the sophistication and beauty of three-dimensional art in the northeast. It compares to the best of cast metal art in Nepal, Himachal Pradesh, Kashmir, and Ladakh.

Barpeta Satra, Assam.

Barpeta Satra interior, Assam.

Barpeta is chosen as the final archaeological site in this overview because of the relevance of its main temple and study center that is dedicated to Viṣṇu, its popularity as a pilgrimage center, the incorporation of local saints into its meaning, and the splendor of its arts. The grounds of this spacious ensemble include a Hindu monastery called *satra* with a large congregational worship hall locally called *kirtan ghar*. A *satra* may be compared to the *maṭh* or pilgrim shelter for holy men that will be discussed in relation to Nepal. There are three *satras* to be noted here: Śri Iśvara Bali Satra, Kawimari Satra, and Barpeta Satra. They are far removed from the *śikhara* temples mentioned above and have far more to do, perhaps, with the indigenous preferences of the Assamese people. The two larger halls are meant for teaching and congregational worship and are places of mass assembly. The teachers are more than respected; they are adored as sources of knowledge and goodness. People fall to their knees before the wise teachers. Yet they can be very approachable and good-natured.

As in so much of the Himalaya, the Assamese sect temple stands as a glorified house. It is bigger and grander than an ordinary dwelling, but a dwelling nonetheless. Within it there may be a palanquin for transporting the local gods on tour, for the "neighborhood" belongs to them. They are recognizable Hindu gods in part, but there are also several "stick" figures that are presumably born of local, animistic forces. Visual strength reveals spiritual might. The *satras* are on consecrated ground in Assam, and the buildings contain large and splendid altars. The buildings are dated by attribution to the fifteenth and sixteenth centuries. The Archaeological Survey of India records that the fame of this site rests on its association with two Mahāpuruṣas (great or eminent men, supreme spirits) named Śaṅkara Deva and Madhav Deva. The sainted reformer Śri Śaṅkara Deva was born in Batadrava (locally known as Bordua) about seventy-five miles from Gauhati, and the shrine that has been built in his birthplace is also especially important to the Mahapuruṣa sect at Barpeta. Barpeta is important because it is the place of Śri Madhav Deva's enshrinement as the master's main follower and descended teacher. It is an extraordinary place.

The newest addition to the Barpeta complex is a plastered cement shrine with hexagonal curved roof, all brilliantly painted white. The large enclosures of both the *satra* and the worship hall are rectangular and covered by overhanging pitched roofs made of corrugated metal. From a distance they appear to be very ordinary, but upon closer inspection they prove to be walled with and enclosed by most remarkable works of relief along with sculpture in the round. Some of these are displaced fragments from earlier buildings, columnar figures of such compact energy and force that they recall the most frontal and direct wooden images of Himachal Pradesh in the western Himalaya.

Examples of carved art on the Barpeta grounds include a single wooden column with floral capital, notched at the top where it may once have supported a beam. It is carved with linear clarity to represent a female with three faces. She stands about four feet tall in her present verandah setting above the compound. There is also a pair of whitewashed females in wood that may represent river goddesses, as in the doorway complex studied above, while they flank a very simple wooden shrine made of latticework with metal roofing and a stone "altar" at its front. The superwomen are clearcut, "primitive" works that seem to be at home in the hills. They share the frontal and solid appearence of the tribal Durgā in the Gauhati Museum that was mentioned above. They are only fragments, but they have the "right" countenance. There also are doors that are made up of solid planks with relief carvings showing Hindu gods within floral frames, presumably waiting for the application of a precious covering as described below.

The interior of the larger of the two worship halls, with its pierced walls to provide ventilation, has some similarly impressive figures. They are backed by huge wooden columns painted white, and they face the wide passage that leads from the entry toward a very large altar that holds three stepped pyramids that are draped in white cloth and garlands of flowers. The triangular construction resembles the figures of deities who are draped in cloth and flowers to be set upon altars like those inside the temple of Hayagriva Mahādeva in Hajo. Neither fits into "normal" contexts of better-known monuments on the Gangetic plain.

The larger worship space holds puzzles as well as familiar characters. To the uninitiated, a colossal carving of Garuda in brown wood as vehicle for Viṣṇu the Preserver is almost cartoon-like. It stands beside a column with its wings widespread to eight-foot width, and a serpent coils around its body. The eyes are wide open and the beak is exaggerated, possibly as a hint of shamanistic reverence for the hornbill bird that is native to Assam, although this is admittedly quite a stretch. Red offering powders are sprinkled over it.

A second large image of the miraculous man-bird kneels with a bright yellow cape over its red body as it looks ahead wide-eyed. A massive wooden image of Viṣṇu himself, holding a conch and a *cakra* disc, drops to one knee nearby. Equally large, at about five feet tall, is a wooden Hanuman,

Boy with wooden Hanuman image, Barpeta Satra, Assam.

Lord of Monkeys and rescuer of Viṣṇu's counterpart, Rāma the hero. Hanuman is shown raising a lime to his furry mouth. At the outer entrance are two brightly painted figures of wood in life-size prominence: the first is of Śiva with his beloved Pārvatī in his lap as he rides upon his bull vehicle Nandi; the second is unusual representation of a small four-armed Viṣṇu in the arms of a woman who may represent his mother.

The freestanding images in themselves do not set Barpeta's buildings apart from any number of folk shrines in the hills. But the bold sculptures are accompanied by more elaborate arts—silhouette screen complexes, detailed polychrome epics painted on exterior walls, and silver tripartite altars

Priests in Barpeta Satra, Assam.

that dominate the main hall. The three step-pyramids are covered with offerings on their table. Six tall oil lamps burn before the altar table, and the base of the table is made of elaborately cast silver with elephants and riders at the corners. Small statues of leogryphs sit at attention on each corner of the three step-pyramids. Each pyramid supports a miniature shrine, finely made of silver and hung with white cloth within. Priests who attend the altar take care to wrap their lower faces in cloth so that their breath or spittle will not be allowed to involuntarily pollute the offerings that they prepare and put in place.

In addition to four brass offering plates on pedestals, there is a huge bowl of grain on the floor in front of the altar. It may be assumed that this is to be later passed out to pilgrims and perhaps to the priests as well. Worshippers dress in white like the priests, kneeling on the outside of the buildings and touching their foreheads to the ground. Again, it is the Mahapuru, a sect of Vaiṣṇavism, that follows these elaborate patterns of worship. The colorful halls are impressive and the sanctity of the spaces is clear, but the most stunning Barpeta arts still remain to be seen.

First, the solid walls of the priest's enclosures are covered with brilliant color on plaster along with relief images made of wood that also are painted. A continuous progression of scalloped niches within rectangular frames leads along the sixty-foot length of one exterior wall of the *satra*. the effect is as colorful as any other Hindu monument in India, equaling even Minakshi Temple with its late medieval polychrome in Madurai, South India. From a short distance the effect is like a comic strip or wildly colored wallpaper. Each niche contains a figure of one of Viṣṇu's incarnations or other Hindu subject, while the wall surfaces immediately above and below these "portrait" niches are made of wood that is pierced or metal that is cast with floral patterns. Most of the illustrated pantheon appear as high-relief sculpture, including a very clear and lively trinity of Brahmā the Creator on his goose, Viṣṇu the Preserver on Garuḍa, and Śiva the Destroyer on his bull named Nandi.

In another scene, Viṣṇu is shown in profile as Varāha, the boar who rescues the earth, as symbolized by a lovely young woman, from the primordial waters that once covered all existence. Another panel shows Viṣṇu as the horrific Narasiṃha, man-lion and lurid executioner of a wicked king. The animated stories are lively, related to arts of the high Himalaya mainly by their meaning. More impressive, perhaps, is a special applied art that is not often seen. Rarely equaled, and only at places like Paśupatinātha Temple in Nepal's Kathmandu Valley and Bhima Kālī Temple at Sarahan in upper Himachal Pradesh, the doors of the Barpeta complex are covered with silver.

Two details of the *satra* in Barpeta may be taken as examples of finely carved wood that is, in the case of the doors, combined with the precious metal. A florid circle on panel with four-armed Viṣṇu at the center and lion/boar heads below, and an entrance column with overall lotus designs, stand for Assam's carved wood. These resemble carved doors and walls that are found in many Himalayan states, and it is just such panels that are sometimes covered over with thin sheets of metal. Brass or other metal may be cut into silhouette pieces that are attached to dark wood, as on a minor door in Barpeta, but this simple method is least often seen. Some cast metal is attached to flat surfaces of buildings, but this, too, is rare. Most often, thin metal sheets are carefully pounded in place as *repoussé* sculpture over a fully carved wooden base.

Subjects rendered at Barpeta include many small portraits of attendant gods and elaborate floral borders but the scenes center on such subjects as Viṣṇu with Lakṣmī as Goddess of Wealth and his female expression. They are shown in a heavenly palace. Another panel shows Viṣṇu with Lakṣmī seated together in an elaborate frame of hooded *nāga* snakes. With painted flowers above and repeated cusped arches borrowed from Islamic art below, the silver vision of the reliefs is glorious but not ostentatious. The glitter of precious materials is simply to be expected as a glimpse of heaven. It is not possible to overstress the dazzling and almost divine perfection that these surfaces of brilliant silver convey. Viṣṇu in his palace with a canopy overhead and Lakṣmī beside him is seated on a throne while Garuḍa and Hanuman join four worshippers who wave fly whisks to honor him. The metal reliefs are a fitting prelude for the silver altars within.

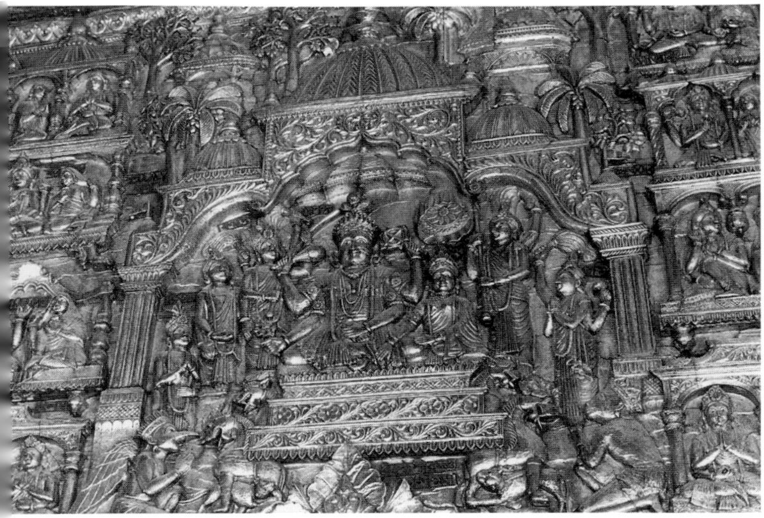

Exterior silver tympanum, Barpeta Satra, Assam.

Inside, priests and worshippers occupy the high-ceilinged worship hall of the larger structure, with subdued light that enters through the foliage patterns of wood and metal while columns end with extended brackets that curve with the same floral patterns of openwork to join the ceiling. There is no procession of *maṇḍapa* porches leading to a small *garbha gṛha* as interior *sanctum;* instead the *sanctum sanctorum* is cavernous in itself. Gupta patterns and those born of the tastes of the medieval age in most of India do not apply. This is not a building of Pāla or Sena inspiration and Mughal details are few.

In total, this Hindu complex in Assam is too unusual to establish patterns that will lead the reader through the rest of the foothills and into the Himalaya region itself. Nor can the temple arts of Assam be used as exact models for any of the arts that appear in the following chapters. But they do provide a preview of the devotion, imagination, and artistic skill that the mountains shelter in many remarkable expressions. They are visionary and inspirational even when basically rough. Perhaps they begin to measure the immeasurable.

3

Sikkim, Kalimpong, and Darjeeling: Tradition and Hill Stations

These hill regions are very different from one another, the first suggesting survival of deeply rooted Asian traditions while the second and third are upstarts, or at least were such in the nineteenth century, upstarts that were born of British interests in the cool and fertile mountains. It is not possible to know the famous hill stations that provided respite to British civil servants without some familiarity with the coming together of east and west, and it is not possible to know the former kingdom of Sikkim without understanding the network of exchange that existed among India, Tibet, and China. Each of these very special places is defined, at least in part, by its architectural tastes and uses.

At 7,000 feet, Darjeeling is reached (appropriately enough for a place of legend) by a lengthy ride on a tiny steam train of only two-foot gauge. The train was opened in 1881, to climb a maximum gradient of 1 to 20. The fifty-one-mile distance from Sukna near Siliguri on Indian plain to Darjeeling is covered in seven hours, with altitudes as high as about 6,000 feet at Manibhanjan to about 12,000 feet at Phalut and Sandakphu. A first glimpse of Kanchenjunga is sometimes gained at Kurseong (4,860 feet) where the mini-train has its longest stopover. Often called the "toy train," this antique conveyance was introduced during the time of the British Raj and still evokes images of that antique period. It, too, is foreign and strange. The economic impact of the railway reached as far as Peking, for the goods that China had traded with Lhasa in Tibet became available from Calcutta, only three weeks' travel from the Tibetan capital. For Darjeeling as "place of the thunderbolt," as well as for lands far beyond, the economic balance shifted.

While ascending the steep hills of northern Uttar Pradesh amid floating mists and clouds, it is not hard for the first-time visitor to free his or her imagination and reconstruct the sybaritic, dreamlike scene that greeted European visitors on holiday in the nineteenth and early twentieth centuries. They came to the mists of the hill station to escape from the heat of the plains below, especially Calcutta. For more than one hundred years, Calcutta served as capital of British rule over India until the architects Baker and Luytens completed their vision of a new and suitably grand capital in New Delhi not long after the turn of the twentieth century. Respite from New Delhi's scorching summer months was then sought in Simla rather than Darjeeling, so much so that Simla became the summer "capital" of the British Raj in India. The impressive pile of stone with castlelike roof lines that served as viceroy's residency there has nothing to do with traditional mountain architecture. Nearby and hardly even noticed during the British period are fine examples of the native buildings in what is called the "Alpine Style."

Darjeeling was and is, of course, famous for its tea, but also for its cool climate. It is almost in the shadow of the white goddess-mountain Kanchenjunga, and the region's traditional orientation is toward Tibet. Several Lamaist monasteries still function there, including the roadside temple of Ghoom, the hillside Bhutia Bustee, and the rather fanciful Aloobari monastery temple with its gingerbread balconies of white-painted wood. The town was planned by Lord Napier of the Royal Engineers, and it grew slowly during the early nineteenth century, when it was part of Sikkim and often attacked by Gurkha forces from Nepal. The Gurkhas, whose home place is discussed in pages to come, succeeded in conquering the Terai as malarial grassy plain to the south and then took part of Sikkim on their way to the Teesta River. They were turned back by British forces of the East India Company and the war of 1814. Then the British reinstated the Rāja or King of Sikkim as an ally, and his territory was joined to Darjeeling in order to form a buffer zone between Nepal and Bhutan. A treaty signed on 1 February 1935 reads:

> The Governor-General having expressed his desire for the possession of the hill of Darjeeling on account of its cool climate . . . I, the said, Sikkimputtee Rajah, out of friendship for the said Governor-General, hereby present Darjeeling to the East India Company, that is, all the land south of the great Ranjeet River, east of the Balsum, Kahail and Little Ranjeet rivers and west of Rungao and Mahanuddi rivers.

The name of Darjeeling is a variation upon *dorje* as the Sanskrit/Tibetan term for thunderbolt or *vajra*. The district is bounded by Nepal to the west, Sikkim to the north, and Bhutan to the west, making this small area one of the subcontinent's most strategic lands. Even in recent years, nearby Kalimpong has been referred to in print as "a nest of spies." The first Europeans to set foot in Darjeeling came in 1829, when a British resident named J. W. Grant took his place there after an early dispute between Britain and Nepal.[2] He worked with Governor-General William Bentick, who anticipated not only economic development but the satisfaction of converting local inhabitants to Christianity. The west had already begun to transform this small part of the east. The center of the hilltop town is Observatory Hill with its Mahākāla Cave, which is sacred to the Hindu god Śiva, beside a Buddhist shrine. Nearby is Birch Hill, the town's main residential area and the site of the Himalayan Mountaineering Institute that was founded by Sherpa Tenzing Norgay after he and Sir Edmund Hillary of New Zealand conquered Mt. Everest on 28 May 1953 in celebration of the coronation of Queen Elizabeth II. Among the people seen walking on Observatory Hill are Nepalese, Tibetans, Bhutias, and Lepchas who may be the original populace of this area. Unlike Gauhati in Assam, Darjeeling is a place of truly Himalayan people and truly Himalayan structures.

One thing that is almost completely absent in the town centers of Darjeeling, Simla, Naini Tal, Mussoori, Ootacumund, and other Indian hill stations—not surprisingly—is traditional Himalayan architecture. But traditional monuments can be found nearby. These include traditions of Tibet that are important to understanding the coming together of two very different cultures. Descriptions of them in early gazeteers and diaries formed some of the first foreign impressions of the Himalaya. Darjeeling's environs provide Ghoom at 8,000 feet and only eight kilometers from the town, as a small settlement at the side of both the road and the railway tracks that climb to the town proper. It is mainly a place of refueling and refreshment, as well as the reputed highest railway station in the world. The traditional structure here is not very old but it is very colorful and is referred to by most people simply as Ghoom monastery.

This structure that is home to monks of the reformed Yellow Hat sect of Tibetan Buddhism contains a fifteen-foot statue of Maitreya, the Buddha of the Future. As will be seen in Leh and elsewhere, it is typical for this Buddha of hope to be represented in colossal size. Ghoom monastery, built in 1875 by Lama Sherab Gyantso and painted in bright reds, yellows, and blues, is larger than the nearby Buddhist centers called Bhutia Bustee and Aloobari, but it appears to be more neglected. As a not especially famous place or one that is home to any major festival, it is maintained on minimal funds that come as offerings. It can provide a shivering stop-off on the way to Tiger Hill, an outstanding viewpoint for seeing the great mountain range at dawn, but the monastery shrine really comes to life only during celebrations of the Tibetan New Year in February and March. Tiger Hill itself is a memorable place as a perch from which to see the great Kanchenjunga (Tib. Khang-Chen-Dzod-Nga), the "untrodden" peak. It is sometimes called the great goddess, a peak that is so respected that it is reported that those who have climbed to her summit have not actually set foot upon its highest point. The mountain rises as a white slash against impossibly blue skies along with its neighbor peaks including Makalu, Kabru, and Janu. Mt. Everest (locally known as Kang Cha-mo-lung "Snow of the Bird Country," Jo-mo-lun-ma "Goddess of the Wind," Chomo-lungma "Goddess Mother of the World," among other names) is rarely seen at a distance of 225 kilometers.

It is perhaps worth noting here that the architectural standard of the Himalayan region as a whole—vertically oriented and multiple roofed buildings with peaked roofs—is sometimes assumed to derive from the bold inspiration of the mountain forms themselves. While some Nepalese structures and some Himachal Pradesh towers may seem to support this attribution, other important monuments do not fit. Tibetan *gompas* (monastery temples) are usually broader and more palacelike than the lofty towers of Hindu edifices of the types just mentioned. Tibetan architecture is immediately tied to the art of Sikkim, Darjeeling, and the small settlement of Kalimpong that lies between them.

Ghoom monastery, properly named Yiga Chhweling, has an especially colorful exterior. One must accept the practical substitution of concrete or cement for wood in many monastery restorations or new constructions, and this is true at this place. Also, corrugated metal has replaced the slanted roof of its second floor. Chinese art is a strong influence upon this nineteenth-century monument, as is indicated clearly by the colossal sky dragons that fly inwards toward the center from both sides of the main floor's upper walls. The dragons are painted bright yellow against sky-blue background and the detail of their prominent white teeth as they snarl is repeated in the heads of *makara* water monsters. These *makara* project out from the two corners of the extra yellow-painted roof that covers the building's shallow porch. The cornice molding of the main floor has dragon dogs with open mouths at each end. All of this seems to describe a technicolor carnival or overblown kitsch, perhaps like Hong Kong's tiresome Tiger Balm Gardens. But in fact, flamboyant color is a long-established and necessary component of Tibetan art that the Darjeeling area has helped to preserve. Color clarifies iconographical story.

Long niches on the front of the building hold prayer wheels by which devotees send their prayers to heaven in infinite number, and the niches stand for the love of polychrome. They are painted yellow on their small roofs, red for the box that holds the vertically mounted metal cylinders that contain written or printed prayers, and blue for the boxes' sills. Anticipating a subject related to Ladakh and Solo Khumbu in Nepal, they form a kind of *mani* wall that repeats the sacred formula, Om Mani Padme Hum or "Hail to the Jewel in the Lotus" with each clockwise spin. Their setting shows a rainbow of primary colors like that found in the silk frames of *tanka* paintings or, in fact, any Tibetan arts.

The glass windowed entry porch at Ghoom is not really traditional, but it is part of art in transition. The multilevel *stūpi* or pinnacle atop the *gompa* is very traditional, as are the cylindrical "banners" made of brass in imitation of cloth that stand five feet tall on the front corners of the main roof. It is a standard Tibet-styled sanctuary in terms of being rectangular and symmetrical, having two full stories with a raised clerestory to light the interior by windows that make up the second level, and because it is so colorful. At the center of the vestibule's roof is a classic triple image of the flaming jewel that shows the radiating truth of Buddha's message. Although the building is simple, it has layers of meaning.

Ghoom monastery is genuine enough to raise any visitor's curiosity about the mysteries and treasures that lie within. As in any monastery, books are its greatest treasure. The essential *Kan jur* and *Tan jur* manuscripts—always the most precious holding of any *gompa*—are carefully wrapped in cloth and stacked on library shelves to either side

Makara/*leogryph as roof corner of Tibetan style.*

of the main altar. There are treasures of visual art as well, perhaps the work of traveling artist-monks who spread their visual language throughout the Buddhist hills. All around the main floor interior are high walls that have been covered with plaster to receive dry fresco paintings. The light on the ground floor level is very dim in spite of the clerestory of the upper floor, and smoking oil lamps have darkened some of the colors, but a visitor makes out the mural art. It is filled with frightening, intense renderings of positive conquerers of evil, as horrible as evil itself, that are involved in the kinds of struggles with ego that characterize the trials of afterlife that one encounters in the Bardo state after death. This is preparation and prologue for *The Tibetan Book of the Dead.* The paintings are dramatic in both their subject and their style as they show the embrace of a multiheaded protector with thirty-four arms as he clutches his female counterpart or *śakti* in *yab-yum* embrace. This combined pose shows the unity of opposites and will be seen again and again.

The paintings also show frightful female characters, in some ways comparable to Western concepts of the Furies and sometimes riding horses and brandishing swords. There is the helmeted Begtse, a red-faced and grimacing god of war who raises a human heart to his mouth while wielding his curved sword, and many other horrific characters as dangerous defenders of the faith. In spite of the impact of color, this is essentially an art of line—and line as flawless perfection. The figures' painted background consists of swirling clouds, plumes of smoke, and explosively twisted flames. Yet at the center of all this there is absolute calm.

Besides the excitement of color and line that one feels when entering a Buddhist shrine room like that in Ghoom, there is the calming quiet of peaceful, controlled balance and harmony. This calm is partly expressed in visual ways. At Ghoom such a port in a storm is provided by the large image that was mentioned above. The smoothly finished and shining statue, with much applied jewelry and the white scarves that Tibetans call "snow flowers" draped over the figure as gifts, as noted, represents Maitreya as the Buddha of the Future.

The prominence of this future form of Buddha as hope and refuge grew along with the second school of Buddhism that developed in India starting around the first century A.D. The second school—called Mahāyāna or "Greater Vehicle" to differentiate it from the earlier school that its successors named Hīnayāna or "Lesser Vehicle"—stressed the importance of the Buddha in various expressions, including that of the Buddha who is yet to come. But the central icon of Ghoom goes several steps farther so that the art incorporates the third and most magical school, Vajrayāna. This

"Vehicle of the Thunderbolt" first developed with much indigenous Himalayan and Central Asian input in the seventh century.

The main figure, made of painted clay, rests at the center of the altar complex and is backed by a very large, openwork halo or mandorla that is made of wood or clay painted in brilliant hues. The patterns of the halo consist of entwined vegetation and animals along with dragons, and there is a large Garuḍa-like bird with a serpent in its beak at the very top. This is the Tantric version of Garuḍa, sacred man-bird of Hindu cosmology who protects and supports Viṣṇu as God of Preservation. Garuḍa is shown subduing a serpent here and throughout the Asian world. White angels that India calls *apsaras* spirits lean out above Maitreya's head.

In front of the main figure is an empty seat, an orator's throne, that is meant to be occupied by the sainted master and high *lama,* whose photograph rests upon it, whenever he comes to the monastery.[3] It is familiar custom, and the presentation of Maitreya is rendered in style and iconography that are also recognizable throughout the mountain regions. The gentle expression of the face and its matte-gold color, along with finely delineated brows and lotiform eyes, are rendered in the way of India's Pāla-Sena dynasties of the eighth through thirteenth centuries and shared with Newar artists of Nepal. The prominent jewelry includes large double earrings and a wide shiny gold crown that is encrusted with coral and turquoise. The rich lapidary effect suggests Nepalese prototypes, but also relates positively to the most revered Buddha image in Tibet. That treasure is the statue inside of the Jokhang temple in Lhasa, the holiest shrine in Tibet, an image whose origin is traced back to the time of King Srong-tsan Gampo in the seventh century, and to his two Buddhist wives who came from Nepal and China.

Although Kalimpong holds no treasure like the Buddha image in Lhasa's Jokhang, it does, like so many Himalayan and foothill areas, have an impressive shrine tower that is made—in twentieth century custom—of concrete. Like Sikkim's famous monastery temple of Rumtek outside of Gangtok, it is completely traditional in every respect except materials. As new monasteries are built at places like Bodhnath in Kathmandu Valley, they are mostly made with the lasting and fire-resistent material of concrete; after painting has been applied in traditional colors both inside and outside of any structure it is absolutely convincing. A Westerner might still be disappointed in the change from the past procedures, but anyone who lives in the constant mist and rain of Kalimpong or Darjeeling, or in deforested parts of Nepal, or in the dry valley of Ladakh with little vegetation, will be quite satisfied with the new way.

The name Kalimpong is derived from the small settlement's former role as headquarters of a Bhutanese governor, for the term Kalim means "king's minister." It is just fifty-one miles from Darjeeling between hills called Durbindara and Deolo. Kalimpong is 4,100 feet above sea level and is the home of the Kalimpong Arts and Crafts Center that produces varied wares of Sikkimese, Tibetan, Bhutanese, and local types. It also is the setting for two Buddhist monasteries. "Tharps Choaling" monastery belongs to the Yellow Hat sect of the Dalai Lama while the new Zang-dog Palrifo Brang on Durpin Dara Hill was completed only in 1975.

A freestanding temple that is not attached to other buildings takes the name *lhakhang* in the Tibetan sphere of influence, and this is to be distinguished from monuments to come, such as the *dzong* or fortified monastery complex that is found in Bhutan and Ladakh. Two other Buddhist monastery halls in the Darjeeling area are Bhutia Bustee, found below Observatory Hill, and Aloobari, which is located three kilometers from town center on Tenzing Norgay Road, past a house called "Step Aside." One way to reach them is by pony, and this may be especially fitting, for the buildings have a picturesque, even theatrical quality about them.

Bhutia Bustee gives the appearance of being perched dangerously close to the edge of a cliff, but in fact it is nestled soundly against its steep hill. It melds with the landscape in a way that many Tantric Buddhist shrines do, the most spectacular of which is Tiger's Nest in Bhutan. As "Darjeeling" means thunderbolt and resting place, Bhutia Bustee implies a secure home for the teachings of Vajrayāna Buddhism, which is also named for the symbol of thunder. It has a longer history than the monastery at Ghoom and belongs to the early Nyingmapa or Red Hat school of Tibetan Buddhism rather than the "reformed" Gelug-pa school that is often called Yellow Hat. It was sacked by the Nepalese in the nineteenth century, collapsed in the disastrous earthquake of 1934, and restored by the Rājah of Sikkim. Its richly colorful interior with walls as fully patterned as silk brocade is like that in Ghoom, and it reminds the viewer of how very different the modes of expression are when Darjeeling at the edge of Tibet is compared to Assam beside the Indian plains.

A typical activity of monks at Bhutia Bustee is making three-dimensional *maṇḍalas* out of sticks and string, objects that represent the geometric centering of concentration and worship that is understood everywhere in the mountains. In his *Tantric Mysticism of Tibet,* John Blofeld treats the *maṇḍala* as derived from the ancient *svastika* with its hooked arms that may hold dots as emanations for the eternal central hub or axis of the diagram. This monastery temple has its own constancy.[4]

Had the Muslim conquests of Muhammad bin Bakhtyar spread from his successes in Bihar and Bengal to beyond the Teesta river, tributary of the Brahmaputra, and become firmly entrenched in "the open country of Tibbat" (Tibet) as he evidently planned, he would have been surprised by what he found there. The crowded spaces filled with human and super-human figures inside of monastic *gompa* monuments would have undoubtedly shocked a Muslim who was trained to reject representational imagery as being profane. It is not certain, but it is possible that Bakhtyar reached a point north of Darjeeling before natural barriers of topography forced him and his army to retreat. The leader died in the Hijri year 602 (1205–06 A.D.).[5] It is helpful to remember that while Islam spread over much of India, often producing iconoclastic destruction of Hindu and Buddhist art, the Himalayan states were usually remote enough to be spared. When the Dalai Lama fled to Darjeeling in 1910 to remain there until after the Chinese revolution of 1911, he was undoubtedly familiar with the wealth of Vajrayāna arts that awaited him.

Aloobari monastery in Darjeeling is one of the most unusual monuments to be treated here, largely because it is a hybrid that mixes several styles. It is not an early building, and it is likely that European/Chinese contact inspired its inclusion of open balconies with metal grillwork for railings. Viewers should not be surprised that the columns have extended capitals that meet to form arches on the lowest of the four floors, but it is remarkable that the arches are of scalloped pattern that is shared with Islamic monuments. Other Islamic elements like the true arch and true dome resting on squinches are not usually found in Himalayan buildings.

As the interior of this monastery is described, it is hoped that one measure of Himalayan architecture is becoming clear—that buildings in the Tibetan tradition may be colorful and even fanciful on their exterior but that the major impact of color and storytelling paintings and sculpture is found, along with sacred books, on the inside. The first and second floors of the Aloobari structure are surrounded by open porches that become extended terraces at the front. Above these are coiled dragon patterns in three dimensions, and the creatures have long snouts like those of the mythical *makara* as beneficial monster associated with water and abundance. The *makara* is also associated with Kāma, god of desire. An early representation of this fabulous beast is found on the railing that surrounds the famous temple of Bodhgaya where Buddha attained enlightenment.

An unusual structural element is a small tower that rests on the second floor's center porch. Like the room below it, the small tower has glass windows and it may function as a private study. Blind windows all around the third floor contain painted carvings of such auspicious symbols as the *pūrṇa kalaśa* or vase of plenty, the endless knot that stands for continuity and cohesion, and the Dharmacakra or Wheel of Buddhist Law. Two very large and cylindrical "banners" like those at Bhutia Bustee that are made of brass top the second roof, and a third banner caps the small study with openwork vegetation as ancient Hindu/Buddhist symbol of the wish-fulfilling vine that brings boons to the faithful. This vegetal pattern is often combined with the *makara,* and the divine animal may disgorge growing things from its mouth. An elongated pinnacle is at the center of the uppermost roof, and this level also supports openwork vines. Because of its white color, its remarkable openness with balconies on all sides, the lightness of its upturned roof corners, and its almost fanciful additions (a large metal peacock spreads its tail feathers at one roof corner), Aloobari is a most unusual building, at least on the outside.

Inside of Aloobari, particularly on the lower two floors, the walls are covered with hundreds of painted images of Buddhas, Bodhisattvas as enlightened Buddhas-to-be, teachers, and saints. They make up a kind of family album or family tree of those who are imbued with the pure truth of the Buddhist way. A prominent place is given to Padmasambhava, the sainted teacher who cleansed the mountains of demons and evil spirits in the eighth century A.D. The central altar has a three-dimensional figure of Avalokiteśvara, as most compassionate of Buddhas-to-be and "he who looks down" with compassion upon the world. He has one thousand arms. The elaborate form is quite usual in the hills, where multiple arms indicate omnipotence and multiple heads show omniscience. It is made of painted clay and graced by a conical offering of rice that is stacked in levels and held in place by enclosing rings of *repoussé* metal, conch shells, and a framed portrait of the Dalai Lama. There is a brass oil lamp on an altar step below the statue and offerings on the altar include *torma,* as symbolic gifts made of butter and dough, and various fruits. *Torma* are colorful as they represent offerings of human body parts, eyes, abstract circular forms, and other meaningful gifts. The carved wooden offering box that rests in front of the altar, painted with vegetation and a protective *kīrti mukha* or face of glory, also is typical. Above all of these is painted a large ceiling *maṇḍala* with four directional colors, like a compass to guide the making and giving of perfectly balanced, eternal art. Some of its details and the golden lotus flower at its center are painted with thick paint so as to stand out in relief and catch the filtered light of oil lamps. The total effect is visionary.

The classic colors of the *maṇḍala,* usually presented in the four quadrants and center of a square diagram that holds five circles, are green to the north, blue to the east, yellow to the south, and red to the west, with white as central color in a circle or smaller square. Symbols that may be shown in each of these color areas are the crossed *vajra* or thunderbolt in the north, single *vajra* in the east, sacred jewel in the south, and lotus in the west, with the wheel of scared law in the center. It is crucial to understand that the *maṇḍala* is much more than a two-dimensional focus for meditation; it is a blueprint for building three-dimensional constructions that are schematic as they imply limitless spatial expandability. Giuseppe Tucci links the *maṇḍala* absolutely with the *stūpa,* called *chorten* in Tibetan context, and with Mount Sumeru (Mt. Meru). The *chorten* may be small enough to rest on an altar as inside Aloobari, large enough to enclose the seated body of a sainted teacher like the precious reliquaries inside of the Potala in Lhasa, or monumental like the memorial *chorten* that honors a former king of Sikkim near Gangtok, the huge but partly hollow structure at Gyantse in Tibet and the most unusual *chorten* that was built in memory of the preceding ruler and father of Bhutan's reigning king.

The mountain as axis is surrounded by four continents with the color yellow to the north, white to the east, blue to the south, and red to the west. Complementing this, a *chorten* is divided into five levels as the five elements. From the flat, square base that stands for the earth, the vertical form rises to a round section that stands for water, a conical section that is fire, an umbrella form that is air, and finally to a mitre-shape or leaf shape that represents ether—the mind, the spirit, and the void.

Aloobari is one of thousands of constructed *maṇḍala* forms. Its interior is spacious and high-ceilinged as it provides halls with room for assembled monks to gather for prayer, chanting, reading the sacred books, and instruction from high lamas.[6] The monks sit cross-legged on woolen carpets with small tables before them that receive manuscripts in the form of unbound pages within two wooden boards as book covers. The language is Tibetan, said to have developed during the seventh century reign of King Srong-tsan Gampo in relation to Sanskrit texts imported from India. The individual pages are removed from the stack one by one and piled neatly in order as the group readings by lamas continue for lengthy periods of the day. Cups of teas mixed with butter are usually poured and set before the lamas on the red-painted tables by young student monks. Each morning the main hall echoes with the hypnotic chanting of lamas in unison and, at times, extraordinary chanting or singing in chords. Such sounds, produced by individual monks, are heard nowhere but in Tibetan contexts. Drums, cymbals, and gongs are kept in the halls. Often stored in *gompas* or *lakhangs* for special occasions are the well-known long horns made of copper and brass that must rest on the ground while the monks blow them during important ceremonies. Their deep drone can be heard for miles in the hills and mountains.

Clarification may be needed here, for while the chanting activities in a Vajrayāna monastery may look to outsiders like habitual repetition of mere rote memorization, the fact is that Tibetan lessons and Tibetan doctrine are always subject to debate and clarification. Ganden Monastery outside of Lhasa, once one of the world's largest, is especially well-known as the setting for spirited contests of monks, contests that require quick wit and profound understanding. During the debates a pair of monks slap their hands together and move in a semi-aggressive way as argument proceeds point by point as if in a boxing ring. A victor rises in status for what he knows. Therefore, interpretive skill is a crucial measure of any monk's advancement through grades that can lead to high lama status.

The extended vestibule or porch at the front of Aloobari's second level leads to the door of the upper hall of worship, as does an interior stairway. One is reminded of the important feature of layering within Tibet-derived sacred buildings, so evocative of the spiritual climb that every Buddhist seeks to make—a climb toward *nirvāṇa* and universal understanding. On either side of the upper entrance are large and brilliantly colored paintings that show the traditional guardian kings of the four directions. This feature, shared with China, is one of the most commonly seen in painting. The guardian kings are elegantly garbed, and they wear armor and chain mail like that which is sometimes found hanging in secret rooms of monasteries. There it is a reminder that monks of the Buddhist *gompas* fought medieval wars, not only against outside invasion but sometimes among themselves.

Wall paintings on the second floor at Aloobari are more active and free that those below. They are brightened by much use of white paint while large centrally placed circles on the wall stand out among crowds of guardians, teachers, and Buddhas in order to emphasize various saints, some of whom are shown in *yab-yum* sexual union with their female *śaktis* while emitting rainbow beams of light. Above all this, the ceiling is lifted and the walls opened to accommodate glass windows,

Buddha with śakti *female principle in embrace. Tibetan woodblock print.*

creating the tower on top of the building. A very small space with railings toward the interior hall is provided with an image of Buddha and attendants.

The main image on the second floor, larger than life-size and made of painted clay, shows Padmasambhava as Guru Rinpoche, who has an evil-destroying sword on top of his golden hat and a three-pronged trident or spear that he carries loosely as another weapon against threats to the faith. The same spear is held by Śiva. His more earthy counterpart, King Srong-tsan Gampo, is sometimes represented with two lovely wives who stand beside him: Bhrikuti as his Nepalese princess and Wencheng as his princess from China. Both women are said to have been Buddhist and to have convinced the king to convert to Buddhism, so today they are both honored as incarnations of Tārā, Buddhist goddess of wisdom and truth. An intriguing question is whether it is true that Bhrikuti was the daughter of King Aṃśuvarman as Nepal's earliest great king.

To the teacher's left is found a mightily expressive representation of Mahākāla in asymmetrical, fighting stance as he holds the *dorje (vajra)* thunderbolt in one hand and the *ghaṇṭā* or bell of truth in the other. Just to the right of this figure is an honored seat for a prominent teacher, as is quite common in the main hall of a *gompa,* but this one is occupied by a nearly life-size portrait statue of the leader. The vibrant guardian above him wears a skirt of tiger skin and a girdle of severed human heads as well as a cape made from the flayed skins of an elephant and of a sinful human. The heads of the two skinned creatures can be seen near the guardian's right knee, and their limbs protrude near his ankles and below his shoulders. The gruesome image is intensified by its placement that presents the blue guardian/destroyer against a red background while the sculptural setting of a large halo glimmers with gold-painted flames. It is a suitable conclusion to this brief introduction to architecture and allied arts in the Darjeeling area as it anticipates the dramatic arts of Sikkim.

On the way to Sikkim the small settlement of Kalimpong, meaning "Minister's Stronghold," that is also called Kalibong or "Black Spur" by local people. At 4,100 feet above sea level, it is 51 kilometers east of Darjeeling and 78 kilometers from Gangtok in Sikkim by way of the Teesta River valley. The land here is thickly forested with the *sal* trees that are basic to Himalayan architecture. As noted, a new *lakhang* made of reinforced concrete was built here in 1975, and the Zangdog Palri Institute of Tibetology also was founded here. Kalimpong's Tharpa Choling Monastery of the Yellow Hat sect with its allegiance to the Dalai Lama is the original worship center here. It is entered through a vestibule that contains an enormous and functioning prayer wheel for any devotee to set in motion, while the wall behind it is painted with the Tibetan Wheel of Life. It is a substantial and well-kept building that is a stopping place for any pilgrims on their way to Sikkim.

The Wheel of Life is commonly found on Buddhist monasteries all through the Himalaya, often being painted on the left side of an entry portico. Such a pattern is said to present the world of attachment or Saṁsāra as delusion and a trap as it centers upon three creatures that stand for the web of crude desire. They are the rooster that stands for greed, the pig that represents ignorance, and the snake that stands for wrath and passion. Next comes a narrow circle that is divided in half with the lower section occupied by unhappy sinners and the upper half with happy people who are evidently redeemed. Around these central figures there are six segments of the total circle that represent six separate parts of existence as they are occupied by gods, *asura* spirits, humans, animals, "hungry ghosts," and the occupants of hell. John Blofeld goes on to explain that the outer rim of the painting has twelve sections, each of which has a picture that relates to the "chain of causality whereby beings are ensnared life after life."[7] The entire wheel is held in the grasp ot Yama, Lord of Death, in hideous form as he wears a crown of five human skulls. Above all of this it is common to find a figure of Buddha pointing to a second wheel—simpler and balanced with eight spokes—as the sacred wheel of Buddhist Dharma or Law within the Wheel of Life.

The former kingdom of Sikkim that is now an Indian state is 2,828 square miles in area, much smaller that its neighbors Nepal and Bhutan. Its varied elevations allow for crops of rice in lower valleys, rice and subtropical crops in Inner Himalayan valleys, and barley, potatoes, and other hardy crops at higher elevations. Copper and timber are abundant and various animals are raised, from goats to yaks. It is a very green and humid environment overall and one of the world's centers of orchid growing. The country was settled as early as the thirteenth century by Lepcha migrants from the Assam hills, and it came into its own as a political entity in 1641.

Sikkim is dominated by the view of Kanchenjunga at 28,162 feet. It is also dominated by Buddhism, which became the state religion in 1641 due to the efforts of the Dalai Lama, who came from Lhasa with two assistant lamas to instill the reformed faith.

The Dalai Lama appointed the first king of Sikkim, popularly called Penchoo Namgyal, and the newly defined kingdom related to Tibet as a kind of vassal state.[8] The third king of Tibet took the throne in 1700 as the "All-Victorious Thunderbolt-Bearer," Chagdor Namgyal. He is remembered as an effective ruler who established the custom of a great masked dance to be performed by lamas, especially at the time of Losar or Tibetan New Year when the dance is given as an offering to the mountain gods. Sikkim was invaded during the time of its fourth king, Chogyel Gyurme (1717–34), known as the "All-Victorious Inimitable King of Religion." The invaders came from Bhutan, and the smaller country was sacked and its citizens forced into slavery. When Chogyel Gyurme died and his young son was crowned, the governmet was taken over by a regent from Tibet. The sixth king, Tenzing Namgyal as "All-Victorious Preservor of Religious Doctrine" (1780–92), saw his country attacked by Bhutanese in the west and Gurkhas in the east so that its territory was much reduced by 1788–89.

Later Sikkimese struggles were with the British, represented by a Resident in Gangtok, and there was tension over Indian presence after India's independence in 1947. Sir Tashi Namgyal as Mahārāja of Sikkim signed a treaty with India in 1950, granting management of external affairs to Sikkim's powerful southern neighbor. Semi-independence was enjoyed by the King (Chogyal) of Sikkim, former Crown Prince Namgyal, and his American wife, the former Hope Cooke of New York City, until 1975. The palace in Gangtok is a large bungalow of basically western design but the royal chapel called Tsuklakhang is entirely eastern. It is a very beautiful monument that preserves Buddhist identity in today's secular country. Tsuklakhang was the setting for the wedding of the Buddhist ruler to Ms. Cooke before the Chogyal was crowned in 1964. The Institute of Tibetan Studies lies just outside the main town of Gangtok.

Sikkim was a hereditary monarchy until 1975, allowing for direct comparisons to the royal identities of Bhutan, and it is inevitable that questions should arise as to how Sikkim's monarchy ended. The king was still alive in 1975, with children to succeed him on the throne. Was he not in tune with the spirits of Kanchenjunga, around whose summit a cordon of respect was drawn so that humans would never trespass? Does the elimination of monarchy lessen the importance of the New Year's dance in which lamas whirl in timeless orbit of the greatest spirits? If the dance no longer takes place beside the Gangtok palace, is the royal chapel still open? Is the dance still performed at all? Official explanation of change tells the outsider that Sikkim "elected to join the Indian Union, seeking representation at the Parliament. India obliged." The special relationship that had been made official with a treaty signed by Jawaharlal Nehru in 1947, granting special status to Sikkim, came to an end.

The effects of changing political status on Sikkimese art could be negligible or they could be great. Today the majority of the population of Sikkim consists of Nepalese, not Bhutias or Lepchas. Where and when is the Black Hat Dance of Lossong (New Year) celebrated and is that Lepcha tradition—along with the Stag Dance, the Skeleton Dance, and various folk dances—still alive? What, if any, is the government contribution to monastery upkeep? Is comparison to Bhutan with its own United Nations representation not pertinent? These are questions of identity. Thus it is especially relevant to note the important features of Sikkimese architecture with its mixed memories of India, China, Nepal, Bhutan, and Tibet.

The name of Sikkim's capital, Gangtok, means "lofty hill" or "hill made flat" in recognition of the building of Gangtok Monastery in 1716. Above the city is Lukshyma hill, the "mother-of-pearl citadel" of the great mountain Kanchenjunga. The land around Gangtok is dotted with *stūpas* as reliquaries and funerary monuments that combine the mound of a grave. *Stūpas* have roots at least as early as the first Aryan contacts with India around 1500 B.C. and the white color and swelling form of an egg.[9] Thus each *stūpa* stands for the union of opposites as life and death. These funerary monuments capture the pattern of verticality and multiplicity that also belong to the Himalayan pagoda tradition. The most noteworthy of these monuments in the Gangtok area are the "Dul-dul" *stūpa* (Tib. *chorten*) that was made to honor Buddha's victory over evil and the *stūpa* that was erected in memory of the noted spiritual teacher Thrul-shik, who died in 1962.

Such representations of the cosmic axis and more are painted brilliant white and belong to a family of monuments that stretches from Ladakh to Colorado and beyond. Generally, a square base of four steps leads to a block of solid masonry that expands at the top in three extending ledges. These in turn support a foundation of five more steps, which underlie the swelling dome-shape of the *aṇḍa* or "egg," also called *garbha* or "womb," that is the swelling life-form of any *stūpa,* anywhere. On top of this bulbous element there is a square, a descendant of the classical *harmikā* or "high pavilion" that is seen on earliest monuments such as Sanchi's Great Stupa founded in the third century B.C. Then there is the spire as *yaṣṭi* as continuous axis often called *yūpa* and contained within the *cattravali* or spire of umbrellas as honorific parasol that takes on particularly Tibetan elaboration. It is made of gold and brass, typically with seven circular rings, then a pierced metal umbrella that first supports a combined sun and moon and then, at the very top, a *kalaśa* or vase/jewel that radiates riches that are the truth of Buddhism.

Adrian Snodgrass best defines the meaning of the jewel, as he does for all elements of *stūpa* design and meaning. He explains that when the jewel is located at the top of the World Axis it is the diamond or *vajra* (which also means adamantine thunderbolt) and that the *vajra*-jewel is both the summit and the summation of the entire axial pillar below. In its special position at the top of the *stūpa* it may be called "the unique Principle of the whole edifice and thus the unique Principle of the whole cosmos."[10] The jewel is at the highest point of the invisible "dome" that encloses the entire monument. Snodgrass adds:

> Having ascended the levels of the *stūpa* in meditation, the *yogin* (practitioner of *yoga*) has reached the ultimate pinnacle of its structure. From here he steps into the Void. He has achieved total Enlightenment and realized the Buddhahood that lay concealed within him. He steps beyond the symbol into Silence.[11]

Sikkimese architecture is important to this study as it shows substantial and spatial construction that results from repetition and expansion of the perfect square of the modular *maṇḍala*. This is a building tradition that is often termed Tibetan, but which has its beginnings, like the *stūpa* mound, in exalted geometry that was first introduced to India by the Aryans in the second millenium B.C.

The Tsuklakhang as royal chapel is impressive from the outside even without reference to symbolism. It is a three-storied, square building with its uppermost level essentially there to serve as a clerestory and provide diffused light to the interior. Its whitewashed walls are slightly battered, and vary in thickness so as to be thinner at the top and thereby slanted on the outside, and there are six large windows on each side, with four at the front that are placed on either side of a large rectangular terrace that, like the windows, is glassed. There are no windows at the back, as suits the shadowed altar areas inside. Thus visitors, having passed through the dazzlingly painted vestibule, find themselves in the kind of deep and spacious prayer hall with altar at the back that is also standard in the Darjeeling area. Again, the underlying reference is to Tibet and India in everything that this art stands for and conveys.

All of the small corners of the yellow-painted roofs turn up in curved pieces of metal, and the center of the upper roof is a vertical pinnacle painted gold. Four very large snow lions made of wood project out at the level of the cornice that connects the upper row of windows. All of the windows have three-dimensional lintel carvings, cloth curtains on the outside like a kind of valance, and a broad curtain sewn of gold and white cloth which covers and protects the chapel vestibule, a space that is filled with dramatic color and story. The windows are surrounded by flat painted enclosures that give the illusion of being frames but are simply black borders. These, like the walls, create a battered and pyramidal design that makes the building look especially sturdy. This feature anticipates the massive impact of Drugyal Dzong in Bhutan, Tongsa Dzong in central Bhutan as the royal family's ancestral seat in that country, and the castle watchtower called Yumbu Lakhang as "Fortress of Life" that towers beside a temple of Tibet's patron saint, Tārā Dolma, in Tibet's Yarlung Valley. This last tower, believed to be more than 2,000 years old, was leveled during China's Cultural Revolution (1966–76), and was faithfully rebuilt by 1985. Once again architecture is the hallmark of a civilization.

Returning now to the Royal Chapel in Gangtok, the evocative structure is especially notable for its vestibule: the *pronaos* that precedes the *naos* as *sanctum* in early Mediterranean terms. Whether or not this place of preparation and transition—as one leaves the mundane world outside for the visionary world inside—is derived from the *maṇḍapa* or porch of early Indian temples is not certain; but it is as essential to the complete temple in Sikkim as anywhere else on the subcontinent. There are three double doors in the vestibule, each painted brilliant red and adorned with horizontal strips of *repoussé* brass and large pierced bosses with ring-shaped door handles. A simpler door to the right side affords access to the upstairs by a narrow stairway.

The walls and ceiling of the ten-foot-deep entry are plastered and covered completely with bright paintings that provide guardian kings, sacred formulae in Tibetan script, plus garlands of gold, jewels, and pearls that are sometimes referred to as a "necklace of the gods." Thick, three-dimensional paint is used selectively, as at Aloobari in Darjeeling, and all three ceiling panels that front the main doors are filled with glowing jewel forms, clouds, and swirling *yin-yang* symbols in rainbow colors. Guardian kings stand to either side of the red entry doors, and there is a painting of an ancestral monastery enclosed by a circular wall that suggests Samye Monastery in Tibet. In all its elaboration, the chapel has the same heavenly references as the simpler *stūpa*.

The grassy lawn in front of the chapel is marked by a circular path of earth that resembles the track of someone learning to ride a bicycle, but that is hardly its purpose. This is the main path of dancing that takes place during the ceremony called Kagey Thuetor as "Worship of the Snowy Range" and the celebrations of the Tibetan New Year. Ideal geometry is expressed here as monks in elaborate Black Hat costumes follow the large circle while whirling their bodies in a tight circle, usually supporting themselves on one foot, in tighter circles around the center. They dance in front of the royal chapel while, in a single story hall to the left of the main building, a religious superior watches carefully while dressed in multicolored brocade and wearing a broad-brimmed black hat. This headpiece has a golden sun and moon at the front, openwork dragons in silhouette on either side, a human skull near the top, and a tall peacock plume with mirror at the center. Just as important is the superbly embroidered apron that he and each dancer wears. It shows the large and glaring face of Kāla, the black visage of time and desire.

Other religious centers in Sikkim provide for more regular and broader uses than Tsulakhang at the palace, which is essentially a temple rather than a monastery for large numbers of monks. They are all in close proximity to Kanchenjunga, their focus of animistic and physical force and there, as in Namche Bazaar on the Nepalese trekking route to Mt. Everest (Sagarmatha), the sound of avalanche is an almost constant reminder of the precariousness of human existence. Madanjeet Singh describes Sikkim as a bowl-like basin barely 60 kilometers wide as it is bordered by two steep transverse ridges in north-south alignment, each about 120 kilometers long. Tibet traditionally refers to Sikkim as Denjong, the "hidden valley of rice." Trade with Tibet took place through the Chumbi Valley that is bordered to the north by the Mimidri or Great Himalayan Chain.[11]

Buddhist connections are mainly to the Nyingma-pa or Red Hat school that also includes Kargyu-pa lineage. Nyingma-pa adherents trace their origin to the miracle-working saint Padmasambhava (Guru Rinpoche), while Kargyu-pa followers trace their doctrine to the teachings of Marpa (1012–97 A.D.) as the master of Mila-Repa (1040–1123 A.D.) and to traditions of Hatha Yoga schools in India. Other subgroupings of the Nyingma-pas include the Karma-pa lineage founded by Tusum Khyen-pa (1110–93), the Drigung-pa founded by Drigung Rinpoche (1143–1216), the Shang-pa of Shang-Rinpoche (1123–93), and others. Most monasteries in the state are Nyingma-pa, but Kargyu-pa exceptions include Phodang, Raland, and the very significant Rumtek Monastery as traditional seat of the Karmapa Lama. All of the schools honor the eighty-four great Siddhas or saints and demi-gods of Tantric belief, and it is noteworthy that these also are revered by followers of the Hindu god Śiva.[12]

It is useful to continue this discussion of Sikkimese art and belief by pausing once more to consider the exalted personage of Padmasambhava. In art the great teacher and savior is usually shown seated on a lotus throne with his legs in yogic posi-

Tibetan woodblock print of the sainted teacher Padmasambhava.

tion. He wears robes of many layers and his broad black hat or crown is of a type that is still worn by his successors. The three-pronged weapon that was mentioned earlier is held against his chest; it is a sign of his victory over all evil beings in Tibet and adjacent Buddhist lands as he preached the doctrine of the *Tantrayogācharya*. He also holds in his right hand the thunderbolt that enables him to cast spells and exorcize evil, and a *pātra* or begging bowl in his lap, the usual vessel of any Buddhist monk who has rejected all earthly attachments. His gaze is intense, even angry, for his function is both most benevolent and difficult: to cleanse the world on behalf of all living beings.

The Siddhas (Mahāsiddhas) are described as Tantric followers who were devoted to psychic culture that enabled them to attain supernatural powers, especially through mental and physical exercises called *sādhanā*. In order to perform psychophysical rites, the Siddhas had to be joined by female forces known as dākinīs. The dākinīs are believed to have written the essential doctrine that Padmasambhava brought with him to Tibet in the eighth century, and in the developed pantheon of Vajrayāna Buddhism they have high status as part of a new Tantric trilogy: Lama-Yidam-Kandroma, which Singh defines as spiritual perception, tutelary divinity, and mystic partner.[13] This is quite different from the three refuges of the earliest Buddhist school: Buddha, Dharma or law, and Sangha or monastic community. This helps to explain why Tantric murals in the hills are so very different from their prototypes at places like Ajanta, where Hinayāna and Mahayāna imagery had a tradition of more than 1,000 years, beginning around the third century B.C. At times they are crowded with calm figures of Siddhas and leaping action of naked dākinīs.

Pemayangtse Monastery was founded during the reign of Chagdor Namgyal, who took the throne upon his father's death in 1700 A.D. The construction is said to have been directed by Jigmi Pao as Chief Lama of the realm, the individual who also supervised the building of Tashiding Monastery in 1715. In both of these places fine clay sculpture is found, showing that even when good quality and durable wood was abundant, Tantric tradition sometimes favored the greater naturalism of clay. Grimacing Bhairava or the awesome Mahākāla, for instance, takes on almost overly convincing naturalism. Sculptures are more than just realistic when they give the illusion of naturally soft, swelling flesh, and strips of drapery fly around them with convincing weightlessness even though the raw material is clay. The images may remind one of Japanese Buddhism's experiments with absolutely convincing "portraits" of supernatural characters like the many-armed Ashura during the Nara Period of 645–794 A.D. At that time in Japan it was deemed essential that otherwordly characters be truly convincing because grandeur and intensity were both important goals. The same may be said of Sikkimese images right up to the present. Like the famous dancing of New

Year's celebrants in Sikkim, these artworks enter our own space so that we feel we are not just observors but participants.

The entry to Pemayangtse Temple is almost as impressive as that of the Royal Chapel, with its great red doorway having metal bands, bosses, and tasseled rings that are just as ornate. This building on its hilltop is believed to be the second oldest in Sikkim, with its forebear called Paimionchi or "Sublime Perfect Lotus" now existing only as a ruin of its former grandeur. From more than a mile away prayer flags attached to tall wooden poles wave their woodblock-printed prayers endlessly as prelude to the experience of the architecture. A visitor walks between two rows of these toward the lofty goal. Pemayangtse is found at an elevation of 6,840 feet and is the superior center of rule and tradition for the other Nyingm-pa monasteries of the country. It evidently did not impress Alexandra David-Neel when she visited the Mahārāja, Sidkeong Tulku, during her wide-ranging travels in and near Tibet. Perhaps feeling superior in her own fine Tibetan robes, she wrote that,

> The monks of Sikkim are for the most part illiterate and have no desire to be enlightened, even about Buddhism which they profess. Nor, indeed have they the necessary leisure. The *gompas* of Sikkim are poor, they have but a very small income and no rich benefactors.[14]

Poor or not, the *gompas* and *lakhangs* of Sikkim continue the wondrously imaginative and powerful arts—especially in painting—that one expects to find within the Tibetan sphere of influence.

Pemayangtse is similar to the Royal Chapel in having two floors with a smaller superstructure as third level. It, too, is covered with corrugated metal roofs that have been painted yellow, and it has a similar distribution of large glazed windows along with its columned vestibule that is topped by a wide porch, itself enclosed by glass windows. There are two side doors on the façade, rather than a passage off of the vestibule as in Gangtok, and the battered walls have their slanting silhouette repeated in painted window frames. Two rather thin columns stand at the front of the vestibule and its ceiling is fairly simple, with gold medallion designs that recall circles woven into Chinese silk. Inside, however, the altar is magnificent as it displays the still little-known artistry of Sikkimese sculpture in clay.

It is recorded that in 1981, six years after the change of government, the twelve principal monasteries of Sikkim still received government grants and that the Sikkim Darbar or center of government had an ecclesiastical department. The influence of the monasteries was dwindling yearly, however, a situation that might be expected when Sikkim became the twenty-eighth state of a secular country rather than a theocracy. Nonetheless, if one considers the tremendous influence that Hindu Devaswam boards in Kerala state of southwestern India have right to the present, perhaps Sikkim can maintain its Buddhist identity. J. S. Lal notes that the last Chogyal, himself an incarnate lama well versed in Buddhist principles, set up a training school or *cheda* for about forty monks and novices; that the Namgyal Institute of Tibetology was established at Deorali partly with the Queen's sponsorship; and that an impetus of a different type was given by His Holiness and Karmapa Rinpoche as renowned teacher and mystic who drew the faithful from all over the world to Buddhist revival. This remarkable, inspirational leader performed the famed and most sacred Ceremony of the Black Crown in many parts of the world, and this writer has seen thousands of Buddhist and non-Buddhist witnesses struck dumb by the sight of the velvet headpiece when it was revealed as the concentrated heritage of Kargu-pa wisdom. Any person who has been received by the late Karmapa Lama, perhaps in his quiet sitting room and study where he often kept cages of his beloved pet birds, is unlikely ever to lose touch with his wisdom, his compassion, and his joy.

Rumtek monastery is the home of the Karmapa Lama, and the hillside complex awaits the miraculous recognition of the current incarnation of the master. The buildings are set against a green hillside a few miles from Gangtok with the dwelling place of the Karmapa Lama set above it and reached by a steep but pleasant walk. The worship hall is very wide in comparison to others that have been noted here, and for all of its careful detail it is a restored and reconstructed building with a frame of concrete, not wood. It is perhaps for this reason that Rumtek Monastery is absent from most studies of traditional architecture in the Himalaya. Such omission is a mistake.

Rumtek is the main site of living Buddhist tradition in Gangtok and one of the important centers of world Buddhism. The Rumtek Monastery temple and seat of His Holiness the Karmapa Lama as great teacher and incarnate Rinpoche is three stories high with an octagonal tower, and all floors have large glass windows, including some of plate glass. The Karmapa Lama has prestige like that of the Dalai Lama and Panchen Lama in the orders of Tibetan Buddhism, and his followers are many in east and west. The Karmapa Lama is traditionally known as a Tulku—a recognized incarnation of departed dignitaries—and this custom of Tibet and Mongolia puzzles even Buddhists of other schools who do not seek out the reincarnation of a particular individual in a child.

The rectangular shrine complex faces its walled courtyard and a breathtaking view across a river valley to the rolling hills of Tibet. The setting is very lush. Further up the hillside are two smaller buildings, one a chapel and the other a subsidiary dwelling. The hillside itself is marked by crowds of vertical prayer flags, with thick forest above them. No structures are found above the second building of the honored leader, and the village of Rumtek and the functional monastery housing of the monks are located below the sanctuary itself. Its very large courtyard is paved with asphalt and stone as it is enclosed by protective walls and by small rooms for food preparation, storage, woodblock printing, and other uses. As in Tibet, the courtyard is essential both as a place for ritual dancing by the lamas and a gathering place for pilgrims.

Eight tapered columns support the second floor of Rumtek temple and allow for an especially colorful and spacious vestibule at the first floor. There are three main doorways and to the right a single small door of access to the second floor with ladder. As noted above, the materials are modern but the sacred symbolism is traditional and intact. Extended capitals have auspicious symbols amid cloud patterns that blend into blue vegetation and blue clouds that "drip" down the red columns like frosting. This is a variation upon established column, capital, and entablature design, and the curving contours of the upper portions almost negate the impression of strong support.

As explained by Thubten Legshay Gyatso, the eighteenth Chogay Trinchen of the new monastery at Buddha's birthplace in Lumbini, Nepal, the standard column elements are defined from bottom to top as follows. The *ka-ba* is a post with lotus-base *bre* above as transition to the capital. This is divided into four horizontal sections, two with small blocks called *bre chung,* below the uppermost section that extends out from both sides as scalloplike cloud forms. These are part of the *zhu ring* or long bow. A narrow beam seat or *gdung gdan* is interjected to underly the main lintel called the *dgung ma*. Then follows a band called *klu thig* in honor of the supernatural *nāga* snakes that are believed to dwell under the ground and in all waters. Continuing upward, it is typical to find a row of lotus petals designated by the Indian term *padma,* then a row of elaborately three-dimensional checkerboard patterns that are called *chos brtsegs* or "*dharma* (law) stacks," but often identified as thunderbolts. A higher, cantilevered level may be painted with flaming jewel patterns and/or lotus flowers and the auspicious endless knot, while proper rafters above these are often given floral (lotus) designs at the ends. Narrow layers between cantilever beams are called *bab skyangs bskums* and ceiling planks or *gral ma* are supported by all that is below.[15] Such order is followed for both interior and exterior columns. Inside, however, the usual order is sometimes obscured by hanging cloth banners and *tanka* paintings that may be displayed all around the study and chanting spaces used by monks. But the elaborate sculptural/structural elements are still deemed to be essential to meaning as well as stability.

Outside, cloth banners are normally attached to the lintels of the three main doors at Rumtek as at any such temple, but the central door has its own unusual and evocative element above the lintel: a row of life-size lion-dogs. They suggest Chinese prototypes as they are painted white, wear double bell-necklaces, and hold in their paws such sacred emblems as the sacred jewel and the conch shell. Their large teeth are very white and their manes are partly painted green. They function like rows of mythical females with exposed genitalia carved above entrances of the Maori, in New Zealand: they keep bad spirits out.

A "portrait" of a great monastery of Tibet that is related by sect and history to Rumtek (presumably one that was destroyed after 1950 and the Cultural Revolution of the 1960s) is painted to show a bright red building of six floors as part of the vestibule murals. It serves as a reminder of the

Kargyupa lineage of great teachers and of historical places that are the foundation of Rumtek. This is a reminder of a sect that highly values asceticism as it traces its heritage back through Mila-Repa, poet-saint of Tibet, to the eleventh century Lama Marpa and his teacher Naropa. Blofeld records that "Many of its members pass much of their lives in lonely caves absorbed in Tantric meditations" and that Kargyupas "tend generally to be austere; they adhere more strictly to Buddhist rules of discipline than do the Nyingma-pas and often practise a type of meditation that is almost identical with that of Zen." He refers to the Sakyapas as tracing their lineage back to the reforming Indian sage Atīśa who spent his last years in Tibet before his death in 1052 A.D. He also states that his Red Hat sect is nearest to the Gelugpa, which has its own great reformer, Tsong-Khapa of the fifteenth century A.D. It was in 1640 that the leader of this sect, His Holiness the Dalai Lama, became king as well as pontiff of Tibet.[16]

Guardian kings of suitable verve are placed around and between the Rumtek entry doors. The small door to the right is attended by a *dvārapāla,* a Sanskrit term for "doorkeeper," who holds a staff topped by a circular banner. The ceiling of the vestibule has a whirling, circular *maṇḍala* at its center, just a hint of the coloristic effects to be found inside. The guardians of the four directions are together called "Gyelchen shi" meaning "four great kings," and their usual placement is in an entry vestibule as at Rumtek. The white-colored guardian of the east is Yulkhorsung, who holds a lute. The south is represented by green Phakyepo, who holds a sword in his right hand while his left hand rests on the weapon's scabbard. The western guardian is Chenmisamng, who is red and holds a small *chorten,* while the northern king Namtoese is yellow as he holds a banner in his left hand and a mongoose spitting jewels in his left. Occasionally all four figures are painted gold.

Chinese-type dragons hang at the center of the entry portals, and one's eye is led upward from this flash of metal to auspicious symbols in *repoussé* metal rondels that are themselves mounted on a wide reddish band below the second roof—reflecting that more traditional Tibetan construction which uses thick layers of reeds, painted maroon red, as insulation under such roofs. The second roof is topped at the center by two golden deer that stand for the deer park at Sarnath in India, where Buddha preached his first sermon. The animals face inward to flank a golden wheel that represents the Dharma or Law that Buddha "set in motion" at that great event. It is a very frequent symbol in Buddhist architecture and is found in Tibet on Lhasa's Jokhang temple as well as on the Potala itself—that awesome replica in Lhasa of the heavenly palace that belongs to Avalokiteśvara as most compassionate bodhisattva. The same symbolism of deer and wheel is part of the carving of Buddha in chunar sandstone that dates from the fifth century and the Gupta period in the Sarnath Museum. The story is one of the most common to be told in the mountains. Finally, the great hall is crowned by a golden *stūpi* of combined vase and jewel symbolism that is pan-Himalayan. There are six cylindrical banners of cloth on wooden frames on top of the building.

The central image on the altar inside Rumtek's main temple shows Buddha seated in a pose of meditation, with so many offering scarves on his body that the exact iconography is difficult to discern. His hair and eyes are painted blue, while his body of twice life-size is made of pieces of pounded metal joined together. The method recalls Nepal and Tibet as well as Ladakh. To his left is a smaller figure of Padmasambhava, and there are attendants to his right side. The usual second floor altar complex that is seen at Sikkim's Pemayangtse and other buildings of more than one floor is here replaced by a raised and draped throne that is meant to be occupied by the Karmapa Lama himself. The throne is fronted by elephant tusks standing on the floor to either side as especially auspicious offerings. Considerable illumination enters this upper space through large windows in the side walls and through the clerestory on the top of the building, next to which there is a room for private worship and study. It is easy to imagine this room as a formal yet intimate place for instruction and prayer.

In total, Rumtek Monastery of the Kargyu-pa lineage is a grand compound and a hopeful sign for the future of Himalayan art. It utilizes modern materials to replace more vulnerable wood and reeds without losing established effects, its paintings by twentieth century artists are of quality as high as those of the past, it is financially secure, and it has become a pilgrimage center for believers from everywhere. The sacred dances still go on, the costumes still are worn, and the face of Yama as horrific force of death and judgment is painted on a small door that leads to the most frightful and most threatening space of all. The latter kind of room will be visited elsewhere in these pages. Rumtek is complete.

A very different focus from the grandeur of Rumtek with its view of all Gangtok on a distant hill is Sikkim's rugged domestic architecture. Examples of houses and sheds built in the Himalayan way could be drawn from any of the regions that this study treats. Sikkim is as appropriate, and as instructive, as any. From nearby Rumtek, from Pemayangtse's compound, and from Kalimpong, three humble structures are chosen. Each one relates absolutely to the structures of temples and palaces but as miniature and much less finished buildings. A very ruined house in Old Rumtek, as the less central area away from the temple is called, reveals half-timber construction that is almost like that of Tudor building in England, for it consists of heavy beams that are visible from outside in a squared complex with fill inside the frame. This fill is of stone for important buildings in Sikkim, as in Bhutan, whereas in Nepal it would be of brick. In the case of this collapsing house the fill is a kind of wattle and daub, as sticks are coated with mud while spaces between them are filled with a mixture of mud and the dung of cows or yaks. Then a smooth layer of mud is put on and finally covered by whitewash. A low foundation of fitted stones supports the house. There is minimal ornament—some carved "thunder" patterns *(chos brtsegs),* boxes and circles cut into the frame of a window—but this is very simple domestic architecture. More "finished" dwellings, each two stories high and walled with rock below their corrugated metal roofs and carved window screens, are found next to the monastery of Pemayangtse as in Gangtok itself.

A collapsing prayer hall of Old Rumtek shows heavy materials that are used to make more substantial and lasting buildings, be they religious or secular. Here, as all through the mountains, the materials are frame and fill. But the more massive wooden beams have stones placed between them, and ornamentation of the exterior columns follows a simplified version of the classic design that is described above. The stone walls are not plastered but are painted over with the usual combination of whitewash and red-orange ochre.

Finally there is a very simple house on the road near the Tibetology Institute in Kalimpong. Its three rooms do not rest on a stone foundation and its walls, painted white and ochre, are made of wattle and daub. It is covered with pieces of metal that are themselves topped by many stones—showing that the winds of the high ranges are always a threat. This same concern leads people of Himachal Pradesh in the west to make shingles out of slabs of slate.

The area occupied by Darjeeling has been shown to be an amalgam of eastern and western tradition while Kalimpong and Sikkim are still whole, or largely so, in terms of indigenous values and goals. Religious leaders of the past seem to be almost as alive and influential as those who speak to the people now. In spite of general poverty, shrines, temples, and monasteries are showered with precious gifts, and references to Tibet and to India are constant. The physical features of monuments great and small are recorded now as insurance against the kind of loss that fire brought to Thyangboche Gompa in the 1980s in Solo Khumbu in Nepal. Perhaps the traditions of form and meaning will continue uninterrupted, for there are some signs of hope. New monastery structures recently put up at Bodhnath in Kathmandu Valley suggest that this is so. The establishment of Buddhist Studies centers in many parts of the world, even the building of new and completely traditional *gompas* and *chortens* on several continents, is encouraging. The rich heritage of Himalayan art is being understood more and more by outsiders. Exhibitions of Tibetan and Himalayan art draw crowds. A large and elaborate *chorten* is being completed now near Fort Collins, Colorado. Foreigners who are exposed to such art must constantly measure their own concepts of artistic judgment against those of the people who made the art. R. A. Stein reminds us in his *Tibetan Civilization* that,

> We should not conclude that the products of these craftsmen fall short of being great works of art, for all their creators' humility and religious preoccupations. Tibetans are certainly capable of evaluating the quality or execution of a work aesthetically. But it is above all the religious subject that they are interested in. So we miss the whole point, of some of the paintings at any rate, if we admire composition and col-

ours that are not due to the painter's free choice but imposed on him by textbooks of ritual. The mandalas, for instance, whose well-ordered symmetry would delight a town planner, are likely to give the European beholder an impression of stylistic elegance or an aesthetic satisfaction that were not intended by the artist, and are not felt by a Tibetan audience.[17]

Perhaps even Sikkim, its Buddhist theocracy a thing of the past and its society marked by newcomers to this small and vulnerable state within the overwhelming entity of India, will somehow survive. If so, its art will help to define its identity.

This brief introduction to Sikkimese art has touched upon the time and place of this tradition, but mostly looked for Tibetan traditions that appear in Sikkim with varying degrees of change. Open floor plans, high ceilings, windows at all levels, and coloristic arts are very different from the rule of sacred sanctuaries in most of India even though terminology and purposes of arts are often related. A *śikhara* temple like that of Badrinath in Dwarahat is almost a stranger, with its vertical projections and massive stonework, while there is a temple at Joshimath as "home" to the Indo-Mongoloid Bhotia people that was built, according to legend, by Jagat Guru Śaṅkarācharya more than 1,200 years ago. Neither of these has the coloristic impact of arts in the Tibetan tradition, however.

Along with the general qualities of open space and colored walls with glittering sculptures in areas touched by Tibet, many exceptions exist that stand solely on their own merits. For example, the grounds of Pemayangtse Monastery hold a small shrine building—the Manilakhang as freestanding chapel of prayer repetition. Its way of repeating prayers is hard to match in any other religious tradition. This is a substantial building made of well-dressed and fitted stones. Roofed with corrugated metal, it rests on a low base of stone and its height is about that of a two-story house. But the building does not function to enclose space; its primary function is to be a solid marker upon and around which well over one hundred metal prayer wheels are hung. As a worshipper circumambulates this monument with his or her right side toward the center, it is easy to reach out one's right hand and launch hundreds, even thousands of prayers in a few moments. This is the height of practicality applied to a mystical purpose. The building goes much further than do "*mani* walls" that rise as stacks of stones inscribed, again, with the sacred formula Om Mani Padme Hum as "Hail to the Jewel in the Lotus" because the invocation is repeated so many more times by using the wheels with prayers inside.

The interior of the Pemayangtse building that is a hanger for prayer wheels does have some murals on the inner walls, but it is essentially a storehouse for clay statues. None of these is of high quality, although one Buddha or teacher on a high shelf is noticeable for its odd hairstyle that is a kind of upsweep chignon not seen elsewhere except, perhaps, as the hair worn by Kannon (Kuanyin or Avalokiteśvara) images in Japan and China. It is not lack of gold or jewels that make the rest of the images, half life-size or slightly larger, seem minor. Rather, it is messy application of paint, perhaps as the result of overzealous renewal, that makes them seem carelessly done.

Perhaps long-term patronage rather than such factors as age or placement determines excellence in monastic arts. Two other fairly recent shrines, at Dubde and Sangacholing, are each two stories high with walls of dressed stone, the second combining cast concrete with wood for parts that are normally made of wood alone, and it has already been noted that such substitution does not necessarily lessen quality. When photographed for this study, Dubde had already received wall murals and their color served as background for a number of clay statues, including a rather disturbing dark figure with crown of skulls that was barely discernible in the darkness. Sangacholing still had unpainted walls to set off its few clay sculptures of mediocre quality. Again, what are the features of impressive clay images if neither of these shrines has any to show? Flat white paint deadens figures while pasted-on ornamentation and overall flatness of a complex image like Avalokiteśvara with 1,000 arms can "kill" the image for a foreign viewer. But perhaps the correctness of iconography is more important than beauty, and a foreigner may come to the art with unrelated measures of aesthetic success.

In spite of the cautions noted above, one may say that Sikkim's Sinon Monastery is very impressive, especially the main altar on its north wall that is shown in a two-page color photograph in Madanjeet Singh's *Himalayan Art,* but the individual figures of the seated Buddha with the *arhats*

Shariputra and Maudgalyayana on his left and right, and eight Dhyāni or directional bodhisattvas flanking them all appear to be frozen. Silver paint on two of the statues flattens their volumes by reflecting light, and the unpainted gray wall behind them robs them of strong color contrast. The photograph seems to have too much light. But is it for the foreigner to criticize aesthetic choices made according to local custom? Is there an indigenous aesthetic at work here to replace measures of excellence that some would call international? The questions remain open.

A very boldly colored painting of Gaṇeśa, the elephant-headed son of Śiva, in the second floor hall of Pemayangtse Gompa near Gangtok is not what might be called a "masterwork" in a study of this kind. It is an icon—not an idol to be worshipped for itself but a symbol of an ideal—and its iconography and iconometry are correct as the deity fans out twelve arms while brandishing symbols of his many powers as Defeater of Obstacles. His vehicle, the rat, is easily recognized at his feet, while both the lotus flower base and the multihued halo are appropriate to Gaṇeśa. Yet the colors, especially the white head on the red body with garland of green, seem quite raw. Even the reflective gold ornaments are too "obvious" for most western tastes. Local devotees may advise that the art needs time to "mellow," for this painting is quite new. Yet its bright colors are essential to full identification of the character shown. Can it be that the viewer has an unrecognized and perhaps romantic need to see such art only with the accumulation of darkening coating of soot and oily residue that come inside a worship space with age? Is there a parallel here to the nineteenth century's search for European romance in a cult of ruins? If so, it has nothing to do with the goals of Himalayan artists. Those young people who now study the making of such images apply clear colors along with classic symbols and measurements just as their guidebooks and teachers prescribe.

Returning to the subject of sculpture in clay, it seems that some widely recognized standards of quality do apply. Examples of successful arts include four clay sculptures that were photographed in a storeroom of Pemayangtse Gompa. The first two represent bodhisattva characters, one with multiple heads, and all seated in relaxed poses on lotiform bases. The other two represent *dharmapālas* as defenders of the Buddhist Law. The second pair take active asymmetrical poses of the kind that is studied by every Tibetan artist. They are perfectly balanced, their proportions and poses having been determined according to a strictly drawn geometric grid. Yet the larger of the two defenders is superior, an image to be treasured, for the perfected handling of clay as the sculptural material. The malleability of clay and its capacity to present pure volumes that are convincing as "flesh" are exploited. Because the face is painted red, it first draws the viewer's eye. One is held there by a grimace, not only of open mouth and prominent teeth below and *three* glaring eyes above, but by wrinkles at the stretched lips and bulging cheek muscles. In other words, the artist has looked at the whole figure from the inside and made everything about it tense and struggling. It is like the forceful fury of protective spirits that the Japanese best captured during the Kamakura Period (1185–1333) with artists like Unkei and his followers.

The active body stance in captured diagonal action of Sikkimese characters adds to their drama, but the "performance" does not depend on the action-packed pose alone. Every line and movement is cohesive as the main protector almost dances. Lines and textures of both clothing and jewelry move across his rotund form and almost freestanding drapery whips around him and up over his head. This is the kind of believable intensity that can make clay sculpture of the Himalaya unforgettable. And so can gentle calm.

The framing of such images, like the figures of Buddha with begging bowl and the sainted Padmasambhava on Pemayangtse's main altars, can make them the center of an almost "noisy" vortex of breathtaking gold and colored accretions, but within all that, the main artistic statement needs to be heard. One of the clearest messages of art in clay is conveyed in the shrine room of Alchi in Ladakh that survives from the eleventh to twelfth centuries. To be found there are marvelous combinations of straightforward presentation and complex iconography. One "listens" to their softly detailed message. But the seventeenth to eighteenth century clay image of Hevajra with his *śakti* at Pemayangtse booms forth its power and beauty.

One final monument of Sikkim will be considered, perhaps not just for exposure but for further artistic interpretation. The place is Enchen. Bhu-

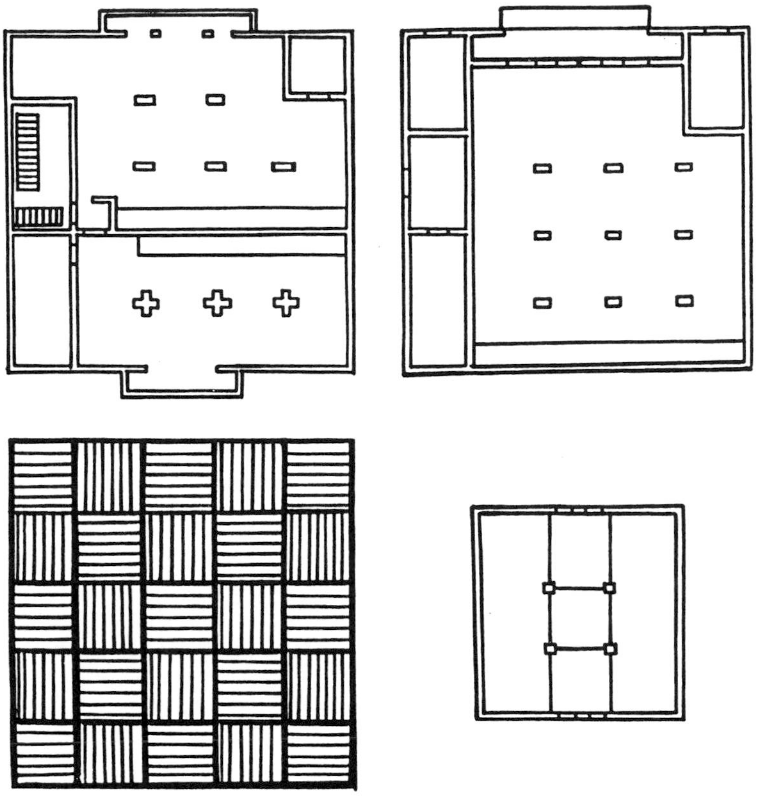

Plan and ceiling pattern of the three-storey monastery temple of Thyangboche in Solo Khumbu, Nepal. The main floor is on the upper left, second floor on upper right, and small tower with windows on the lower right. Modular ceiling pattern also shown.

tan, Tibet, Nepal, and Sikkim became havens to Tantric Buddhist monks and other refugees from the plains as Muslim invaders came to the Himalayan borderlands during the twelfth century and later. Philip Rawson notes in *The Art of Tantra* that Nepal is a special case because Hinduism survived alongside Buddhism in that country, while the other places of refuge integrated earlier and shamanistic faiths like Bön Po with Buddhism. In fact, Nepal did the same. The real point may be that the amalgam of centuries of cross-fertilization and scholarly debate is responsible for both the iconographic intensity and the special force of monastic art in the Himalaya. Enchen Gompa is an example as it stands three full stories high, with a fourth level that is a roofed clerestory to provide light to the spaces below. It is a living monument in every way, and very large numbers of men, women, and children come to Enchen for teaching and blessing by high lamas. The modular design, based on the multiplication of perfect squares, has allowed the *gompa* to expand, but even so it is necessary for a large tented area to be extended from the front of the monument when mass instruction occurs. Rapt attention greets the preachings of honored men at this place. And prayer flags on strings are hung from trees and bushes all over the temple grounds and beyond.

The vestibule of Enchen is home to some of the most skillfully painted representations of directional kings that are to be found anywhere. One—Yulkhorsung as guardian of the east—strums his lute with an expression that is both serious and serene. His armored partner wears red-orange clothing that flashes against a background of gold. The most ferocious protector vibrates in dark blue skin color against red flames. Jewelry is precise and three-dimensionally detailed, and the treatment of faces shows the easy touch of a master artist. Gruesome features, like offering bowls containing tongues, eyes, and a human heart, are rendered as delicately as Easter baskets in the West. Even though the walls of the main floor have minimal paint of their own, the sculptural groupings that are set up against them on altars have entwined detail that is striking. Somehow, Sikkimese Buddhist art needs to appear in a jewel box setting in order to look its best.

The altar on the second floor at Enchen is subdued, with a single seated figure of Buddha that is attended by two fully round *arhats,* but the walls above and around this threesome, even a step of the altar in front of them, hold so many *tanka* paintings framed in silk or under glass that they produce the kind of flat patterns of contrasting colors that are usually supplied by murals. Perhaps such accumulative effect is essential to Himalayan arts, for the arts of Vajrayāna Buddhism are widely expected to be colossal, multiple, and precious. This is part of their definition.

On the main floor the groupings have stronger impact. Sculptures of teachers, saints, and four bodhisattvas attend Buddha here, the central icon being blue-haired, wrapped in cloth, and painted brilliant gold. The treatment of his gentle face is the result of Gupta/Pāla-Sena/Nepalese inventions and tastes, and the image could be called "classic." But two other sculptural complexes at Enchen may be said to literally outshine this first group. A triple-headed Heruka is life-size and shown in *yab-yum* pose with his *śakti* almost crushed against his body. Heruka is the beneficent Vajrasattva bodhisattva in wrathful form, and a being that is taken on by an initiate along with the exacting and dangerous use of *sādhanā* teachings that bring about the union of wisdom and means. With his *śakti* in his embrace, Heruka stands for this marvelous union or *yab-yum*. He glares in all directions but, even more forcefully, his spread wings are like sword blades threatening destruction in all directions. If sculpture were sound this would be a shriek. Perhaps only Balinese images of Garuḍa, the man-bird support of the Hindu god Viṣṇu, can match this three-dimensional intensity.

Much "quieter" but equally memorable is the main altar grouping in Enchen that presents Padmasambhava, Guru Rinpoche, as a golden mentor with four attendants in a mandorla that is, like the Buddha's own, made of shimmering gold. Structural columns rise above the altars and disappear into the darkened ceiling area, carrying all of the symbolic meaning that is defined by Thubten Legshay Gyatsho. The monument is whole. It is iconographically correct. It is international. It is traditional. And it is very much alive.

4

Palaces and Monasteries of Bhutan

When a country is remote and difficult of access, and even purposely closed to visitors, it takes on a certain mystique. When such a country opens at last, even if to just a few groups of visitors each year, it is an important event. But the world-weary traveler who seems to have seen everything twice may be disappointed, or even say of the new destination, along with Gertrude Stein, "There is no there there." The wait to enter the green Himalayan land of Bhutan is worthwhile. Bhutan most definitely is a unique destination, and it is an unmatched reality. The green rolling hills and high peaks of this Buddhist country that was only recently seated in the United Nations are marked by colorful and imposing buildings that are more than mere copies of Tibetan or any other neighbor's art. Architecture takes special directions. When combined with palace structures, a temple can be part of a fortress, a *dzong*. The recently constructed and majestic palace complex in Bhutan's capital city of Thimpu is, perhaps, overshadowed only by the Potala in Lhasa. There is a remarkably independent architectural context for the cultural life of Bhutan, the "land of the peaceful dragon."

The government of Bhutan is centered in a brilliantly colored palace compound with watchtower that is like a castle keep and, like the associated monastery that sprawls below the palace, it rises, painted white and red with a great many glazed windows, in its winding river valley. It is not only the seat of the country's rulers but also a school, worship center, and dwelling place for hundreds of monks who belong to the Drukpa sect. A Bhutanese enters the compound only with a special sash draped across his chest and shoulder, for this is the most formal government compound in the country. Nearby is the dwelling of the king.

Thimpu Dzong and many other brilliantly painted structures occupy the 18,000 square miles of territory that are the land of Bhutan. The buildings vary from the *lhakang* or individual temple that may be very simple or very elaborate to colossal fortress-monasteries like that in Thimpu called *dzong (rdzong)*. Some of the finest structures are found in Punakha at an elevation of 5,170 feet, Paro at 7,750 feet, and the recently designated capital of Thimpu at 6,087 feet. None of the buildings is an exact copy of Tibetan art, but ties to Tibetan civilization are basic to understanding this special land and its history. Five passes lead into Tibet from Bhutan while India is just to the south, with road access from the subcontinent as a whole afforded mainly at the dusty trading town of Phuntsoling. The country is still sheltered today, but Bhutan's recorded history begins at least as early as the sixth century B.C. To quote Vincent A.

Smith as regards Himalayan rulers:

> It seems to me almost certain . . . that the Saisunagas, Licchavis, and several other ruling families or clans in or near Magadha were not Indo-Aryan by blood. They were, I think, hill-men of the Mongolian type, resembling the Tibetans, Gurkhas, Bhutias, and other Himalayan tribes of the present day.

The crucial period of the sixth century B.C. was, as Smith further notes, "a time when [people's] minds in several widely separated parts of the world were deeply stirred by the problems of religion and salvation."[1] This stirring began a century earlier, partly as the inspirational teacher Vardhamana, the son of a Licchavi nobleman who is usually known by his religious title of Mahāvīra, established his reform movement—Jainism—centered upon non-violence toward all living things. Mahāvīra died circa 467, but his religion is still kept very alive by many thousands of believers in South Asia, including a major and influential settlement in Bombay. The Himalayan people, however, were not particularly moved to adopt the Jain way.

Gautama, called Śākyamuni or "Sage of the Sakya people," was the son of the Rāja of Kapilavastu in the Terai plain of Nepal. Also a reformer, he rejected attachment to the earthly world in favor of striving for higher values and the truth and understanding that is *nirvāṇa* or enlightenment. He became known as Buddha because of his supreme knowledge of things *(bodhi)*. After he preached his first sermon at Sarnath in northern India near Varanasi, his word spread throughout Asia, including to Bhutan, the land of the Bhotiya people. Buddha died circa 483 B.C., and the histories of the Hīnayāna (Theravāda) and Mahāyāna schools developed until, by the eighth century A.D., a new impulse toward proselytizing and a new Buddhist presence in the land transformed the religion and the people of Bhutan. That presence was Padmasambhava, Guru Rinpoche, the eighth-century teacher and saint whose miraculous appearance is recognized throughout the Himalayan lands. Some say that this revered teacher was born in Kashmir, where he became familiar with the magical powers of sorcerers. If so, knowledge of spells may have helped him accomplish his greatest mission in the Himalaya: to free the people from the evil clutches of demons. The most prominent place in Bhutan to remember that exalted teacher and that important time is Taktsang, Tiger's Nest.

Having dedicated his book, *Bhutan—Land of the Peaceful Dragon,* to the memory of His Majesty, Druk Gyalpo Jegme Dorje Wangchuk, King of Bhutan (1952–1972), G. N. Mehra goes on to note that,

> Perhaps the most exciting and vital aspect of the Bhutanese tradition as inherited by us is found in its art. Everywhere one is amazed by the natural and untainted sense of beauty, line, and colour which the Bhutanese artists preserve in their painting, sculpture, applique work and carving. One must, however, recognize that in Bhutan there is no such thing as art for self-expression, or art for art's sake . . . The Bhutanese tradition maintains that making images of deities is a pious act leading to salvation. In its evolution and development, therefore, Bhutanese art . . . is in the nature of Sadhana. Further, since according to Buddhism the Self does not ultimately exist, self-expression is of no real value. Beauty has no meaning apart from divine life whose attribute it is along with Truth and Goodness (Sastyam, Shivam, Sundaram).[2]

Such is a crucial reminder to those who come to Asian arts from other traditions of their own that the artist is truly without self or ego as sacred visual traditions are continued. We are sometimes told that there is no word for art, that art is simply life. Yet there are specialists whose talents are sought after, monks or secular artists who travel widely to give their best efforts to projects like mural painting inside of monasteries. They are like the itinerant portrait artists who brought their miniature painting skills to all of the states of Rajasthan and beyond, as researched by B. N. Goswamy of Punjab University. When they finish their work they do not sign their name. Much more important than taking individual credit for the art that they make is that such talented individuals must pass on what they know to others. Therefore it is appropriate to look at the artistry of Bhutan or any of the Himalayan lands as if the art was made according to the guild system of medieval and later Europe, or as a community project that benefits a settlement as a whole. In today's Tibet one witnesses the heart-rending spectacle of poor people carrying stones, one at a time, to re-erect great monasteries that dynamite and repression have erased from their land. Art is meant to be eternal, or so it seems. Traditional Bhutanese art survives to a remarkable extent, yet its art is vulnerable too, as are whole societies that become overwhelmed by outside pressures. No modern leader is more aware of the vulnerability of people and art than His Majesty Jigme Singye Wangchuk, the present king of Bhutan.

Bhutan is like Sikkim in that even the transmigration of tribal groups, especially people from Nepal who may make up as much as 60 percent of its population, has led to little intermingling, so that the land and social fabric is highly compartmentalized in ways that favor the "retention of tribal and cultural individualities."[3] People native to Bhutan belong to the Mongoloid type that is dominant in the Great Himalayan valleys rather than to the Indo-Aryan element that belongs especially to the Terai and Duars regions to the south. That these groups still retain their identities is to be expected after many centuries of selective interior development and very little contact with the outside world. It may be remembered that Nepal opened her doors to foreigners only after the revolution of 1950; Bhutan came later. Paul Grimes of *The New York Times* was the first American reporter to enter Bhutan, and then only in 1960.[4] He came to a land that is traditionally called Lho Mon Kha Shi (literary name: Lho Mom Kha Bshi). The name *Bhutan* is derived from the Sanskrit *Bhotana,* to mean the end or limit *(anta),* that is the borderland of Tibet (Bhota). As Michael Aris notes in his introduction to *Views of Medieval Bhutan,* which he bases upon the diaries and drawings of Samuel Davis in 1783, the seemingly frozen surface of Bhutanese society is in fact based on 350 years of turbulent change, with relative stability beginning only in the seventeenth century with the establishment of a theocracy similar to that of Tibet.

Today the ethnic groups who populate the country are mixed but distinguishable. Those in the west, past the Black Mountain Range, are mostly of Tibetan origin although they have lived as Buddhists in Bhutan for centuries. In the east the people are mostly non-Tibetan and related to peoples of Assam and Nagaland but they, too, are Buddhists. People of Nepalese origin are found all through the southern foothills and adjoining the Duars plain of India, and they are mainly Hindu. It is sometimes said that there is inherent instability in this group's settling in the Buddhist country of Bhutan,[5] even though the Buddhist/Hindu mix that has long been the rule among Nepalese people themselves is generally without strain. The cultural mixture anticipates the unique character of much Bhutanese architecture.

The Bhutanese call their country Drukyel (literary name: Hbrug Yul), as the land of the Druk school of Buddhism that is named for the *druk* or dragon. Present-day Bhutanese belong primarily to the Nyingma-pa and Kargyu-pa sects of Buddhism, but it may still be said that the national Buddhist church of Bhutan is founded on the Drukpa sect. That fact sets this Buddhist country apart. Isolation is a factor that keeps coming up as a proposed reason both for things that have lasted in the Himalaya and things that have never happened there. As supposed isolation is addressed, it is useful to remember that trade always went on in the mountains, and very wide-ranging trade for at least two thousand years since the opening of the Silk Road by China's Emperor Wu during the Han Dynasty (206 B.C.–220 A.D.). That exchange provided at least some knowledge of very distant people and places, and recent discovery of a silk thread in Egypt may push the beginnings of east-west trade to even earlier times. It must also be remembered that religious doctrines traveled across all of the Asian continent with the help of teachers and missionaries. Political/military happenings in the Himalaya, including invasions by Tibetan forces, the Gurkhas, Muslims, the British, and others, left indelible marks on the native cultures that were encountered. Refugee movements changed the balance of populations in the mountains, especially during Islamic campaigns of expansion. Often the refugees were priests and monks who fled north from such important centers of learning as Nalanda in northern India, center of art and culture during the Gupta Dynasty (320–650 A.D.). The hills have always been a refuge for lowland peoples and they continue to be today.

And there are miracles. Abundant accounts survive of extraordinary deeds that saved humans and all the world from calamity through divine intervention. Padmasambhava as Guru Rinpoche is the foremost figure in such accounts, and it is fitting that his image greets visitors who reach the first Bhutanese temple that is met upon crossing the border from India at Phuntsoling. The statue is precious and painted gold.

Although remoteness is a consideration, it must be said that isolation is much less important than translation as the accomplishments of Himalayan civilizations are measured. This fact is true in all of the mountain regions that are considered here. Bhutan offers a rare illustration of a culture's development from medieval to modern times during a single generation. The art of Bhutan is like that of any culture that is strongly influenced by Tibet, but there is often invention, and syncretism is characteristic. R. A. Stein develops this point in his *Tibetan Civilization* as he states:

> Syncretism, or simply using different styles side by side, has never shocked the Tibetans. An attempt was even made, in the beginning at least, to combine styles from the great neighboring countries, whose cultures they were aware of borrowing, with the Tibetan style, just as the fusion of Buddhist tales with indigenous tradition had been encouraged. When Samye temple was built, the lower part is said to have been done in the Tibetan manner, the middle with a Chinese roof and the upper part with an Indian roof . . . The same tradition also claims that a castle built by King Mutik Tsenpo south-east of Samye had nine turrets and three floors. The ground floor, it states was Tibetan; the two-roofed first floor in the style of Khotan, was built by Khotanese carpenters; the second, in Chinese style, by Chinese carpenters (with three roofs); and the third, in Indian style, by Indian carpenters (also with three roofs).[6]

Stein also advises in his epilogue that:

> Many travellers and writers have used words like 'mediaeval' and 'feudal' when describing Tibet. Often it has been just a rather vague expression, but sometimes a pejorative one. We have not the slightest inclination to copy that. A civilization is an objective fact which the historian has no cause, and no right either, to judge, especially in relation to the supposed 'values' of the one he at present belongs to.[7]

With the last warning in mind, it still seems fair to say that Bön (Bön Po) religion is especially vexing for westerners to understand. It is useful to remember Stein's explanation that Bön is only one of the components of the religious world in Tibet and the Bonpos only one of ancient Tibet's varieties of priests.

The biography of Padmasambhava begins with the prophecy of his birth being made by Buddha himself, according to *The Tibetan Book of Great Liberation* as edited by W. Y. Evans-Wentz. The child was lotus-born beneath a rainbow of five colors in a lake where he appeared independently and "self-born." This recalls the legend of the appearance of a golden lotus in the midst of the Nepalese lake that once covered Kathmandu Valley at the place where Svayambhūnātha *stūpa,* the "self-existent" stands today. This theme of miraculous forthcoming, especially from waters, is found in places widely separated in the mountains and beyond. After living an earthly life and experiencing worldly happiness, Padmasambhava, like Buddha, rejected attachments to this world. Legend recounts that he preached about the impermanence of life, and that the guardian kings of the four directions prostrated themselves before him, as did the four directional *dākinī* females as powerful and horrific forces. Padmasambhava is said to have meditated and taught in cemeteries, where he subdued the threatening spiritual beings that surround any place of death and made them subservient to him. Before traveling north he worshipped at Bodhgayā in India, where the Mahābodhi tower temple that attends the place of Buddha's enlightenment beneath the spreading Bodhi Tree may not have looked much like its reconstructed state today. His impact in the north was tremendous: His appearance in art is almost constant throughout the Himalaya, from Kalimpong to Kathmandu and on to the west.

In his *Modern Bhutan,* Ram Rahul outlines Bhutanese history in terms of conjecture about post-Gupta instability in India and the vulnerability of Bhutan after the death of King Bhaskaravarman of Kamarupa, later Assam, in 650 A.D. He terms Bhutan "exposed" to incursions from the north that led to ultimate occupation by Tibet. When the central authority in Tibet collapsed, beginning in 840, the Tibetan presence was already so entrenched that Bhutan retained its colonial definition, so that in the thirteenth century the Muslim historian Minhaj-us-Siraj characterized the invasion of Bhutan in 1205, by Muhammed bin Bakhtiyar Khalji, as a military campaign against Tibet.[8] The invasion did not extend further than one valley in southern Bhutan because the Muslim armies were effectively resisted by hillmen who were equipped with armor, bamboo lances, helmets, and shields.[9] Rivalry between various sects of Buddhism was also known, with strain between the Lhapa Kagyupas, who brought the *dzong* system of fortified monasteries to Bhutan from Tibet, and the Drukpa Kagyu of Ralung lasting for more than four hundred years. The fortified bulk of monasteries throughout the mountains is a continuous reminder of frequent warfare that marks so much of the Himalayan past. Tibet was by no means the only aggressor.

That Himalayan lands have always been physically isolated in no way diminishes the importance of their geostrategic locations. For example, Bhutan lies between the Tibetan plateau and the Assam-Bengal plains of India, a position as important as any other in Asia. Its rulers were able to control access to and traffic through their lands, and this remains true today. And so the kingdom of Bhutan, 18,000 square miles in area with its capital of Thimpu first having been reached by road from India only in 1963, is important—important for its location between China and Tibet and India but also for its language, diverse crops, official Buddhist religion, monarchy, natural beauty, resistance to drastic change that might come as part of "modernization" with too-rapid exposure to the West, and fine arts.

The most significant cultural and political centers of Bhutan are, again, Thimpu, Paro, and Punakha. Phuntsoling has been noted as it, along with Sarbhang and Samdrup Jongkhar, serves as an important border town providing entry from India. Bhutan's monasteries themselves have been political and cultural centers, including such prominent places as Wangdu Phodrang, built in 1578. Karan and Jenkins note that during the past five hundred years numerous Tibetan lamas from Kampa have settled in Bhutan and established monasteries and forts that date as early as 1500, with Punakha founded in 1527.[10] They also point to an influential traveling lama of more than three hundred years ago, Sheptoon La-Pha, who became the king of Bhutan and acquired the title of Dharma Rāja, Ruler of the Law. His ascendence is crucial to later Bhutanese history.

The office of a righteous rule in Bhutan serves as a reminder of devoted kings of India during the early days of Buddhism and is a model that was passed on to the mountains: the ideals were people like Emperor Aśoka of the Maurya Dynasty (322–185 B.C.), Kaniṣka of the Kushan Dynasty (50–320 A.D.), and Chandragupta II of the Gupta Dynasty (320–650 A.D.). To be a king who follows the tradition of the "perfect" way was admired in medieval times and still is today. Such a leader is a *cakravartin,* a ruler of the sacred law or *dharma.* The king is important as prime patron of the arts.

Performing arts are just as integral to Bhutanese culture as to any of the Himalayan world, and royal patronage is as important to such art as it is to religion. Dance is an illustration of Bhutanese history, and sometimes the only illustration. A Royal Dance Troup and an official orchestra were established by the father of the present king. The favored instruments are the flute *(zulim),* four-stringed violin *(piwang),* xylophone *(yangci),* and seven-stringed lute *(dranyen).* The last is recognized by having the head of a stag, horse, or *chusin* equivalent to India's *makara* water monster) at the top. Sixteen dancers wearing animal masks and carrying tom-tom drums and sticks perform a dance called Dramitse *(dramitse ngachem)* after the place of its beginnings. The dance deals with the story of a monk who lived in the monastery of Dramitse in eastern Bhutan and who was related to the saint Pema Lingpa (1450–1521). He is said to have been transported in a vision to the celestial palace of Guru Rinpoche where he saw this dance performed. It shows victory of Buddhism over demons. And it is quite literally part of, not just a periodical decoration for, Bhutanese sacred and royal architecture.

The kind of Black Hat Dance that is part of Sikkimese New Year celebrations and is associated absolutely with the Karmapa Lama in Sikkim takes on different meanings in Bhutan. Francoise Pommaret-Imaeda and Yoshiro Imaeda explain in *Bhutan—A Kingdom of the Eastern Himalayas* that in Bhutan the dance commemorates the assassination in 842 A.D. of the wicked king Langdarma who opposed Buddhism in favor of the native Bon religion, and that it also propitiates the deities of the earth. Bon survives in many ways, however, and the great mountains of Bhutan—Kulha Kangri at 24,784 feet, Gangkarpunsum at 24,600 feet, and Chomolhari at 23,997 feet—are considered to be the seats of Bon gods. Important references of the New Year celebrations called Losar are made to these peaks, which are also sacred to Tibet. The pattern of Sikkimese festivals is repeated in Bhutan.

Bhutan also presents *durdag* dances in honor of masters of cremation grounds, *tungam* dances of the fearsome but ultimately positive guardian gods, *raksha mancham* dances of judgment of the dead, and more. When dances are performed under official patronage there is always an overseer, a Red Shawl officer known as the Chamai Chichap or "Master of dance."[11] The greatest presentation of dance in recent memory was surely the enormous efforts that attended the coronation festival of His

Majesty Jigme Singye Wangchuk in June of 1974, including events that were held in the great courtyard of Tashichho Dzong in Thimpu. The dances are performed in monastery/palace compounds with their geometric patterns once more emphasizing the circle as dancers' path that complements the rectilinear plans of surrounding structures.

Much is familiar in the visual arts of Bhutan, especially in painting, architecture, and sculpture, even while much is intriguing for its variance from Himalayan norms. The four guardian kings who are painted at Dungtse Lhakhang in Paro as well as numerous other sites in Bhutan are the Gyelchen shi or Four Great Kings, and they are the same directional protectors that have already been noted in Sikkim. Namtoese guards the north while holding a banner in his right hand and a mongoose spitting jewels in his left. Chenmisang is the protector of the west, and he holds a small *stūpa* (Tib. *chorten*) in his right hand. Phaksepo guards the south and holds a sword in his right hand while resting his other hand on its scabbard, and Yulkhorsung protects the east while he plays his lute. Directions of the universal *maṇḍala* as both compass and gyroscope in three dimensions are shown again. Individual guardian variations of pose, costume, expression, and more are always possible. These attendants of the Buddhist word are remarkable.

Some of the arts are colossal. Especially memorable in Bhutan is a giant *thondrol* applique that shows Guru Padmasambhava; it is displayed on the outside walls of Paro Dzong on the fifth day of the Paro Tsechu festival that falls in March. Often published in recent years, it is another artwork that enlivens its setting as it portrays the triumph of good over evil. The calendar that determines the date to display this rare work is itself based upon the calendar of Tibet, its beginnings traced to a year equivalent to 1027 A.D., when the great *Kālāchakra Tantra* or Way of Life determined by the Wheel of Time was introduced to Tibet.[12] The style of the huge composition is very Tibetan. Paintings and applique along with unique weavings in red, maroon, yellow, orange, black, and white are in themselves worthy to make Bhutan's mark on the map of world art history, but there is much more. Hardest for a foreign audience to comprehend may be that the concept of beauty has no meaning apart from divine life, whose attribute it is along with Truth and Goodness (Satyam, Shivam, Sundaram).

In the vast corpus of Himalayan wall murals, especially *maṇḍala* paintings, there is none to equal the large cosmic *maṇḍalas* that are found at Paro Dzong and Simtokha Dzong in Bhutan. The square within circle *maṇḍala* on the ceiling of the Tshogdu assembly hall in the royal *dzong* at Thimpu is truly awesome. Tradition requires that such a prominent work must be directed by chief masters of painting who are called Khyilkhor Lobpon or "teacher of the *maṇḍala*."[13] Such a master is equal to the leader of a guild.

The great ceiling circle, more than thirty feet in diameter, is suited to the place where momentous decisions are made for the people of Bhutan. Beginning with perfect line followed by indigenous mineral and vegetable paints that government training centers preserve and cultivate, the Tshogdu Hall painting shows Buddha seated in meditation posture at the center of a rainbow halo. Sixteen *arhats* radiate around Buddha in their own circle of lotus petals, a square "palace of heaven" enclosure with one of the previously mentioned guardian kings at each T-shaped "door," and auspicious symbols are in the remaining space before a final circle of colors that shows the boundaries of the universe. Because the huge circle is set within an octagonal frame in the pattern of a lantern roof made to fit within the square assembly hall, there are four remaining corners that have smaller directional *maṇḍalas* painted within them. The total is a cosmic map once more: a perfect scheme of the world at large.

Remembering that the word *dzong* refers to a fortified monastery, one can imagine monks and their teachers in such a setting, engaging in classical debate while analyzing the messages of paintings that, to outsiders, may appear to be completely abstract. Or are they never the subject of formal debate? The Imaedas explain that the powerful paintings convey classic Buddhist cosmology. More specifically, a cosmic *maṇḍala* from Paro Dzong, with its four quarters of existence filled with swirling directional colors, shows the four continents within a circle that stands for the Buddhist cosmos. A second painting of a perfect expanding circle in gray, white, yellow, and gold is less clearly representational, but a beautiful abstraction from Simtokha Dzong presents symbolic mountain ranges as yellow concentric squares while circles in different colors stand for the twelve months of the year. The path of the sun is represented by an ellipsoidal line in brick red, and moons are there as well.

As in the case of Navajo sand painting, the full meaning may be unexplainable except by the artist who made it. Also, the great wheel may be rendered on a flat surface in dry pigments that are both mineral and organic. Such work has been created at the American Museum of Natural History in New York and elsewhere abroad. It is always temporary and it must be perfect.

Two truly remarkable *maṇḍalas* from Paro Dzong have now been published in color, and they raise the interest of viewers everywhere. Both relate to the important *Kālachakra Tantra,* a very significant Tantric text about what translates as "The Wheel of Time," which is said to be one thousand years old. If the authors mentioned above are correct, the four wide concentric circles of different colors that are painted in these *maṇḍalas* stand for the four elements: air (yellow), fire (red), water (light blue), and earth (dark blue). Mount Sumeru (Meru) is found in five parts in the center of one mural with interlocking circles while the other Paro painting shows the sacred axis-mountain in vertical elevation. The works call for study in light of John Blofeld's analysis of the *maṇḍala* diagram, of Philip Rawson's discussion of Hindu and Buddhist cosmograms, of Ajit Mookerjee's many studies of Tantra art, and of Giuseppe Tucci's *Theory and Practice of the Maṇḍala,* among many other works.

If this chapter seems to link many elements of society together, perhaps without much advance preparation for the reader, it is because the art and the culture are one. As Robert Goldwater clearly states, the art is part of the function, not merely its later illustration. Roy Sieber adds that works of art have the amazing ability to move us, even when presented totally out of context in the very artificial setting of a museum. In Bhutan the art still has its own context around it—three ecological zones that are defined "horizontally" along the east-west length of this varied land and are explained below. G. N. Mehra prefers to designate four zones—northern, central, eastern, and southern—because of the important divisions from the foothills upward that are due to the country being criss-crossed by valleys and ranges that are themselves extremely variable.

As in Sikkim, Bhutan is cut into slices by mountain chains that run north to south. Yet all of the regions are inhabited by Drukpa people, all speaking Tibeto-Burman languages. Their earthly *maṇḍala,* corresponding perfectly with *maṇḍalas* in art, is integrated absolutely with the cosmic diagram of perfection. As regards Mary Shepherd Slusser's analysis of historical, religious, cultural, and other features that define *Nepal Maṇḍala,* there is a Bhutanese equivalent. Bhutan's worldly diagram is both secular and sacred. No feature of the land is more important than holy Chomolhari peak. At 7,315 meters high, it is the Bhutanese equivalent of Kanchenjunga and was first climbed by an Indo-Bhutanese expedition in 1970.

In terms of other visitors, the first westerners to enter Bhutan were probably Father Cabral and Father Cacella, Portuguese Jesuits who came in 1627 and described Shabdrung Ngawang Namgyal as "the King and at the same time the chief Lama."[14] They reflect the Portuguese explorations of Alfonso de Albuquerque who reached India in 1510, but more especially the proselytizing of another Jesuit who reached out to Asia: St. Francis Xavier (1506–52), *apostolic nuncio* to the East, whose body rests in a glass casket in the Basilica of Bom Jesus in Goa. Perhaps foreign visitors sensed that only part of the Bhutan's national *maṇḍala* is found in the earthly features of the land.

As with Sikkim and Nepal, the country is divided climatically and geographically into the high Himalaya (where the border with Tibet was closed in 1959), the inner Himalaya, and the foothills. Thus it has three climatic zones—alpine, temperate/monsoonal, and tropical. The valleys within these zones are most important to the economy of the country. The Haa Valley is in the far west and produces wheat, barley, millet, and potatoes. It is not far from the trade center of Yatang in Tibet even though contact has now ceased. The fertile Paro Valley with the Pachu River is further east with its more temperate climate and lush vegetation. Beyond this to the east are the valleys of the Wang district including that of Thimpu, the capital. Punakha Valley is northeast of Thimpu, and above it is the valley called Gasa, which is known for its yak herds and its butter. South of Punakha are the rich grazing lands of Sha district, and east of this is Mangde Valley with its famous Tongsa Dzong as fortified monastery. The richness of the fields is reflected in the elaborate monastic arts.

As has been noted, all of this varied land first became a unified state in the early seventeenth century, and its history is wed to politics and religion. This happening is due in part to the force of personality that belonged to Shabdrung Ngawang Namgyel (1564–1651), the first unifier of Bhutan who is also known as Du-gom Dorji, and his association with the powerful mystique of the Drukpa School of Tantric Buddhism. The union of church and state was and is complete in Bhutan, although the tradition of dual rule—by a Dharma Rāja to govern religious affairs in the theocracy and a Deb Rāja to manage state affairs including revenue and foreign affairs—ended in this century, after being established in 1616. The Dharma Rāja had to be a holy incarnation and exhibit supernatural attributes before he could be accepted as the "chosen one" to guide the country along the path of Buddhism.

In 1907 hereditary monarchy was established and supreme authority was placed in the person of the king alone. The first king of the present dynasty was Sir Ugyen Wangchuck, former governor of Tongsa, who was elected to be the first supreme ruler. He and his successor, his son Druk Gyalpo Jigme Wangchuk who took the throne in 1928, ruled from Tongsa. After his coronation in 1952, King Jigme Dorje Wangchuck shifted the full-time capital to Thimpu, a very beautiful place in a high green valley that had previously been a summer capital only. Tashichho Dzong or the "Fortress of the Auspicious Religion" still dominates the place; it is claimed to be more than 800 years old, although as noted above it has been restored and rebuilt considerably in order to house today's general secretariat and headquarters of the Central Monk Body, along with the headquarters and gilded throne room of the king. A short distance away is a memorial to King Jigme Dorje Wangchuk, an extraordinary *chorten* that is familiar to this study only in its exterior form.

The Drukpa Kagyu sect was introduced by Lama Phajo, and the sect was strengthened by Shabdung Rinpoche who gave the faith its own special values and patterns of worship. As background, it is useful to review that Bhutan shares much with Tibetan Buddhism, most commonly called Lamaism after its monks or lamas. The religion of Bhutan, again, has several divisions, of which the best known are the Kadampas, who developed into the "new" Kadampas or Gelukpas (as yellow hats), the Kagyupas as a group of the larger red hats group of the Nyingmapa order, and the Sakya-pas. All of these can be traced back to the Nyingma school, which is credited with being introduced to Tibet by Guru Padmasambhava himself in the eighth century after he preached through the foothills to the high peaks (which helps to explain the frequency of the Guru's depiction in Sikkim as well as in Bhutan and Nepal). The Drukpa Kagyu sect is identified most of all with Bhutan, where the local name for monks is *gelong*. These somehow distant, even unreal "facts" come very much to life at one of the Buddhist world's most remarkable places: Taktsang or "Tiger's Nest."

The oldest temples of the land of Bhutan are said to have been founded in the seventh century A.D. G. N. Mehra chooses to emphasize the Kyichu Lhakhang in Paro and Jampa Lhakhang in Bumthang, and associates both with King Srongtsan Gampo of Tibet. Bumthang is associated with the belief that Padmasambhava meditated there and dispelled harmful spirits. Kurto Senge Dzong in eastern Bhutan is where a *dākinī* and consort of Guru Padmasambhava named Yeshe Tshogye performed a *pūja* or worship honoring Dorje Phurba, the combined thunderbolt and dagger.[15] The Tangu and Cheri temples near Thimpu are close to the memory of Shabdung Rinpoche, the first building credited with some of the finest murals in the country. Dramitse monastery in eastern Bhutan, one of the largest in the country, belongs to the Pemalingpa sect. Nagendra Singh refers to the Kyichu Lhakhang in Paro and the Jampa Lhakhang dedicated to Maitreya as Buddha of the Future in Bumthang, the principality that was enlarged by an Indian refugee prince, Sindhu Rāja. He presents these monuments dating from the seventh century A.D. as Bhutan's earliest temples. G. N. Mehra attributes both temples to patronage by Tibet's King Srong-tsan Gampo. He adds that Padmasambhava meditated at Kuje Lhakhang near Bumthang, where he was welcomed as Guru Rinpoche, the "Precious Teacher." He traces this belief to members of the early Nyingmapa sect.

The eighth century also saw the making of "rock monasteries" such as Thowada at Tang to the north of Bumthang, Sengge Dzong in the northwest district of Kurto, and Tiger's Den Monastery of Taktsang high above Paro valley. Each of these incorporates a natural cave or rock grotto, but no other place of worship in Bhutan outshines Taktsang.

It was at Taktsang or Tiger's Nest/Den near Paro that one of the eight manifestations of the Guru Rinpoche Padmasambhava is said to have meditated and vanquished evil spirits that terrorized the land. The tight complex of small buildings hangs on to its very high cliffside niche with confidence, even as visitors struggle to make a two-hour climb from the plain below. Small squared buildings have been added to the front of a natural cave, while a prayer wheel turns by the power of a rushing stream below, and a tiny hermitage for meditative withdrawal from the world perches like a bird on a sheer cliff up above. The buildings are simple shrines, with small glass windows, and their prayer flags, prayer wheels, and bells are all additions that are to be expected. The building of the present structures is credited by Mehra to the fourth "Deb Raja," Tendzin Rabgye (1638–96). Records show that the main shrine structure went up in 1692, while legend has it that Tendzing Rabgye cut off his hair after praying to Guru Rinpoche and threw it into the abyss below. From those locks of hair rocks sprang up the underpinnings of the temple.[16] And within the small cave itself a surprising work of art—a surprising, "living" presence—waits.

Made of clay and painted brilliantly in the way of images that have already been discussed in Sikkim is a more than life-size image of Padmasambhava in a most horrific, violent form as he stands as demon-destroyer on the back of a pregnant tigress that is sometimes said to be flying. This is the incarnation of the great teacher as Dorje Trolo, and the frightful image is as awe-inspiring as the steep precipice that supports the shrine complex three thousand feet above the plain as it clings like a spider to the rocky cliff.

The prominent architectural monuments of Bhutan fall into the categories of *dzong* or fortified monastery that may have palace/government functions, *lhakhang* or individual temple, and *chorten* as Tibeto-Bhutanese version of India's *stūpa* or Buddhist relic mound. The first group includes Wangdiphodrang Dzong, which was built in 1638 by Shabdrung Ngawang Namgyel in remote eastern Bhutan where it houses a fearsome entity often kept from sight but suggested by black windows painted with skeletons and grinning faces; Rashigang Dzong, the most eastern monastery of all, founded in 1656; and Tongsa Dzong, built in 1543 in the center of the country where it was enlarged in the mid-seventeenth century and then restored after a severe earthquake of 1897. Paro Dzong is one of the country's most picturesque monuments in its riverside setting, and a circular watch tower or *ta dzong* with many floors on the slope above Paro Dzong now serves as the National Museum of Bhutan. Punakha Dzong stands at the confluence of the Pho and Mo rivers where it was founded by Shabdrung Ngawang Namgyel in 1637. Until the 1950s it was the *dzong* of the winter capital of the country, and it is still the home of many monks who go there to escape the harsher winter of the new capital in Thimpu.

Then there is Drugyel Dzong at the northwestern end of Paro Valley, a largely ruined complex that was built in 1647 by Shabdrung Ngawang Namgyel in celebration of his victory over the armies of Tibet. Its name means "Dzong of Victorious Drukpa," and it is near the sacred mountain Chomolhari. Fire caused by a butterlamp ravaged it in 1951, but its former grandeur is still indicated by large processional doorways, high battered walls, massive beams, tight enclosure of window frames and cornices between courses of dressed stones, and a high observation tower for security.[17]

Rather than great size and massive ramparts, applied arts and treasure-box preciousness may remain as indelible impressions for first-time visitors to Bhutan's *lhakhangs*. They anticipate small but never humble structures that are found in Ladakh as well as in Tibet. A selection of these smaller but no less significant complexes in Bhutan includes the aforementioned Kuje Lhakhang in Bumthang, Kuje meaning "the impression of Guru Rinpoche's body." Believed to have been visited by Padmasambhava before he continued his journey from India toward Tibet, the compound has three buildings at the place where the master meditated to discover the "vital principal" of the legendary King Sentah, and its two main buildings date from 1652 and 1900 while a third was added in the mid-1980s by Her Majesty, the Queen Mother of Bhutan. Sheltered here is the largest statue of Padmasambhava in Bhutan.

Dungtse Lhakhang is not as imposing as Kuje Lhakhang, and it is unusual in that its overall form is much like a *chorten*. It is not, however, a death monument or a reliquary. Like the watch tower turned museum above the *dzong* in Paro, it shows that Bhutan sometimes reinterprets established forms in unexpected ways. Dungtse Lhakhang has been attributed to the fifteenth century and the time of the sainted Thangtong Gyalpo (1385–1464). This leader is said to have had the monument erected in order to subdue a serpentine force that lived under the mountain at the foot of which this building stands. It was restored in the nineteenth century by order of the twenty-fifth supreme religious leader of Bhutan, Sherab Gyeltshen (1772–1848).

Proper *chortens* include the very large and remote Chendebji Chorten, built in the eighteenth century reportedly to subdue the dangerous spirit that guarded its valley, and it has a long *mani* wall beside it. Such a wall rises here, as in Ladakh, Tibet, or Nepal, as inscribed and often painted stones are left by pilgrims and other travelers who seek blessings by donating an honorific stone bearing the sacred words "Om Mani Padme Hum." The monument rises as a solid hemisphere with substantial circular tower on top consisting of four terraces as radiating squares. A second solid construction is Chorten Kora in the region of Tashiyangtse north of Tashigang, a "gigantic" pile that is of unknown foundation date but was restored in the first half of the twentieth century. Legend conveys that a Bhutanese brought home the model for this monument carved from a turnip. It is enclosed by a low stone wall that is crowned with eight directional *chortens,* and the hemispherical *aṇḍa* rests on three squared steps that are punctuated at the lower four corners by miniature *chortens*. The five-part plan is like that of the *pañcāyatana* design of such Buddhist and Hindu monuments in India as the aforementioned Bodhgaya's Mahābodhi Temple of the Gupta Period and Deogarh Temple of about the early sixth century, each standing for the great mountain at the center of the universe, Mt. Meru, and four lesser peaks around it. Comparisons as far away as Cambodia and China may also be made. The top of the *yaṣṭi* parasol-axis is a golden pinnacle with metal umbrella banner. Most noteworthy in terms of this study is that both of the *chorten* monuments in Bhutan are painted with directional eyes on all four sides of the *harmikā* as base for the *yaṣṭi*. These all-seeing eyes, commonly identified with Ādi Buddha as premordial Buddha-energy, are most closely associated with Nepal. They provide one more element of continuity across the varied lands of the Himalaya.

Ram Rahul outlines the following chronology of people and events that is useful to review here in abbreviated form as it relates to Bhutan:

1616	Ngawang Namgyal from Tibet's house of Gya of Druk and Ralung and the head of the Druk school of the Kagyupa sect arrives in Bhutan and proclaims a theocracy with himself as spiritual head under the title of Shabdung
1629	Shabdung Ngawang Namgyal establishes Simtokha Dzong
1637	Shabdung Ngawang Namgyal establishes Punakha Dzong
1639	Shabdung Ngawang Namgyal defeats the invading Tibetan army of Depa Tsangpa
1641	Shabdung Ngawang Namgyal constructs Tashichho Dzong on the ruins of the old Dongon Dzong
1642	the Mongol Gushri Khan invests Dalai Lama V with power
1644	Gushri Khan sends Mongol-Tibetan troops to Bhutan
1646	Shabdung Ngawang Namgyal establishes Paro Dzong and reaches a territorial agreement with Tibet
1648	Mongol troops again invade Bhutan
1657	Tibet invades Bhutan again
1676	Bhutan invades the Chhumbi region of Sikkim and receives estates in western Tibet from Ladakh
1700	Bhutan invades Sikkim and the Chhogyal of Sikkim flees to Tibet
1708	the Chhogyal returns to Sikkim
1714	Tibet invades Bhutan[18]

Later in the eighteenth century Nepal invaded Sikkim as part of Gurkha expansion that is personified by King Pṛthvī Nārāyaṇa Śah, and Warren Hastings became the finest representative of the Crown to affect Himalayan history. But perhaps the above happenings are enough to suggest that relationships among the Himalayan kingdoms were not always happy ones. The kinds of contact mentioned here have direct bearing upon the history of art and architecture.

The last architectural form to be studied in detail here is that which is most particular to Bhutan—the *dzong*.

The general definition of the term *dzong* is "fort or castle; seat of religious and administrative hierarchy of a particular area." This study has used the definition "fortified monastery" in order to emphasize the massive impact of its geometric design and the ever-present religious character of its art. Like any building that is shared by the Tibetan tradition, it is modular. That is, the expandable and infinite repetition of squares that is seen in ceiling beam patterns determines the size and geometric form of any enclosure rather like the *tatami* mats that are the determining factor of room sizes in Japan. Also like Tibetan structures, the Bhutanese *dzong* encloses many interior spaces both small and large, and it normally consists of three or more stories. Yet the *dzong* is set apart from monastery art in the Darjeeling area and Sikkim by its more solid fortifications, its tall but often narrow windows, and the occasional use of defensive bridges as the only way of entrance.

The most prominent *dzongs* in the country are the Tashichho in Thimpu and the Punakha, Tongsa, Tashigang, Wangdiphodrang, and Paro, which is approached by a covered bridge that is supported by massive, cantilevered beams of wood like those that support the public bridges of Srinigar in Kashmir. The walls of all these large complexes are painted white. A wide band of red is painted all around each structure at one or more upper levels. The uppermost roof of each is crowned by a *stupi* pinnacle of brass or gold. All roofs were traditionally covered by shingles made of slate or other material that are typically weighted down with stones, as at Wangdiphodrang. Today, however, most roofs are covered with metal painted red, including the great Tongsa Dzong and Tashichho Dzong. The design of all is strongly horizontal, and they impose regularity and rational balance upon the green landscape of Bhutan. Even though the *dzong* is a relatively new kind of monument, having been introduced to Bhutan from Tibet only in the seventeenth century, it is well established and consistent in its many expressions. One summary description is especially concise:

> The dzongs are built as variants of a basic model: a quadrilateral of buildings enclosing one or more courtyards. A central tower called the *utse* often marks the division between the religious and the civil quarters, which are strictly separated. The wood carvings and paintings that decorate the dzongs are often outstandingly complex and subtle.[19]

The structure of the *dzong* is basic, as a trabeate building made up of post-and-lintel wooden frame for interior spaces and piled stone blocks for exterior and interior walls. Comparison to medieval European or Japanese construction might be useful, but structural method is of only superficial importance if architectural symbolism is studied. Again the writings of Thubten Legshay Gyatso of Nepal's Lumbini Buddhist Monastery are especially useful, for his *Gateway to the Temple* is a manual of wide-ranging Tibetan monastic customs, art, building, and celebrations. The manual prescribes the way to establish temples, beginning with examination and taking possession of the building site, and its precise steps recall directions of India's *Śāstras* as architects' guides that are followed throughout the South Asian sphere of influence. Choosing a site depends upon practical, astrological, and other considerations, such as not disturbing the serpent earth deity while seeking the spot on its body that yields special attainments. Among physical features of the earth that yield "miseries" are steeply inclined slopes, thorny brambles, cinders, ant hills, alkaline soil, and insect infestation, while a good setting will have good water, trees with fruit and leaves, water which flows from right to left, and earth "which is an intense, brilliant white in hue."[20] Besides physical tests of the land, the *Tantras* direct purification by means of *mantras* that may be spoken over it. When the land is pure one should activate a "protection circle" through meditation. Other rites allow the consecrator to "take control" of the land. It is necessary that one examine, test, appropriate, and tame the land, for "no matter how one proceeds there will be the danger of obstacles and obscurations."[21] Limitless benefits derive from constructing a sacred place, and the *Saddharmasmṛtyupaṣthana Sūtra* explains that:

> The virtue of correctly erecting a temple and install-

> ing in it shrines, and offering a dwelling, bed, and refreshment to the monastic assembly, increases ever more and more, and will not become exhausted even in a thousand million aeons.

A second *sūtra,* called in Tibetan *Phags pa legs nyes kyi rgyr dang bras bu bstan pa i mdo,* in which the causes and effects of good and ill are taught, quotes Buddha as saying:

> Any being who in this life sponsors the building of the Tathāgata's *stūpas* and assembly halls will without a doubt in the future become a king. He will rule over many subjects, and all will obey his word.

Finally, Thubten Legshay Gyatso quotes the *Visesastaya* as stating:

> Those of the Nirgrantha ascetic school say that to build such things as a pleasant dwelling-enclosure is a cause for moral fault. But you, Omniscient One, have declared it to be the cause of merit.

The Lumbini author himself explains the "puzzle":

> Accordingly, if a patron should build a religious structure following the dimensions and size prescribed by the basic texts, his mental stream will become endowed with vast merit. This is because founding a temple will contribute in part to the spreading of the jewel of Buddha's Teachings, because the monastic assembly will be able to dwell there free from anxiety and thus be able to perform the practices set forth in three wheels of the Doctrine.[22]

Building sacred monuments as a means of acquiring merit is a constant value as Himalayan art is encountered, with roots that extend back in time to at least the second millennium B.C. and Vedic prescriptions in India for making such offerings as altars of fire. *Gateway to the Temple,* however, precisely describes Tibetan and mountain means of sacred construction. They are not always unique to those places but rather part of the totality of Asian art.

Traditional construction procedures that are followed once a suitable site has been chosen are common to Bhutan, Sikkim, Nepal, Bengal, Himachal Pradesh, Ladakh, and Tibet herself, whether the goal is to build a standard *gompa* as monastery or a fortress-like *dzong.* The time for building is set by the monastic community, and size is a major consideration as the design is determined. To be more complete, this analysis turns to the six steps of erecting a monastic chapel as outlined by Thubten Legshay Gyatso:

1. Examine and take possession of the building site
2. Decide on the precise building scheme
3. Determine ways to conduct the attendant building festivals
4. Choose the arrangement of murals in the temples
5. Determine the origin of pictorial representation
6. Determine the basic line measurements of sacred images

Thubten Legshay Gyatso notes that the *Vinaya* is consulted for the size of wooden temple spans, with one and one-half standard spans being *one span of the Buddha.* A temple interior should normally be seven or twelve of the longer spans in size. Alternate measures, depending upon the number of resident monks, also are made. The *Vinaya* goes on to state that a temple should be square, with courtyards on three sides if desired. In front of the temple there should be a covered walkway, and the center of the temple interior should be a chapel where the "Great Teacher's" image dwells. This space among many other recesses is most highly "charged" and most anticipated by worshippers as they enter a complex building. Any visitor to Tibet who has had the good fortune to enter the famous inner rooms of the Jokhang or Tsulhakang Temple in Lhasa remembers the good-natured excitement and awe of believers who ritually encircle the jeweled image of Śākyamuni, a dazzling statue that is believed to have been given to the temple by King Srong-tsan Gampo's Chinese wife Wen Cheng in the seventh century A.D. It occupies a perfect, constant space, and the metal image is covered with a blue-green snowstorm of turquoise in a design overstatement that seems somehow logical in this mountain world of visionary and magical arts. It seems appropriate that the vestibule of the temple is crowded with prostrate worshippers who humble themselves before the divine entity that the statue, and all of its attendant arts, represents. The chanting of sacred formulae is constant and the Jokhang is eternal, untouchable, the center of the center.

Bathhouses and ambulatory spaces, like the cloisters of European Christian pattern, are prescribed in the *Vinaya* along with meditation cells, kitchen, storehouses, a heated room for warming

Children beside a brass-plated door, Barpeta Satra complex, Assam.

Carved and painted outer wall of Barpeta Satra, Assam.

Ghoom Monastery outside of Darjeeling.

Guardian figure inside the upper floor shrine, Aloobari Monastery, Darjeeling.

Aloobari Monastery, Darjeeling.

Detail of upper floor murals, Aloobari Monastery, Darjeeling.

Manilakhang behind Pemayangtse Monastery, Sikkim.

Reconstructed Rumtek Monastery, seat of the Karmapa Lama, Sikkim.

Detail of the entrance door frame, Rumtek Monastery, Sikkim.

Drugyel Dzong, Bhutan.

Distant view of Paro Dzong complex, Bhutan.

Kharbandi altar in Phuntsoling, Bhutan.

Tashichho Dzong complex, Thimpu, Bhutan.

Tiger's Nest shrine to Padmasambhava, Bhutan.

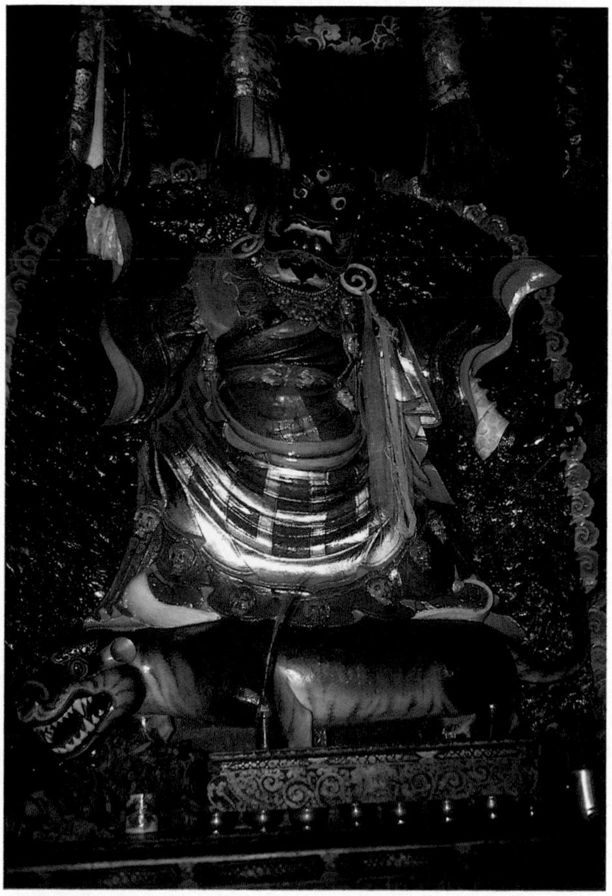

Replica of secret image inside of Tiger's Nest, Bhutan.

"New" Palace at Nawakot, Nepal.

Nyatapola temple, Bhaktapur, Nepal.

Detail of Naka Bahīl shrine entrance, Patan, Nepal.

Thikse Monastery, Ladakh.

Altar complex inside the dukhang, *Alchi Monastery, Ladakh.*

Detail of entrance, Mosque of Shah Hamadan, Srinigar, Kashmir.

Carved strut figures, temple of Indreśvara Mahādeva, Panauti, Nepal.

Carved and painted strut figures of Changu Nārāyaṇ temple, Nepal.

Temple of the goddess of Chatrarhi, Himachal Pradesh

Palace tower in Hunza, Northern Pakistan.

Gondhla tower near the Rohtang Pass, Himachal Pradesh.

by a fire in winter, various reception rooms, studies for high lamas, the main instruction space, various kinds of altars, library shelves to hold sacred books, and more. The largest courtyard will be directly in front of the two-story entry portico, and this court will be the setting for ritual dancing. A second open space is sometimes found on the monastery roof around a raised construction that may be a clerestory for the spaces below. The reception hall and/or study of the highest lama may also be found in a rooftop setting.

In the words of the Lumbini expert:

> Tibet's own pure tradition of temple architecture is a system that incorporates the good and harmonious from among various architectural features of the celestial palaces described in the tantric divisions of scripture. In that tradition one begins by collecting and organizing all the materials needed for building both the inside and outside of the temple. Then on the plot of land, whatever its size may be, the outlines of the individual structures' floorplans are laid down. In conformity with those outlines, expert carpenters and masons measure the lines, keeping them perfectly straight and true, and the floorplan is definitely fixed.

These are the many parts and concerns that bring the most complex Himalayan buildings to functional life.

The measuring and outlining that are described so briefly above are of utmost importance. The same is true of the creation of a mural or a statue or a *tanka* painting or a three-dimensional *maṇḍala* as a work of art that is also a prayer; the art must be perfect. David P. Jackson and Janice A. Jackson provide the clearest definition of the steps of iconometry that are part of Tibetan *tanka* art in their *Tibetan Thangka Painting—Methods and Materials,* and the rules apply to all sacred arts of Tibet and related cultures like Bhutan. This may be the world's most precise art, and the wonder is that it is so alive, so intensely expressionistic. Units of measure are divided into two main types: small units called *cha chung* and large units called *cha chen* that relate to each other in a ratio of twelve to one. These units have no absolute value but instead are used to indicate proportional relationships within each sacred composition. Proportional classes are themselves varied according to the subject of a work of art from Buddhas down to the level of humans.[23] Once again the ultimate goal is perfect balance. A hierarchy of importance is found in architecture as well, in order to capture good and harmonious architectural features that originate in celestial palaces as they are described in classical tantric literature. Tibetan buildings have nothing in common with the clay and stone *śikhara* towers of Assam and only a very general similarity to the spacious *satra* buildings that are also found in that state, but have everything in common with monastic structures of the northeastern hills from Darjeeling to Sikkim. The relationship continues throughout the Himalayan states that remain to be considered here.

A newly constructed "cathedral" in Tibet will have a main assembly hall of from about fifty to more than one hundred columns, and no other structure of the hills surpasses this inclusion of interior space. The middle of the main hall will have from two to thirty-two longer columns for a central area that will have balconies and a raised roof above it. A large roofless courtyard is usually built, and the most elaborate woodcarving will be found on the cornices along the inner faces of its balconies, all brightly painted. Inclusion of active exterior space also is stressed more here than in other Himalayan building traditions.

Thubten Legshay Gyatso explains that since the woodwork in this area may be on an "excessively grand scale," it is compensated for by changing the normal configuration of beams. There is a custom of putting two *'ben-log* beams on top of the bow capital, and on this there should rest five or seven small blocks. He also notes that the interior of the assembly hall with its ornate sanctuary or chapel requires long pillars only. The first columns within the sanctuary provide an especially elaborate portico; these may be eight-sided or sixteen-sided, their rich painting making them lustrous as well as "facetted." The latter term applies both in the sense of the facets of jewels as the column surfaces reflect the lights of flame lamps and in the architectural sense of the poles having raised planes between the columns' flutes. The Lumbini author describes interior supports of the main hall that vary in number from only four to sixteen, each being carved and drilled in the most ornate manner possible. Elaboration upon this plan is possible, of course.

To a believer, structural methods are much less important than monastic symbolism. The vestibule that leads to the interior symbolizes the "three doors of liberation." To the left and right side of the main chapel there may be other sanctuaries as well. Frequently, these include a major protector god on the right side. Among little-known details that are revealed by the Buddhist writer in Lumbini is the traditional use of "filler material" in the form of cloth, silk, grain, and the "five precious materials" to fill spaces above the main beams that are gaps between projecting cantilevers. Modern practice uses these only in small amounts but adds printed blessings and small pressed-clay images called *tsha tsha* that show Buddhas, bodhisattvas, gurus, protectors, and more.

The impact of Tibet-related architecture is, foremost, an impression of mass, and second, an impression of celestial color. It is not surprising that construction festivals take place as various steps of the process proceed, for the monument itself is a celebration. In anticipation of monuments to be seen in Ladakh, it is important to briefly note the arrangement of "extra" or applied arts that are given to the temple interior. Each building has its own special qualities and each is meant to be very *full,* but some basic rules do apply. For example, the sacred image of Buddha that is housed in the inner recess of the building should be painted with pigments or made of gilded copper or other metals. Beneath this is a "vast and copious" throne that should be supported by a lion, elephant, horse, peacock, and two *shang-shang* birds with human torsos, like India's compound *kinnara* birds. The three-dimensional arts find complement and contrast in the painted walls that stand behind them. Mural paintings are often repetitive, always detailed, and themselves dynamic as framing devices.

Above the throne is a background design as a kind of halo or mandorla that consists of the "six ornaments" that are, from bottom to top, two elephants bearing a butter lamp and an incense container, then two lions holding two winged horses while standing on the backs of the elephants, then a winged horse or *sha-ral* unicorn on each side or possibly *sharabha* compound creatures that are Garuḍa-lions. This exhausting multiplication continues in the form of two small boys who hold conch shells in one hand and the beam of the painted backdrop in the other. The beams end as intertwined jewels that are draped in silk, according to established requirements. Then there is a "voracious water reptile," India's *makara,* on either side, resting on its back legs while its tail curls up into the "eternal knot" pattern. Above these are *nāga* snakes on both sides and finally, at the very top, a snake-eating Garuḍa as beautiful combination of human and bird. Decorative additions include strings of pearls, flowers, rainbows, and clouds. Truly, this is one of the world's most developed and varied visionary arts. The possible meanings of this particular altar design include the "seven diversions" that should be eliminated from the path toward truth, the four "gathering things," the six perfections, the strength of ten powers, the "stainless," and the "clear-light."[24] Mural painting, origins of the arts of painting and sculpture, precise messages of carving, and more will be discussed as other cultures within the Tibetan sphere of artistic influence are considered. But it is appropriate to quote here from the epilogue of the scholar Thubten Legshay Gyatso to the source that we have used:

> May the merit of this work and my and all other beings' store of virtue, which is the river flowing down from the blessed realms carrying along with it the gold dust that benefits the Doctrine and sentient beings, all reach the sole destination, the Ocean of Perfect Wisdom, so that even a tiny current of virtue will not be lost.[25]

Signs of virtue that are found in a single column summarize the heavenly references of *gompa* or *dzong* architecture. The slightly tapered timber that makes a column for a portico or interior hall is slightly tapered from bottom to top. Then it reaches a block-like *bre* as a kind of base for the capital. The capital itself is extended with scalloped arms that reach out parallel to the cornice above, which it supports. Its lowest level is the *'ben log,* its second horizontal section with alternating blocks is the *bre chung,* its third horizontal section with cloud-curve edges is the *'ben log* once again, and then capital is topped by another row of wooden blocks as *bre chung.*

Above the four-section capital is the *zhu ring* or long bow that extends out in billowing cloud design to underlay the cornice proper. The cornice is divided horizontally into eight or more levels with narrow bands between. The lowest is the *gdung ma* or beam seat, the next is the *gdung ma* as main beam or lintel, and then a *klu thig* or *ñaga* line of the spiritual serpent is found. The remaining five bands that rise toward the ceiling planks of

Capital and column inside of Pangboche Monastery, Solo Khumbu, Nepal.

gral ma are especially colorful and nearly always found as described below.

The thin *nāga* line is topped by a wide band that is painted with petals of the *padma* or lotus, followed upward by another thin dividing line. The next of the remaining cornice bands is filled with a three-dimensional checkerboard that is called the *chos brtsegs* or *dharma* (sacred law) stack. A cantilever is normally found above this, often painted with the sacred jewels of Buddhist Truth. A narrow division, the *bab skyangs bskums,* is interjected before the next cantilever level, which may be painted with such meaningful elements as open lotus flowers alternating with endless knots as a sign of complete perfection. After one more narrow division band, the rafters *(lcam shing)* are reached, and these may alternate with painted floral patterns as *lcam rtsa.* No more varied and meaningful architectural element can be found in the Himalya.

The kind of carved and painted storm that has been hinted at here is unequalled outside of the Tibetan tradition but matched in three-dimensional terms by the "shimmering" wood-carving of architecture of Nepal. Both traditions are based upon oral and literary accounts of the crystal-walled palace of heaven that sacred architecture seeks to duplicate on earth. Perhaps it is the jewel-like glow of these arts—their transcendence of the earthly plane—that inspired the painter Svetoslav Roerich to say that, "Beyond all conflagration and strife, beyond all destruction and violence, stands the eternal concept of spirit." The embrace of sacred carved and painted design belongs not only to temples but to houses and palaces as well. The texture of any building is as important as its size and function. Bhutanese structures fall into the consistently Himalayan method of using frame and fill—that is, timber and stone in Bhutan, Sikkim, West Bengal, Ladakh, and Himachal

Pradesh, but timber and brick in Nepal plus the unusual Kashmiri preference for combined timber and more timber.

This overview of Bhutan and Bhutanese architecture will conclude in part with references to the diaries and drawings of Samuel Davis that date from 1793, works that are most effectively discussed by Michael Aris in his invaluable *Views of Medieval Bhutan*. Relevant information also is drawn from *Bhutan—The Early History of a Himalayan Kingdom,* a second important work by Michael Aris, and one that he introduces with his own memories of being private tutor to the Royal Family of Bhutan for more than five years. These sources will be combined with the present author's recent experiences in the field. Understanding Bhutan is as much a challenge today as ever, but monuments serve as effective touchstones. The following comments will help to review the contents of this chapter as Bhutan reveals her special identity.

The first Buddhist temples of Bhutan are reidentified by Aris (whose classical spellings for terms and proper names are used here) as sKer-chu lHa-khang in the sPa-gro valley and Byams-pa'i lHa-khang in the Bum-thang province, and he states that they not only fit within the known character of the most ancient temples of Tibet but that sources place them within the elaborate system of temple construction that was devised by King Srong-tsan Gampo who ruled Tibet from circa 627 to 629. He provides a scheme based upon geomantic principles that reportedly were introduced to Tibet from China by the famous seventh-century princes Kong-Jo as an aid to conversion to the new faith. The pattern consists of three squares, one inside the other, that surround a circle that is labelled as lHa-sa: 'Phrul-snang (Jo-khang) as "heart-blood." The corners of the three squares as they proceed from the outside in are designated (in clockwise order beginning at the upper left): left foot, left hand, right hand, right foot/left knee, left elbow, right elbow, right knee/left hip, left shoulder, right shoulder, right hip. This reference to body parts suggests comparison to earliest temple and city plans of ancient India that are based upon proportions and parts of the first being: Puruṣa. The temple diagram from Tibet suggests India's Vāstupuruṣa Maṇḍala but also the six concentric squared zones of China according to the *Yu Kung,* realms of existence that range from cultureless savagery on the outside *(huang fu)* to the Imperial center *(tien fu)* that is deep within.[26] It is entirely possible that both ideals were known in Boutan, and that both relate to the evolution of the *maṇḍala* that is referred to throughout this study.

Looking to much later times and to monuments that still survive, it is useful to consult the careful records of Samuel Davis, a young lieutenant who accompanied the embassy that was sent to Bhutan by Warren Hastings in 1783. Davis served as draftsman and surveyor, while making drawings of the country that he saw. He was, as Michael Aris points out, the first foreign artist to paint in the Himalaya and the only one of distinction ever to work in Bhutan. Of Buddhist temples and images Davis writes:

> The priests have no separate buildings erected purposely for the exercise of religious ceremonies, in the manner of our churches, the pagodas of the Hindoos and Chinese, or the mosques of the Mahometans. Their devotions are always performed before altars erected in large apartments appropriated to this use in the palaces or castles where the Gylongs are lodged—these residences themselves being, in fact, the temples.

He also writes of the Dharma Rāja and Deb Rāja, the peasantry, the monks, and in one special reference, the nuns:

> These villages being always well built, and the houses lofty and whitewashed, are often beautiful objects when viewed from the road in travelling through the country. Each of these fraternities has its chapel, altar, and Lama-groo/-guru, or chief priest, who presides, and sees that the duties of the profession are regularly and properly discharged. There are besides a few who, in the character of faquires, pass their austere and solitary lives in lonely places high up among the rocks and jungle; and in some parts of Bhutan are said to be religious societies of female devotees or nuns, who, like the priests, have their superior and other officers, but all of their own sex. Provisions and necessaries are supplied to them, but no man dares be found after day-light in the precincts of the place, on pain of severe punishment.

And Davis comments upon the architecture that is common to use by both nuns and monks:

> In architecture, I think, they make the best figure: there is boldness in the design of many of their castles when they are not considered in the character of military buildings; and, with a little more attention to uniformity in the disposal of windows and doors,

and such as, perhaps, *they* think unessential points, these might without partiality be thought perfect in their kind. The projection of the roof is extremely well proportioned to the extraordinary thickness of the slope of the walls, and the large projecting balconies are much better adapted than windows to fabrics of so great an area and height. The apartments are lofty and of good size, and the method of getting into them by ladders, instead of stairs, seems to me the only peculiarity that admits of improvement . . . their timbers and planks are hewn, the use of the saw being altogether unknown. The beams are put together with mortises and tenons, and the boards by a piece let in across and dovetailed. Not a nail or bit of iron is to be seen in their buildings, nor even a wooden pin; yet their work is not deficient in firmness or stability.[27]

With the above early observations in mind, we turn to Bhutanese arts as they exist today. Tashicho Dzong in Thimpu has been much enlarged, as noted earlier, but it still conveys the impression of unified grandeur that struck Samuel Davis. Its courtyards are plentiful and large; its buildings have many stories; its windows with glass are numerous; its rooms have multiple uses. Because this one feature can no longer be readily found in Tibet, we emphasize that the monastic community is large and that its strict organization from highest lama to youngest novice is whole and undisturbed by outside forces. Davis gives his overall impression:

The palace of Tacissudjon really surprised me by the regularity and grandeur of its appearance . . . It is oblong, hundred yards in front and a hundred in depth, divided within two squares by a separate building raised in the center, more lofty and more ornamented than the rest. In the latter the Rajah and some of his principal people reside; and upon the top appears a square gilded turret, said to be the habitation of one of the lamas. One of the squares comprehends the chapel and apartments of the priests, and the other is allotted to the officers and servants of the government.[28]

Aris uses an engraving by J. B. Allen to illustrate the size and grandeur of the complex in Thimpu,[29] with its strongly horizontal statement amid the high green hills that are its background and its more delicate, uplifting, and very "Chinese" pagoda roof above the freestanding and central building as it stood before it was enlarged and otherwise modified during the 1960s. More than any other building complex outside of Tibet proper, the *dzong* in Thimpu captures the enormity of the Tibetan vision in combination with the refinement of local artisanship. One need only point to the colossal animals that stand on top of the central tower to prove that borrowing from Tibet has been both selective and inventive in Bhutan. As far as basic "nuts and bolts" are considered, there are none, but Samuel Davis informs us that,

The windows of the upper chambers balconies project of a size to hold fifteen or twenty persons; but there are no windows below, as they would not contribute to the strength of the place. The walls are of stone and clay, built thick, and with a greater slope inwards than is given to European buildings. The roof has little slope, and is covered with shingles, kept down by large stones placed upon them in the manner the Portuguese fasten the tiles of their houses in Medeira:—it projects considerably beyond the walls . . . The only singularity that strikes at first sight is the ladders instead of stairs; but the steps are broad, and after a little use are not found inconvenient . . . Most of the floors of the palace are boarded; and from the great breadth of some of the planks, we judged the trees to have been of much greater size that any we had met with. They also have floors composed of pebbles, well cemented together. The walls are whitewashed, with a stripe of red all around, a little below the roof. Upon the top of every chapel, or other place where there is an altar and service performed, a small cylinder is placed, five or six feet long, usually covered with white cloth, with a broad ring of red, bordered by two of blue round the middle of it. Those upon the palace, and other houses belonging to the Rajah, are gilt, and become a showy ornament.[30]

The comments of the eighteenth-century visitor are exact and well-tailored even to the Thimpu monument as it stands today. The castle of Chuka with two towers on its hilltop does indeed make "a very respectable appearance" in the watercolor that he made and his sketch of the village of Muricham hints at the solid, practical, and beautifully decorated appearance of prosperous families' houses even as they continue to be built today. A bridge of chains (called *lCags-zam*), also at Chuka, is very accurately rendered in an engraving by James Basire after Davis. It is an ingenious kind of construction that was invented by Thangtong Gyalpo (1385–1464) whom Nagendra Singh judges to be "the first and only pioneer-engineer of Central Asia and the eastern Himalayas." Some of Gyalpo's original chains are still kept in his family monastery on the road from Paro to Thimpu.[31]

If bridge technology is admired, so is the design

of the sheer and the strong, the thrusting towers of "Kapta/Chapcha/Castle" painted in 1783 but probably built during the late seventeenth century. These towers are impressive in their "bleak but beautifully romantic situation" that is remarked upon by Samuel Turner in his own nineteenth-century journals, and they compare well to the castle towers of Himachal Pradesh and Lahaul. Equally grand is the tower in Nomnoo, even though it is shown to be attached to a house rather than a castle. Bhutan's towers are as impressive as the temple storehouses called *bhandar* in Himachal Pradesh, and they reinforce the importance of the Himalayan emphasis upon verticality, impregnability, solidity, and visual excitement. They are less delicate than the tallest towers in Kathmandu Valley and Nawakot. Towering buildings among towering mountains are unforgettable; they are magnetic to those who climb ever higher to reach them. Perhaps Gondhla Castle in Lahaul, Dubde in Bhutan, Pemayangtse in Sikkim, and Nawakot in Nepal best reveal the impact of nearly every building that is discussed in these pages.

William Daniell chose to illustrate "The Palace of Wandechy—Bootan," after an untraced original by Davis, and in direct frontal view. It serves to show that the lofty impact of Bhutan's architecture comes from frontal symmetry as well as multiplicity and dramatic setting. The monastery of Simtokha, one of Bhutan's most important centers of learning, also has the dignity of symmetrical design in its hilltop setting. The wide stairway that leads to a three-part entrance below a broad projecting balcony at "Wandechy" is equalled in formality by the mood and stability of Simtokha. The fortress-like security of the active study center suggests the timelessness of Buddhist learning, and the boys who practice Tibetan calligraphy with chalk on pieces of slate will be its carriers. This *dzong* was built in 1618 and is the oldest Drukpa fortress in the south of Thimpu Valley. Some of the subjects that Davis illustrated are still difficult for foreigners to see. Davis writes,

> I was greatly mortified and disappointed in not being permitted to see the inside of the palace; a stern porter kept the inner entrance; and, in consequence of an order given during the late tumults, obstinately refused me admittance: nor could I by any means prevail upon him to relent.

The writing of Samuel Davis is richly supplemented by journals written by Samuel Turner,[32] and foreign readers must be thankful for such early accounts written by other outsiders with all of the exactness and truth that make even diaries invaluable to later scholarship. There is no room for theory or interpretation until the essential facts have been recorded and so, even near the end of the twentieth century, we continue to look back to the writers of the nineteenth. The *dzong* at Punakha, built by Sabdrung Ngawang Namgyal in the winter capital in 1667, stands today after repairs that were carried out in 1781, and essentially as it was seen by Samuel Davis in 1783. With a total of eighteen temples, it is still there and it is still difficult for foreigners to enter.

The above story is familiar to any foreign investigator who might occasionally forget that he or she is only a visitor. This writer has been devastated by the firm closure of doors at Paśupatinātha temple in Nepal, stern priest-guardians at Nepal's Changu Nārāyaṇa temple, an overly zealous attendant at the temple of Markula Devī in Udaipur, H. P., and a formidable Hindu priest of the Devaswam Board in Trivandrum, South India. They are all worthy players and sometimes opponents in the game of knowing Asia.

It is perhaps appropriate that *dzongs* have been most stressed in the previous pages, for they are the special accomplishment of Bhutan. Nagendra Singh points out that it was in the seventeenth century that the first big fortresses of *dzong (rDzong)* type were built, making them relatively young monuments in comparison to other buildings in the mountains. However, they "became the spiritual and administrative centres of every district" and "included within their tapering strong-walls the buildings of the main monasteries as well." As has been stated but is worthy of review, the "head monastery of Bhutan where the Head Lama had his seat was the Tashicho Dzong (bKra-shis-Chos-rDzong) of Thimpu, the capital." Wangdiphodrang Dzong (dBang-hdus-pho-brangr Dzong) is southeast of Punakha, and in the west stands Paro Rinpung Dzong (sPa-gro Rin-spungs r Dzong), totally and exactly rebuilt after a fire in 1905. Tongsa Dzong marks the border of eastern Bhutan and is the ancestral *dzong* of the royal family.[33]

It is widely known that Padmasambhava worshipped at Bodhgaya, the place of Buddha's achievement of Enlightenment with its famous

Mahābodhi temple of the fifth century A.D., and he is said to have multiplied his body, sometimes looking like a herd of elephants and sometimes like a crowd of *yogis*. He decided that he should go to learned teachers in order to study the Three Secret Doctrines, and he realized that future generations would need spiritual guidance. He became a master of astrology, medicine, languages, arts, and crafts—and some say that he was well-acquainted with the ways of sorcery, possibly learned in Kashmir. He took the vow of celibacy at Asura Cave and, according to tradition, was ordained into the Buddhist order by Ānanda, the chief disciple of Buddha. He is believed to have studied with Ānanda—in spite of the thirteen centuries that separate these two figures—and he went to a cemetery where he encountered Mahākāla, the "Great Black One."

Mahākāla personifies the masculine or *śakta* aspect of the disintegrating forces of the Cosmos while Kālī, the "Black Female One," is the feminine or *śakti* aspect. Mahākāla is the Lord of Death and the wrathful incarnation of Avalokiteśvara (Tib. Chenrazee) who is incarnate on earth in the form of the Dalai Lama. It is recorded that Padmasambhava taught the dangerous female *dākinīs* and then went out into the world to preach, including spending five years in Kashmir and five years in Nepal. As has been mentioned, he is said to have conquered the forces of evil at Tiger's Nest in Bhutan and at many other places, leaving behind hidden texts and treasures to be found by others when the need for them is greatest.

Of special importance to this study is that, after a return to Bodhgaya, Padmasambhava decided that the time had come for him to go to Tibet and to strengthen the hold of Buddhism there that had been established in the seventh century under King Srong-tsan Gampo. Padmasambhava made it possible for King Thi-Srong-Detsan to build a monastery of circular plan at Samye by subduing evil spirits that had prevented its construction, and tradition holds that miracles attended the consecration of the site. Later, animistic Bön Po believers—the original "clergy" of Tibet—were defeated in public debate and ordered into exile. Buddhism was spread throughout Tibet, and the Mahāyāna Buddhist *Kanjur* and *Tanjur* were translated from Sanskrit into Tibetan, with Tibetan script based, at Srong-tsan Gampo's directive, upon the classical writing methods of India.

The eighth century saw the departure of Padmasambhava after he had "remained in Tibet one hundred and eleven years" and he continued his travels to Persia, Sikkim, Bhutan, China, Sri Lanka, and India. As he left Tibet the great teacher is said to have instructed his followers that "Hereafter, the Doctrine will be disseminated by Avalokiteshvara." This statement may have referred to the Dalai Lama as preeminent expression of the great bodhisattva. The first historical representative of the Most Compassionate One was the Grand (Dalai) Lama named Geden-dub (1391–1475 A.D.), nephew of Tsong-Khapa, the founder of the Gelugpa Order. So the entire world of late Buddhism in the Vajrayāna tradition, including the Nyingmapa lineage, looks to Padmasambhava for inspiration. And his image is everywhere.

Two illustrations after Samuel Turner are a fitting conclusion to the overview of British contributions to our study of Bhutanese art and culture. First there is a wash-drawing after Samuel Davis for an engraving by James Basire: "The Dwelling of Tessaling Lama, with the religious Edifice, stiled Kugopea." It is published in Samuel Turner, *An Account of an Embassy to the Court of Teshoo Lama in Tibet,* plate 12, and reproduced in Michael Aris' *Views of Medieval Bhutan,* page 24. It shows a tower that is two and one-half times as tall as it is wide, entered by a tripartite door and porch, painted at the top with a wide band of presumably red color, and crowned by two metal-covered roofs with raised ribs, *makara*-like monster heads at the roof corners, a lotiform pinnacle at the very top, vertical banners of cloth on frames, and roof silhouettes that are lightened visually by their upward curves and bells that hang below the roofs. It is an international design. Its solidity belongs to Tibetan and Tibet-related structural methods, its emphasis on animal heads may be due to local preference (comparison to Kalash carvings and roof-top animal forms in northern Pakistan is interesting), its ribbed roofs belong to both Tibetan and Nepalese prototypes, and its axiality that culminates in a spire *(qubbah)* is born of India or Pakistan.

The second work of art is also an engraving by James Basire, again after Samuel Turner, in his *Account of an Embassy,* plate 11, and it presents a subject that is not unique to Bhutan but shows the powerful mix of cultures that is continuous through these mountains. "The Mausoleum of Teshoo Lama" is shown against the background of a towering cliff with an essentially monastic and residential-type building having six prayer banners and a large doorway in the foreground, and a building of one of the region's most extraordinary structural types in the background. Turner called it a *kugopea* and Aris provides the Tibetan term *Gos-sku-spe'u* or "cloth-image tower." Its remarkable purpose is to provide a place for hanging a gigantic cloth artwork, sometimes called tapestry but, as noted above, actually painting or applique of a type that may still be seen today, even at the Potala in Tibet. There is an example of such a display wall at Tibet's Shigatse monastery complex. The battered tower rises seven stories high and tapers toward its wedge-like top. It is white below with additional color (red?) only at the very top story. To Americans, it is like the screen of a drive-in movie; to believers it is a blank surface that they know will come to life at festival time. There is no stronger statement of the colossal in the mountains. Other such structures are found in Thimpu in Bhutan and elsewhere in the sphere of Vajrayāna Buddhism. It is architecture as drama, substance as dream. As buildings crumble and fall, hopes and prayers continue to rise, even in Tibet.

Finally, a monument that belongs to the present in terms of reinterpretations of established forms and meanings: the memorial *chorten* of King Jigme Dorji Wangchuck (1952–72) that was erected in Thimpu under the rule of the late king's son, His Majesty Jigme Singye Wangchuck. It is fantasy made concrete and imagination preserved. Bhutan today is moving forward with close attention to the needs of her people, and with membership in the United Nations Development Program along with the World Health Organization, UNESCO, and UNICEF. The young monarch has a Royal Advisory Council (Lodoe Tshogde) consisting of a chairman who is appointed by the king, five representatives of the people, two representatives of the clergy, two representatives of the southern Bhutanese people, and a women's representative. The National Assembly (Tshogdu) consists of 150 members including elected representatives, appointed government officials, and ten members of the clergy with the Je Khenpo as its head. Eighteen districts are governed in this, the only country in the world that has Mahāyāna Buddhism as its state religion. In this remarkable place is an unparalleled monument that preserves the visionary and dream-like impact of Vajrayāna cosmology while it honors the memory of the past king and his lineage.

While *dzongs* have been stressed in this overview of Bhutan, it is also important to understand the *chorten* as "receptacle of offerings" and northern Buddhism's interpretation of the Indian *stūpa*. The Great Stūpa at Sanchi in India, dating from the third century B.C. through the first century A.D., is a prototype that allows for both circumambulation in a clockwise direction and ascension up its curved stairway onto the body of the monument, and up to a height that allows the elaborate iconography of story that covers its *toraṇa* gateways to be read at eye level. The Thimpu monument compares to this multilevel effect of a climb into sacred space, but its spiral rise takes place *inside* the *chorten* rather than on the exterior.

Symbolically, every *chorten* as northern version of the *stūpa* consists of five basic parts which represent the five elements of existence—earth, water, fire, air, and ether. It is also said to consist of five colors—yellow, white, red, black, and blue. These in turn are associated with the five Buddhas of the Matrix World and the directions—Samkusamitararaja at the south, Mahavairocana at the west, Ratnaketu at the east, Divyadundubhimehanirghosa at the north, and Amitabha at the center.[34] The stepped based of a terrace-*stūpa* and the storied pile of the tower-*stūpa* both stand for Mt. Meru at the center of the universe, which is identified with the World Pillar of unity that is the axis of all things. This exactness of meaning is expressed through structure wherever a *stūpa* or *chorten* is built, and the visual elements themselves are usually abstract—a mound that is topped by a *yaṣṭi* (staff or flagstaff) as central column, possibly with a *chattra* umbrella as honorific covering at the top.

Tsarak Pema Namdol Thaye, who was born in 1966 and began drawing at the age of four before being trained in the traditional ways of a master artist by Master Sherub of Kham Sanen Rekhi and Master Yeshi of Bha Lingkha Shey, prescribes the drawing of an ideal *chorten* on a grid measuring 40 by 68 squares, for a total of 2,720 units. As with measurement for any image, painting, temple, and *maṇḍala,* the design is defined and guided by horizontals, verticals, and diagonals in absolute balance for perfect iconometry. Even the gently smiling mouth of Buddha is constructed within a rectangle of twelve sections with crossed diagonals to determine its mathematically determined center. For those who would understand and perhaps draw such perfect designs, Pema Namdol Thaye of Kalimpong has published the *Concise Tibetan Art Book*.[35]

All of the standard rules were followed to create the memorial *chorten* of the late King in Bhutan, but with one very important variation. The mound, painted dazzling white, is hollow. This in itself is not extraordinary—Burma is just one of several cultures that creates a semi-hollow *stūpa,* mainly to provide inner shrines and perhaps a circumambulatory passage within. Medium-sized hollow *stūpas* to hold the body of sainted teachers are found both inside the traditional sanctuary of the Potala in Lhasa and in a modern shrine recently constructed near Bodhnātha *stūpa* in Kathmandu Valley. But the Thimpu *chorten* is completely hollow in large size, having much more sculpture inside than is provided in four small window shrines that expose directional Buddhas on the outside. Its two-story interior is filled by a mammoth cone-shaped mountain as the center of existence, with all the occupants of heaven and hell rendered in full color and full action. Sakyamuni and the multiple Buddhas are shown in plaster over a rubble base, as are male and female bodhisattvas and terrific powers like the wild and grimacing Heruka, who are often shown in *yab-yum* sexual union. Demons to be conquered are present along with spiritual ideals, and it is as if one has entered the Bardo world of the after-death plane as one climbs a spiraling staircase that encircles the colossal sculpture. As much as in any other work of tantric art, color is overwhelming, and the iconography is astounding.

The Thimpu *chorten* could be compared to Bhutan's cylindrical temple of Tamcho Gompo on the Thimpu-Paro road that is known as the "Monastery of the Iron-Bridge Builder" after the temple architect Thangtong Gyalpo, or to the cylindrical tower of Dungtse Lhakhang or "Temple Erected with a Cylindrical Wall" to the west of Paro Dzong, a structure that is credited to the same architect. But no other monument is filled with such a varied and expressive microcosm of the macrocosm as that found in Thimpu.

The preceding discussion has touched upon monuments in order to trigger thoughts of definition and comparison and analysis. But it must be remembered, even in the overwhelming presence of the giant cosmic diagram described here, that the physical works of art are secondary. Art merely serves as catalyst to reaching understanding of higher things and higher values. All is illusion in the physical world of mundane attachment, but art can lead to escape. And so we return to the astounding temple complex as Taktsang, Tiger's Nest, high above Paro Valley. In *Ancient Bhutan,* Blanche C. Olschak writes:

> To the right of the path, high up in the mountain ranges on the north side of the river Pachu, there are perpendicular rock formations. Built into their walls can be seen the many-storeyed constructions of the monastery and its adjoining buildings. They look quite inaccessible . . . Before reaching the Tiger's Den Monastery, one first comes to a little Lhakhang built on a rock plateau overhanging a drop of several hundred feet. This is the temple of Urgyan Tsemo (U-rgyan rkTse-mo). From here the Tiger's Den buildings can be seen on the opposite side of the gorge, clinging to the sheer sides of the mountain and called by the particular name of Zangdo Pari (Zangs-mdog dPal-ri), the "Copper-coloured Mountain Paradise of Padmasambhava." It does not take much imagination to realize that here, before its consecration as a holy place, a tiger demon had to be subdued.

And so Bhutan is defined by its monuments.

5

Late and Early Arts of Nepal

THE BOWL-SHAPED VALLEY OF KATHMANDU, AN ELliptical space that measures only about twelve miles by fifteen miles and which can be walked around by its *pradakṣiṇā patha* or pilgrimage route in a single day, is lush. It is quite far from the looming snow peaks of the high Himalaya that are visible only during the dry season, roughly October through March, and it does not receive snow at its altitude of 4,500 feet. The walls of the valley have been terraced over the millenia into a landscape of the human hand and simple tools. The valley may be considered here as a kind of geographical and sacred *maṇḍala*. Its life lines are its rivers, notably the Bagmati River, but life lines are also defined by human movements. Definitions and interpretations of those movements as ceremonial pilgrimage routes that link a network of temples and the sites of miracles are offered by Ulrich Weisner, Niels Gutschou, Giovanni Scheiber, and Mary Shepherd Slusser, while the painstaking measurement, drawing, site planning, and other details of physically recording the valley's buildings have been carried out by foreign specialists like Carl Pruscha and Wolfgang Korn along with the skilled Nepali crew that is employed by His Majesty's Government of Nepal. John Sanday and other foreign advisors have offered valuable insight as monuments receive special designation and protection or are even rebuilt from the ground up. Specialists like Deepak Shimkhada and Gautamvajra Vajracharya have brought their unique knowledge of their own country's accomplishments in art and literature to the United States. With all of these investigators, the art of Kathmandu Valley has become better and more widely known than that of any other Himalayan area.

The following pages are meant to convey the special identity of Nepalese architecture, first in the northern region of Solo Khumbu that preserves Tibet-related arts in the way of Bhutan and Sikkim, along with local invention, and then approaching Gorkha and Nawakoṭ as stations of the Hindu king Pṛthvī Nārāyaṇa Śah on his way to conquer Kathmandu Valley in 1768–69 in order to set the scene for Gurkha/Newari confrontation and cooperation. The valley itself will be treated in terms of selected monuments in its three major towns—Kathmandu, Patan, and Bhaktapur—along with illustrative temples and *stūpas* in village settings. The author will draw upon his earlier works *Temples of Nepal* and *The Nepalese Pagoda—Origins and Style* to define the main categories of temple and palace arts, all with special concern for preservation of what some would call the most developed civilization that ever existed in the Himalayan region.

Typical house of Newar farmers with three storeys and construction of wood, baked bricks, and clay tiles.

The often heard description of Kathmandu Valley as holding 2,000 temples and shrines is not an exaggeration, and the belief still holds that the valley was created after a miraculous lotus flower with jewelled parts bloomed above the primordial waters that once covered the land, and when the Bodhisattva Mañjuśrī cut an opening in the valley wall with his magical sword. The land was populated and, legend recounts and Mary Shepherd Slusser repeats, Mañjuśrī was helped by the "heavenly architect" Visvakarman to create a populous city, today's Kathmandu, that was patterned after the form of Chandrahas, the miraculous sword. Hindus may credit Kṛṣṇa with draining the waters away, but the story remains essentially the same. It is a story that is repeated for many parts of Asia, sometimes—as in peninsular Southeast Asia—involving a royal ancestor who opened the way to civilization by "drinking up" the flooding waters and marrying a local princess. The tale matches perfectly the antique account of Viṣṇu taking the form of Varāha, partly human and partly boar, and lifting the world, as personified in a woman, out of the waters. It is a suitable role for the God of

Tree shrine with roots around Varāha image of Visnu as a bear, Dhum Vārāhī, Nepal, fifth century.

Fifth-century stone image of Viṣṇu in his boar incarnation as Varaha, Dhum Varahisorine, Nepal.

Preservation, and a stone image of Varāha is shown saving the world in a wayside shrine at Dhum Varāhī, probably dating from the sixth century.

Earliest sculptures from Nepal are comparable to Indian art of the Kushan (50–320 A.D.) and Gupta (320–650 A.D.) dynasties. Paintings of such early times are lost in Nepal, but murals and portable manuscript illustrations show ties to the Pāla and Sena dynasties of the eighth through thirteenth centuries. The earliest surviving architecture, notably Kāṣṭhamaṇḍapa in Kathmandu and the temple of Indreśvara Mahādeva in Panauti, dates from the twelfth century. Along with physical remains, the dynastic history of Nepal is well documented, and this is a rich record that no other Himalayan civilization possesses, with the possible exception of Kashmir. Mary Shepherd Slusser gives the following carefully determined sequence of seven periods:

Licchavi	ca. 300–879 A.D.
Transitional	ca. 879–1200 A.D.
Early Malla	1200–1382
Late Malla	1382–1769
Shah	1769 to the present, but interrupted by loss of power for a century
Rana	1846–1951, when a local family usurped the power but not the throne of the Shahs
Shah "restoration"	1951 to the present

There is another kind of setting that is even more important than historical sequence, and that is the religious setting of Buddhist and Hindu belief coexisting in remarkable harmony so that the life of any individual is shaped and directed by concerns with the divine. Mary Shepherd Slusser states in the first volume of *Nepal Mandala* that,

> For most Nepalis, even the sophisticated, the vast concourse of deities, an invisible host inhabiting the Kathmandu Valley, is still paramount. The traditional devotion is rendered with undiminished fervor. This is expressed in daily worship *(pūjā)* and in the collective observance of a seemingly endless cycle of family, local, and national festivals. The life of most Nepalis is not only circumscribed by the physical limits of their milieu—in the Kathmandu Valley a diminutive oval of terrain—but by their traditional values and institutions. Moving between temple and *vihāra,* deity and sacred site, each linked to each in an ancient web of interrelations, the Nepalis worship their gods in traditional ways under the influence of traditional beliefs colored by legend, and by the pervasive influence of tantra-derived mysticism and magic.[1]

So this study cannot begin to interpret arts of the past without taking account of the still-viable religious context of a believing populous whom we move among and learn from today. Nepal abounds in treasures, both earthly and divine. All of the "attractions" of late twentieth century life are known to the people of Kathmandu Valley, and there are many outsiders and many insiders who bemoan the loss of more "innocent" times. But the observer should remember that to walk only a few miles beyond the valley can lead one back centuries in time, and that Nepal is still a land of

Ritual cleaning, repainting and dressing of Matsyendranātha image made of wood. Sveto Matsyendranātha temple, Kathmandu, Nepal.

farmers while maintaining communication among its peoples remains one of the government's most daunting tasks. Can it be true, as this writer was told in 1966, that some of these people have never seen a wheel?

Having glimpsed the remarkable architecture and allied arts of the Darjeeling areas, Sikkim, and Bhutan, it is familiar territory that we visit in the mountains of Nepal. Of the 400-mile length and the 100-mile width of the Nepalese kingdom, no region is more spectacular in geography and beauty of Buddhist art than Solu Kumbu, home of Sagarmatha or Mt. Everest, Mother of the World and the Abode of Snow. A sense of the magical hangs over the great peaks almost like the clouds that so often cling atop their summits. This is the top of the world. As Mt. Everest is shared on maps by Nepal and Tibet, the architecture of Solo Khumbu reflects both Nepalese and Tibetan invention as it shares two traditions of domestic and sacred construction. A village like Namche Bazaar (as if there *could be* another village like Namche Bazaar) belongs to the Sherpas, and its buildings show the Tibetan orientation of this northern culture. Although Tibet's economy has been termed a closed one, trade has always reached into Nepal—the drive from Kathmandu is only about one hundred miles long—and onward to India, China, and Mongolia. Christoph von Fürer-Haimendorf explains that the name "Sherpa" is derived from the Tibetan *shar-pa* that means "easterner," which is puzzling since Tibetans view Sherpas to be southerners from their homeland in the north. Still, the name distinguishes the Sherpa people from other Bhotia groups.

The principal populations of these people are found in the three regions of Khumbu, Pharak, and Solu, although the name Solu Khumbu is sometimes applied to them all. The Khumbu region as a whole stretches from the Tibetan border to the confluence of the Dudh Kosi and Bhote Kosi rivers, and its villages are found at average elevations of 12,000 to 13,000 feet. Summer settlements and grazing grounds, however, are found as high as 16,000 feet.

Caravans carried Tibetan wool to India where it was admired for its sheen and strength while rock salt, borax, and carpets were brought to Nepal and Kashmir. Tibet sought the silks, gauzes, and damasks of Chinese weavers in order to make the robes of monks and officials, while cotton, hats, wool, and more "ordinary" goods were acquired from Nepal and India. In his *Tibet—Land of Snows,* Giuseppe Tucci appropriately moves beyond the tents and yurts of nomadic Tibetans to describe architecture that is "average," not that of the very rich or the very poor. He speaks of the mansions of nobility along with ordinary dwellings, for there is no important difference between them beyond size and accouterments. Power is expressed as height, in Tucci's words, and this is especially true in the case of castles, with the height of Ladakh's seventeenth-century palace in Leh reaching nine stories into the sky on its hilltop setting. Tibet's Potala of the fifth Dalai Lama, completed in 1694 A.D. and still standing in Lhasa—thanks to the efforts of Chou En-Lai to keep it from being part of the mass destruction of sacred buildings that happened during the Cultural Revolution of the 1960s—is a combined palace-fortress and temple. It stands for imposing grandeur at its fullest expression in the Tibetan world. Tucci relates that,

> Like a new mountain built over the one it stands upon, and imitating its solidity and boldness rather than imposing premeditated rhythms of its own, details of the craggy truncated pyramid are swamped in the hugeness of its impassable walls, with their stairways that seem to reproduce the zigzag patterns of mountain ledges.[2]

Indeed these comments capture the taste for overpowering volume that characterizes some Tibetan architecture, including palaces, but it must be remembered that the lhakhang as much smaller and much simpler temple is far more common, and so is the much smaller and simpler house. We may credit, as Tucci does, the trans-Himalayan house as the starting point of Tibetan and much neighboring architecture including that of Solo Khumbu. He calls the massive rectangular houses an "imposing display of strength" as they are made of stone or big, oblong, sun-baked bricks on a foundation of rock. As the houses taper upward to a flat roof that is used for laundering and drying clothes as well as for many other purposes, they are said to have "a certain rude dignity."[3]

The present author might disagree that there is a rude or rugged impression to be drawn from the domestic structures that he was housed in while trekking the Solo Khumbu region of Nepal, for the interiors of average or slightly better-than-average houses are spacious and comfortable, with at least some glazed windows and polished wood floors. The ceilings are low but appropriate to the short and stocky physique of Sherpas as well as heat conservation, but there can be a problem of smoke from stoves that are stoked inside of the house. The subject of wood smoke brings up the desperate state of deforestation that imperils Solo Khumbu and nearly all of Nepal, with solar cookers offering one of several alternatives to traditional cooking and heating.

A poor family will have a house of only one floor, and sometimes that is hardly more than a lean-to. A more prosperous family will have a house of two or more stories, with the lowest level being used for storage and sometimes to shelter animals. One notices well-proportioned windows set into frames that are made of painted wood, with both the side beams and the lintel often being brightly painted while the sill is plain. The window's carvings may harmonize with a carved entablature above them, and certain Tibet-oriented areas show a thick layer of reeds that are placed horizontally and perpendicular to the outer wall surface as an effective blanket of insulation. This last element is widely spread through the Himalaya, and it is as appropriate to sacred structures as to domestic ones. The blanket of reeds may be two feet thick or more, and it is usually painted a dark, red or maroon. If glass is not available, and certainly it is not in most Himalayan villages, paper may be glued to the frame of a window which then becomes a translucent source of light as it protects from the elements. Accumulation of snow is generally not a problem on the flat roofs, for intense sun at high altitudes melts it quickly, even in the cold. The roofs offer pleasant work spaces and, in a place like Namche Bazaar, a bird's eye view of the village and its dramatic surroundings. The sight and sound of avalanches are most impressive from such a vantage point. Such a village has the appearance of consistency due to the mostly uniform height of its buildings and, whether or not there is a layer of vegetal insulation, there is normally a band of dark red color that goes all around each house below the flat roofs and a low wall on top of it to enclose the rooftop work area.

Christoph von Fürer-Haimendorf is impressed by the uniformity of Sherpa architecture, with all dwellings made according to a single basic plan with stone walls that are plastered and whitewashed on the outside while roofs, supported on a framework of heavy timbers, are covered over with broad wooden slats that are weighed down with stones. He points out that Sherpa houses, most of which are two stories high, are made without nails. Inside of a Sherpa house the second floor normally consists almost solely of a living room measuring 25 to 40 feet long by 10 to 12 feet wide. This layout is almost always the same and includes a hearth for cooking and heating, a broad bench under the windows with a long, low table in front of it, the seat of the house owner next to the open fireplace, and the place of honor next to the host. The anthropologist also notes that the walls of the room are usually panelled with wood and that one corner of the room usually holds the wooden bedstead of the house owners; others sleep on the floor. Almost any part of the room may function as a sleeping area, with rugs on the floors normally being unrolled for the night. Cupboards and trunks are used for storage, including storage of folded clothes, and a domestic shrine may have its own space along the walls in a sleeping room or "study." The kitchen of any house with its open hearth is normally very clean and, if the owners can afford them, vessels of copper, brass, or aluminum will be found neatly lined up on shelves where they are a proud display that often includes a woman's dowry and wedding gifts. A wooden churn for tea is an important item in any kitchen, and a churn may also be kept for brewing *chang* as a potent kind of wine/beer that tastes a bit like sake. Wooden bowls, metal utensils, and chopstick-like sticks with metal caps that may be carried in a quiver-like tube of wood or metal are also part of the domestic scene. Access from one floor to another may be provided via narrow stairs or a notched log that is set up as a ladder.

Domestic structures, like all Tibetan-style buildings, utilize a heavy frame of timbers whenever they are available, and the walls are more likely to be made of stone covered with plaster than of *terre pise* or rammed earth. Tucci redirects his focus from houses to monastic *gompas* made of the same materials, and he states that, "The same quality of line, made more impressive by their monumental scale, is found in sacred buildings." He proposes that, "There is a distinct cleavage in monastic architecture between masonry—simple, silent, jealously protecting the sacredness of what it encloses—and ornament, gay and garrulous by contrast."[4] To this observer, however, the structure and the symbolic additions that Tucci calls "ornament" are of a piece. Both are straightforward and very bold. Neither element can stand alone.

An additional kind of structure that has already been called widespread, even universal in terms of the Himalaya, is the *chorten*. Those that have already been mentioned in Sikkim and Bhutan are joined by Nepalese monuments like the multiple structures in front of Thyangboche monasteries and the countless votive *stūpas* or *chortens* that are gifts of faith made by pious Buddhists and sometimes repositories for the ashes of honored teachers and monks. Closely associated with *chortens* are *mani* walls, mentioned earlier as accumulation places of prayer, blessing, and commemoration that are often gifted with inscribed stones when a journey is commenced and/or finished. One of the rarest types of *chortens*, and a variety that is especially relative to Nepal-Tibet exchange in Buddhist art, is the "*chorten* with many doors" called *go-mang chorten*.

The most impressive monument of this kind is found at Gyantse in southern Tibet, near Shigatse with its great Tashilunpo Monastery, and not far from the Nepalese border. Gyantse is a large monastic complex that was spared extensive damage during the Cultural Revolution and other Chinese campaigns, although the huge fort that once stood on the hill above the town was completely destroyed. It is on the main trading and pilgrimage route between Darjeeling/Kalimpong/Gangtok and Tibet's trading town of Shigatse. The prominent four-story structure that supports a hollow tower is a reminder that it was to Tibet that a young Nepalese artist was summoned to build a major *chorten* in the thirteenth century. The artist, Aniko, was a Nepalese specialist in bronze-casting but his work in Tibet began with architecture. He affected the history of Tibetan sculpture as well, and this is evident as Nepalese features are seen on the many wooden figures that still fill the monastery shrine hall next to the Gyantse *chorten*. Any such combination of sculpture, painting, and architecture is likely to honor his contributions. Gyantse has probably the most elaborate *chorten* ever seen in Tibet. Called the Ne-nying Gompa, the shrine-filled monument is one of many that keeps alive the name of a seventeen-year-old youth who came to Tibet upon the recommendation of Phakpa ('Phags pa, 1235–80), a religious teacher who initiated the Mongol emperor Kubilai Khan into the mysteries of the Hevajra cycle of Tantric Buddhist ritual. Aniko, whose impact on Tibetan art is recognized by Nepal's own Rishikesh Shaha in *Heroes and Builders of Nepal* as well as by others, was brought to the developing Chinese capital at Beijing where he was made director of Imperial Manufactures in the Mongol Court of China's

Yuan Dynasty (1280–1368 A.D.). It is not surprising that the first paved road that was opened between Nepal and Tibet in the 1960s is called the Aniko Highway.

The Ne-nying Gompa is quite unique in its layering of radiating and expansive square terraces and the inclusion of multiplied shrine rooms from bottom to top (further research is needed to compare it to the *chorten* "with many doors" that is illustrated but not precisely located in Tucci's *Tibet—Land of Snows,* plate 32). David Snellgrove and Hugh Richardson refer to a relationship between tiered-roof temples that are now lost in India but still survive in Nepal and sacred structures like the gSer-khang (Golden Temple) at sTod-gling in western Tibet that was first described by Tucci and is "built in the form of a *mandala,* the mystic circle or divine palace, representing the center of existence dominating the four quarters of the compass."[5] The subject of a divine palace built in the earthly realm should be kept in mind throughout this study, as should the Tibetan concept of five-part sections of a *chorten* relating to the five elements of existence (earth, water, fire, air, space or ether). These associations are as appropriate when discussing a simple gateway with *chorten* form above it, as when approaching the rich complexity of Gyantse, dated to the fifteenth century by Snellgrove and Richardson as they refer to the huge tower as *sku-'bum* or Great Great Stupa.[6]

Sixty-four shrine rooms crowned by a circular tower with four more doors contain clay images of various Buddha incarnations, disciples, many bodhisattvas, guardians of all kinds, traditional teachers and saints, *dākinī* goddesses, and more. The top two levels that crown the monument as square superstructure supporting circular rings above the *chorten* body, itself descended from the *aṇḍa* or "egg" as the *stūpa* hemisphere of India, have shrines to the cardinal directions and the "all-seeing eyes" that Nepal associates with Ādi-Buddha as premordial Buddha principle. The eyes, in double-curved lotiform pattern that derives from Pāla-Sena dynastic art of India as it is interpreted in Nepal, are painted on all four sides of the square *harmikā* as next-to-last structural element. Above this hollow pedestal is the *yaṣṭi* or crowning parasol in the form of an eleven-stage cone of metal rings on a lotus-petal base that supports a pierced metal umbrella with a *stūpi* in vase-of-plenty and sacred jewel form at the very top.

The structure is as imposing as an ancient ziggurat, but it is lightened by the many openings that make the monument both more open and perhaps more inviting than most *chortens*. It animates the earth around it like any *chorten* marker, and it animates visitors by drawing them into the chambers of its inner secrets. Our brief look at the Gyantse *chorten* and the wood sculptures in its shrine hall returns this investigation to international themes. Carving and metalwork are also discussed by Snellgrove and Richardson as showing elements that once existed in Kashmir and that still are found in Kathmandu Valley. Tibetan woodwork of "old neglected temples" in western Tibet is said to still preserve the style and meaning given to art by Kashmiri craftspeople. The present researcher would like to expand that sphere of interaction to include the arts of China and, especially, the Silk Road. Aniko had tremendous impact upon the development of both Tibetan and Chinese arts. He introduced a fluidity of line and surface to bronze art—an image of a bodhisattva in the Newark Museum's Chinese art collection is one example of his affect on other artists—that had never been seen before. Yet it is not enough to trace the pattern of Nepali and Kashmiri influence in Tibet alone. One can begin to broaden the search to include Khotan and Mongolia in Central Asia, as well as all of the other cultures along the Silk Road, even as far as Tun-huang where China's part of the Silk Road opened into northern and southern branches.

Gompas in Solo Khumbu are all "international" in terms of tastes and skills that determine their impressive totality. The Buddhists of Khumbu follow the Nyingma-pa sect. The *gompas* of Khumbu are fairly recent it seems, with that of Pangboche said to be the oldest. Its foundation is credited to a legendary holy man, Lama Sanga Dorje, who could be called the "patron saint" of Khumbu. Devuche is a nunnery of fairly recent foundation date according to von Fürer-Haimendorf, who found twenty nuns there in 1957. Thami is a small but dramatically situated *gompa* on a steep mountainside and it is said that a family of married *(gyupi)* lamas has cared for a small temple that was originally established by Lama Sanga Dorje.

Thyangboche is the best known monastery, with much of its art said to date back to the fourteenth century, although von Fürer-Haimendorf

Thyangboche monastery, Solo Khumbu, Nepal.

attributes its beginnings to the twentieth century. Any monastery or nunnery in Khumbu, including Kumjung Gompa in the village of Kumjung that is one of the highest towns in the world as well as home to the famous Kumjung artist named Kumjung Kapa Kalden Sherpa, relates to Thyangboche as standard of elaboration. That monastery, like any in these mountains, may seem to explode and implode with Tibet-related mysteries expressed by color and line and flame and shadow. It is an understatement to say that the art of such places is "full," yet it is unfair to say that the mural paintings, *tanka* paintings, and sculptural assemblies show a sense of *horror vacuii,* or fear of empty spaces. Both would be foreign value judgments. Rather, artists like Aniko try to hint at the immensity of an essentially unrepresentable universe while including as much of its limitless populous as they can. Tucci observes that "motifs of differing origin and baroque exuberance of workmanship are underlined by a certain heaviness of design and the concern not to leave any space unfilled." Yet if space must be filled, it is for reasons of iconography—telling the full and awesome story—not merely visual fullness. Tucci tells us that,

> Even the shape of Tibetan utensils and furniture is overblown. The bulging teapots, rather short-necked, with their high domed lids, have none of the lightness of the Persian or Chinese ones.

He relates how Tibetan goldsmiths find,

> Endless ways of showing off their expertise: the auspicious signs and symbols . . . floral whorls, and tendrils—the whole decorative heritage of craftsmen expert at their work but of limited invention.[7]

Tibetan art has always engendered controversy, from the Jacques Marchais Museum on Staten Island to the *tanka* paintings shown on New York City's Riverside Drive to places even further from Tibet's solid sphere. Beauty is always in the beholder's eye, and so the art of Tibet's technicolor vision is left behind once again, to resurface in Ladakh, as this analysis proceeds toward Kathmandu Valley and the art of the Newars.

Before considering Nepalese art from its earliest expressions in Kathmandu Valley to its full flowering in medieval times, and after examining its development as part of the Tibetan cultural sphere of Solo Khumbu, this analysis turns to fairly late military and political events. These treat the meeting of Hindu invaders and Buddhist dynastic rulers in ways that affected not only the country itself but all of its neighbors. The subject demands that we begin by leaving the Valley aside as the "center" of Nepalese culture in order to first look to a very different area in the western hills. That place is Gorkha.

Ludwig F. Stiller, S.J., in *The Rise of the House of Gorkha,* notes a tendency toward political fragmentation in Nepal along with divisive aspects of nature and economy, and such factors are found throughout the mountain areas under study here. He speaks of "petty rājas" who ruled the "ministates" and the alliances into which they grouped themselves. He sees Rajput infiltration from the Indian plains and Punjab as affecting greater Nepal before the Gorkhali conquests that would succeed in unifying the whole country for the first time. He considers a broad area of about 700 miles from east to west and 100 miles from north to south (again, the present extent of Nepal is about 400 miles by 100 miles) as he explains that political fragmentation accounted for there being an independent state for every 850 square miles, some small and some large. Whatever their size, these states were protected from interference from the south by the thick jungles and malarial threat of death to all who would cross the region of the Terai; that is, the lowland between the hills of Nepal and the Gangetic plain of India. Yet for those who had ways to circumvent the most pestilential parts of the southern border, Kathmandu Valley was renowned as a center of trade, just as it was famous among the traders of Tibet, China, and Central Asia. Two independent kingdoms, Bijayapur and Chaudandi, were once located to the east of Kathmandu Valley, while Makwanpur was an independent state found to the south. Central Nepal was ruled by twenty-four princes, while Mustang was independently ruled to the north. The Baisi Rājas were twenty-two princes ruling their own principalities in the west. Beyond the Kali River lay Kumaon and Garhwal and beyond the Sutlej River lay Kangra, all to the west of Nepal. Any of these areas was constantly changing in terms of its rulers and alliances.

Although Gorkha is singled out here, it was not by any means the first substantial kingdom to grow up in Nepal. Epigraphy and geneologies are part of the substantial records that reconstruct earlier times. Any consideration of Kathmandu Valley history must begin with the important Licchavi Dynasty of 300–879 A.D., its gradual decline, and the later dynasties to rule Kathmandu Valley and more. Stiller points to the Malla kingdom of Jumla to the far west, studied by Giuseppe Tucci and others, that was founded in the twelfth century and may have been created by joining the interests of the kingdom of Guge in western Tibet, Parang in southeastern Tibet, and Ladakh. The Malla kingdom of Kathmandu Valley dates from 1200 to 1769, and it is the most important time period for this study that concentrates upon the valley's cultural developments. The Sen kingdom in central Nepal extended its borders to the fullest during the reign of Mukunda Sen I (1518–53) but, like the western Malla kingdom, it lasted for about two hundred years—from the mid-fourteenth through mid-sixteenth centuries. Like Perceval Landon and other early researchers in Nepal, the present author is most concerned with the more famous and more influential Malla kingdom of Kathmandu Valley, with its outstanding development of art and culture during what has been called the "golden age" of the Newar people.

While the valley kingdom of the Mallas was not always fully unified during the years of its growth, it is well documented that it had strong influence over many parts of central Nepal. In terms of the present study, the Malla Kingdom of the valley and the architecture of the Newars are credited with providing a high point of Himalayan art and civilization. This fact was well recognized by Sylvian Levi, whose early work *Le Nepal,* published in three volumes between 1905 and 1908, remains a basic source on Nepalese history. All western researchers owe a debt to Giuseppe Tucci, David Snellgrove, Pratapaditya Pal, Luciano Petech, Stella Kramrisch, Henry Ambrose Oldfield, Brian Hodgson, James Fergusson, A. L. Basham, and others whose work is pioneering in spite of their cultural distance from Nepalese scholars like Hem

Raj Sakja and other authorities whose names are found in the following pages. The best study of the cultural history in Kathmandu Valley is undoubtedly *Nepal Mandala* (2 vols.) by Mary Shepherd Slusser, and that outstanding work is consulted in sections to come as it is added to the present author's own field observations.

Our primary concern is to compare Nepalese architecture to that of the other mountain cultures that are presented here and to look for what is special about it and about its creators. Alliance by marriage and by family ties in general was crucial to the growth of Nepalese culture, and this study will refer especially to medieval arts of the Mallas and late medieval arts of the Śah family with its branches—not only in Gorkha but in Nawakot and elsewhere—as extensions that were most often achieved by the actions of Śah rulers who took over the thrones of existing states.[8] While the family subgroups of conquered dynasties did not always cooperate fully with Śah usurpers, they did lend backing to the advances of Gurkha conquest that changed the history of Nepal and surrounding regions forever.

The prominence of the lineage based in the hill kingdom of Gorkha should be examined with some reference to another royal line—that of the Rājput kings of India. During the fourteenth century, Rājputs gradually moved into greater Nepal, seeking refuge from attacks upon their North Indian strongholds, including Chittor. They came to be very influential in the military and "foreign" affairs of the hill states of Nepal, but not in the day-to-day procedures of government.[9] Rājput presence is important to recognizing developments in Nepalese art and in Nepalese political history right up to the present moment. Rājputs are crucial to the development of art in the Pahāri hills of Northwest India, but also in other Himalayan and foothill areas. The natives of Rājasthān and the Punjab Hills reached a long way to affect Nepal, but they succeeded. To some extent they, like European kingdoms, provided models for the extravagant kind of monarchy and associated "royal" families that ruled the country from 1769 through the mid-twentieth century, when certain political changes affected the continuity of relationships between prime ministers and kings, between Ranas and Śahs, that lingers to the present day.

We refer to Stiller once again as he writes of the "Dream of Unification" that drove the Gurkha armies and their leaders to unite some eighty small kingdoms of greater Nepal and to give the land national identity. Their methods were often harsh, their ruthless military skills were unquestioned, and their advance was seemingly unstoppable. The author quotes the first and greatest conqueror-king, Pṛthvī Nārāyaṇa Śah, the Gurkhas' unquestioned leader, as he arrived at the edge of Kathmandu Valley to say:

> From Chandragiri's top I asked, "Which is Nepal? They showed me, saying, 'That is Bhadgaon, that is Patan, and there lies Kathmandu.' The thought came to my heart that if I might be king of these three cities, why, let it be so."[10]

And king he did become. The process of unification was lengthy and difficult for it affected the military, political, judicial, administrative, cultural, and religious elements of life in Nepal. Geography, as always, was an obstacle to Himalayan cohesiveness. Pṛthvī Nārāyaṇa Śah's own history, *Dibya Upadesh,* records the dying king's last words regarding the country of Nepal as, "my little, painfully acquired kingdom."[11] It has been suggested that he felt much affection for his subjects, even for those who had fought his entry to Kathmandu Valley. Yet memories of Gurkha attacks, especially upon other peoples of the western Himalaya, suggest cruelty beyond measure. The final aims of the Gurkha leaders were political and economic rather than religious, and they did not generally destroy the temple arts that are the focus of this study. They took palace design to new heights both literally and figuratively. The most effective leader of the Hindu invasion is still an enigma after more than two hundred years.

Pṛthvī Nārāyaṇa Śah had ruled the house of Gorkha since the age of twenty, and he was always ambitious. Francis Hamilton in his pioneering work of 1819, *An Account of the Kingdom of Nepal,* describes the king as,

> a man of insatiable ambition, sound judgment, great courage, and ceaseless activity. Kind and liberal, especially in promises to friends and dependants, he was regardless of faith to strangers, and of humanity to his enemies.[12]

If the question is raised as to how Gorkha, of the many mountain kingdoms, was the one to triumph over its many neighbors, it may be, in

Stiller's words,

> Because Prithvinarayan Shah of the House of Gorkha provided the vision and the leadership that galvanized this state to concerted action and sustained it to the moment of victory. The story of the unification of Nepal did not unfold entirely during his lifetime, but it began with him, simply because he boldly took the first step on that long journey of conquest.[13]

A miniature watercolor portrait in Nepali/Rājput style of the famous founder of the Śah Dynasty is found on the upper floor of the National Museum in Kathmandu Valley. It shows a profile view of a seated man who is small and thin, looking remarkably weak, a "chinless wonder." That picture is seldom reproduced or published, however. Much more often seen is a large-scale oil version of the king's portrait painted in romantic European style, showing a stalwart man in full battle attire who strides straight toward the viewer while carrying a sword in one hand and raising his other hand in victory. This is presented dramatically against an illusionistic background with imposing throne, victorious lion, blowing double pennant as the Nepalese flag, and the waving plumes of the king's Greater Bird of Paradise crown. Perhaps the identity of the real man is to be found somewhere between these two images.

The king of Gorkha, like his Gurkha soldiers, was a Hindu. Kathmandu Valley was essentially Buddhist under its Malla Dynasty rulers, although Hindu and Buddhist elements have long been more thoroughly mixed there than in any other Asian locale. The forces of Gorkha were supported by the goddess Kālī, bloodthirsty and horrific female *śakti* who is noted above as the consort of Mahakala. She is the fiercest female form of Śiva as Lord of Destruction. Soldiers believed—and may still believe—that Kālī would actually fight beside them on the battlefield if they needed help. Every soldier paid his respects to Kālī's shrine, hung with red flags of victory, in the hilltop palace at Gorkha. If possible, a soldier or his family will hang a photograph of the fighting man on the outside of the temple porch.

Kālī's unquenchable thirst for blood is associated with the *khukhri* knife, a weapon that every Gurkha wears at his waist in a black leather sheath, that he clenches in his teeth in the midst of battle, that is slightly curved so as to better sever the head

Gorkha Palace, Gorkha, Nepal.

of a sacrificial buffalo in a single swing, and that everyone knows should not be returned to its sheath without drawing blood. Gurkha loyalty is also unquestioned, even when the soldiers are hired as mercenaries, and so they are the romantic subject of Kipling and countless other British writers even as they form a personal bodyguard today for Queen Elizabeth II. But a more important subject of this study is the impact that the Gurkhas had on Nepalese art and architecture.

The first phase of Pṛthvī Nārāyaṇa Śah's move toward Kathmandu dates from roughly 1744–54 and includes the taking of Nawakot as a former provincial capital of the Malla Dynasty. The main monuments of the small hilltop town are a pair of strongly constructed palace buildings, one towering and defensive and the other of lower, domestic design. They are made of hard, red-orange brick and have well-integrated wooden elements including string-courses, windows, doors, and brackets that are recognized as being distinctly Newari.

The Mallas had, of course, employed their own Newari artisans to make such buildings, but Newar art was already familiar to the Gurkha invaders and the sacred and royal structures in Gorkha also reveal Newari workmanship in their use of brick, wood frame, tile roofs, and carved wood. Shantaram Bhalchandra Deo slights Newari art when he attributes it with having "fanciful decoration" when in fact every part of an important building has symbolic meaning, but he is correct in his concise analysis of:

> The architectural peculiarities of wooden structures of Nepal [that] comprise the use of heavy wooden framework, ingenious arrangement of load distribution with the help of struts and bracket capitals, projecting or balconied window groups, multi-storeyed receding roofs, massive pillars and elaborate window and door frames. A little imbalance in the wooden frame or disintegration of wood contributes to the weakening of such constructions.[14]

It is useful to remember that the Newars are known not only for delicate wood carving and refined metalwork but also for massive and lasting architecture in spite of Deo's cautionary note regarding disintegrating materials. The buildings in Gorkha and Nawakot have very heavy walls that are at least three feet thick. These are opened to light by windows with telescoping frames of multiple lintels that reach higher as they go into the building. Projecting balconies with floors supported by extending beams of the interior storeys are found only at the highest and most impregnable part of the palace. The tower is otherwise a "closed" building while the nearby resthouse has an open porch for rest and quiet work, with low-ceilinged rooms above. The contrast of vertical thrust beside horizontal resting place is common throughout Himalayan architecture. Both Nawakot and Gorkha display basic Nepalese building skills.

Window in a resthouse courtyard below Gorkha Palace, Gorkha, Nepal (copyright His Majesty's Government of Nepal Department of Archaeology).

Detail of Gorkha Palace, Gorkha, Nepal (copyright His Majesty's Government of Nepal Department of Archaeology).

The most common kind of "open" building is a pilgrimage stop or laborer's resting place, called *sattal* in Nepal, while towers belong to palaces like those in Kathmandu Valley, to watchtowers that recall that at Gondhla in Lahaul, or temple storehouses that are as large as that at Sarahan in Himachal Pradesh. A timber frame that can reach as high as twelve stories in Nepal is solidly filled with bricks that are fired at high temperature in a tall brick kiln. This kiln is fired by wood after the clay itself has been mixed—at least for important buildings like palaces and temples—with a vegetable substance similar to molasses that makes them especially hard and long-lasting.

It is important to note that Nepalese building is always simple trabeate, composed of horizontal and vertical "piled" elements that are supported by their own weight, with the only angled elements being sloping roofs and diagonal brackets or struts that are braced against lower walls as they reach up to support them. Access to upper floors is afforded by steep, ladderlike stairways as in Bhutan, and there are often trapdoors to close one level off from others. Wooden screening of balconies and windows offers a view of the surroundings while effectively hiding the viewer. They are like the *jhali* windows or doors of India, and perhaps related to the Rājput tradition of limited *purdah* or protection of women from the sight of strangers. The roofs are covered with interlocking hard-baked tiles, and they may have decorative or protective symbolic additions on houses or palaces, while they must have them on temples.

Pṛthvī Narāyān Śah tried diplomacy before force when he sought to take Nawakot. Nawakot's commander, Jayant Rana, was originally from Gorkha and so Śah sent him a letter stating that they should join forces, but the commander stated that he would remain loyal to the Mallas and a battle was thereby assured. On 26 September 1744, about one thousand Gorkha soldiers quietly crossed the Trisuli River at night to completely surprise the enemy. The road to Kathmandu seemed open from that point forward. Pṛthvī Narāyāṇa Śah met resistence there, but only after he had defeated Kasi Ram Thapa, leader of Malla forces sent by King Jaya Prakāśa Malla of Kathmandu to take back Nawakot. Thapa paid for his failure with his life.

The Malla king negotiated with Pṛthvī Narāyāṇa Śah at Nawakot, giving various lands to the attacker's allies and two important forts at the east side of Kathmandu Valley to the invader himself. This loss is one reason the king was dethroned in favor of giving the kingship to his eight-year-old son, Jyoti Prakash. Taudik Kazi became minister and held the real power in his hands, a pattern that would later become traditional through alliance of the powerful Rana family with the ruling line. The kingdoms within the valley had their own territorial disputes, including for control of the villages of Sankhu with its important temples and Changu with what may be the earliest of Nepalese temples, Changu Nārāyaṇa. For a time the Gurkhas, also called Gorkhalis, remained in their forts. But they soon controlled the ridge that forms the western side of Kathmandu Valley even as Jaya Prakāśa Malla managed to return to take government control in the valley in 1750 while allowing his son to remain on the throne. The ten years between 1754 and 1764 saw other rulers of hill regions rise up in objection to the rapid advances of the house of Gorkha and act to keep the Gurkha armies in check. Even Jaya Prakāśa Malla had some success, for he took the fort that Pṛthvī Nārāyaṇa Śah had built at Shivapuri on the edge of the valley.

The Gurkha leader negotiated with Tibet for needed funds and, in 1757, returned to attack Kathmandu Valley. His focus was on Kirtipur, an important town that occupied a strategic hilltop. Other citizens of the valley came to fight with Kirtipur, and the Gurkha forces had to withdraw. They took their revenge in 1765 when, after having failed in 1764, they finally crushed the resistence and punished the vanquished, legend tells us, by cutting off the noses of many if not all residents of the hilltop village. In popular lore, the town was henceforth known as Naskatpur after the Sanskrit term *nasa,* "nose."

With the gradual but complete accession of the three main kingdoms of Kathmandu, Patan, and Bhadgaon (Bhaktapur) and many neighboring villages, Pṛthvī Nārāyaṇa Śah fulfilled his dream of taking the entire valley. Kathmandu fell quietly, as the Gurkha leader entered the city during the Newar festival of Indra Jātrā on 26 September 1768, and seated himself on the royal throne that was set up in the palace square while King Jaya Prakāśa Malla escaped to Patan. On 6 October that royal city also fell. And the fiercest fighting of all took place in Bhadgaon before it fell.

It is the applied arts of metal and finely carved wood that most clearly separate Nepalese architecture from the *gompas, chortens,* palaces, and ordinary domestic structures that have been noted in Sikkim, Bhutan, Tibet, and the Darjeeling area hills. It may be appropriate to begin with details as Kathmandu Valley building arts are approached, especially the details of wood construction and finishing that create the wooden window and balcony complexes for which Nepalese art is famous. They are what first drew the present author to Nepal and Kathmandu Valley and, after more than twenty years' comparison of this art to other Himalayan traditions, he remains convinced of the importance of their very special accomplishments.

Shantaram Bhalchandra Deo served as professor of Ancient Indian Culture at the Indian Aid Mission in Nepal from 1963–65, and his study of Nepalese woodwork is a pioneering one.[15] After outlining the sequence of Nepalese history in terms of rule up to the time of the Śah (Śāha) dynasty he begins, on the very first page, to define the cultural synthesis that is reflected in every sphere of Nepali life. He reflects upon the early periods that left "a legacy of culture which is a fascinating blend of Hindu, Buddhist, Tantrik and local elements." The amalgam of cultures that has created the civilization of Kathmandu Valley, and especially of the Newar people there, must always be considered. Sandwiched between the great land masses of India and the plateau of Tibet and between latitude 80° and 88°E and longitude 27° and 30°N, Nepal consists of great topographical variety as well as many distinct populations. Mustang and Dolpo are just two of the remote areas that have received serious study in recent years. But the cultural center is unquestionably Kathmandu Valley.

Professor Deo notes a fabric that is imaginatively woven from threads of later ritualistic Buddhism with its vast pantheon and of tantric Shaivism with its emphasis upon Shiva and his family amid more than one million deities plus local characters. It is not hard to find evidence of the latter. For example, nearly anyone in Kathmandu city can direct a visitor to the public "toothache tree," a big timber that projects from a humble building into the public lane where anyone can pound a nail and coin into it and thus end the torment of a toothache. Such a lane is part of a network that is invisible to the naked eye but crucial to stability and well-being of any town—the *maṇḍala* of human movement is sacred activity, a kind of *pradakṣiṇā* or pilgrimage circumambulation that gives merit to individuals while maintaining group identity and social cohesiveness. There is more than sympathetic magic. Lanes that look like simple alleys can be just as important as processional avenues as this net of symbiotic exchange between the worshipper and the worshipped is maintained. It may be that no physical map of such routes exists, and their logic may be known only to the *pujārī* or priest, but they remain crucial and whole. They are the "invisible" plan of Nepalese town architecture.

To return to an impressive art that is likely to be found along or near any of the paths of town organization, the wooden relief sculptures and screens are unmatched elsewhere in Asia. Unmatched in terms of their structural integrity—the

Street near Indra Chok, Kathmandu, Nepal.

Shrine with carved doors near Yatkha Bahāl, Kathmandu, Nepal.

Window of a shrine near Yatkha Bahāl, Kathmandu.

frame of doors and windows extend at their bases to look into the brick wall matrix that surrounds them—they are also matched in terms of their complexity. The rippling rhythms of wooden parts are created by their almost nonsensical multiplication. An opening will have not one but thirty, fifty, or even more narrow lintels to cover it. They are not individually supportive but found as a "shimmering" group. It is perhaps not an overstatement to say that multiplied cornices, lintels, and vertical frame elements are kaleidoscopic in the way that they surround an opening and make it visually vibrate, even oscillate all around. Some of the border motifs are shared with Tibet, others with India, and some are unique. While a typical artisan might provide no explanation of the wooden finery other than "that is how it is done," there is in fact a firm basis in precise literary guides that are drawn from the *śāstras*. There is also direct relation to elements of the sacred *maṇḍala,* and this is described in such classical texts as the *Guhya Samaja Tantra* of Tibet.

The *maṇḍala,* already mentioned several times in the preceding pages, is at the heart of architectural form and meaning throughout the Himalaya as it is in India and Tibet. In religious context it is explained by Nelson I. Wu in relation to "perishable plurality" versus "eternal unity" so that the sacred diagram is seen as follows:

> In the two-dimensional design of the Buddhist *mandala* . . . there is a double spatial relationship: the plan is seen from above and the figures from the front. As the Buddha faces the viewer forever, he is facing any direction from which he is seen. This problem of portraying the omnipotent religious energy is a very real one in temple architecture of an axial plan.

Wu goes on to say that,

> The temple is at once the notion of God, the dwelling of God, the body of God, and the holy act of man utilizing tangible substance to realize all these abstract ideas. Thus its basic plan is not the abstract and eternal rimless circle, but the vastupurusamandala (Vastu, the Site; Purusa, the Essence; Mandala, the Form), whose manifestation is a square.[16]

That square radiates energy and light and truth, thus the wooden parts of a Nepalese building also radiate and seem endless in the multiplicity of

A painted Tibetan maṇḍala *from Darjeeling.*

structure and symbol. The panel in the center of a *maṇḍala,* the Brahma-sthana, is equal to the inner room or *garbha-gṛha* of a Hindu or Buddhist temple in Nepal, and it is the exact center of a *maṇḍala*-based building plan. The designated location of the most important image or symbol to be honored is determined by the intersection of diagonal lines drawn from the corners of this inner room. In his forward to *Living Architecture: Indian* by Andreas Volwahsen, Walter Henn raises an intriguing question:

> Modern architecture is sometimes reproached for being poorer than that of earlier eras, since most buildings are constructed on the basis of a grid plan. Yet by contrast Indian architecture does not seem to have suffered any kind of limitation upon its wealth of forms by using such grids, even figures so rigid and unyielding as squares. Is it possible that this profusion was only able to develop 'because' it was based on a grid?[17]

The grid has been called the module of monastery building in Sikkim and in the Tibetan sphere of influence. It has the same importance in Buddhist Nepal, and for Hindu-Buddhist "pagodas" of Nepal it gives rise to the vertical repetition of multiroofed towers, not only temple towers but palaces as well. Such points are made in harmony with the pioneering research of Stella Kramrisch in *The Hindu Temple* (Calcutta, 1956) and the useful review compilation of George Michell in *The Hindu Temple* (London, 1977). In the latter work, the outward direction of energy is shown as proceeding from the center of the temple sanctuary, with important secondary images of the deity housed inside appearing on the exterior of the building. The reader may integrate the universal use of the *maṇḍala* in temple design with another centering procedure: the use of *sādhanās* or specific visualization rites that are taught individually to a

The temple of Śiva Maṇḍir in the Palace Square of Kathmandu.

A constructed maṇḍala *made by monks at Nepal's Svayaṁbhunātha* stupa *temple, courtesy Christopher George.*

person according to his or her personal characteristics. Yet both provide a context to bring the body, speech, and mind into play for integration, balance, and calm amid the distractions of the earthly life. That Vajrayāna, as the Tantric school of Buddhism, utilized visualization as early as the third century A.D. is, according to John Blofeld, proven by Lama Govinda, Benoytash Bhattacharya and other authorities.[18]

After such considerations of geometry, the grid, and the *maṇḍala* as its source and its product, it is useful to return to the subject of woodcarving of doors, windows, and balconies in Nepal. They are, of course, international in many respects, but one connection remains puzzling. That is the proposed tie to South India that is referred to by Deo as he writes,

> It is noteworthy that the impact of South Indian culture on Nepal is not insignificant. Nanyadeva, the founder of the Tirhut line at Simraongarh in Nepal, was a feudatory of the Chalukyan ruler Vikramaditya [and] V. [Luciano] Petech remarks that "somehow such a connection had existed, since many of the Chalukyan inscriptions boast of a suzerainty over Nepal." Even Kalachuri Bijjala himself seems to have patronized South Indian Brahmanas. The descendants of the king also took pride in their Karnataka origin.[19]

If specific similarities to South Indian carving are difficult to define—and they certainly are in the

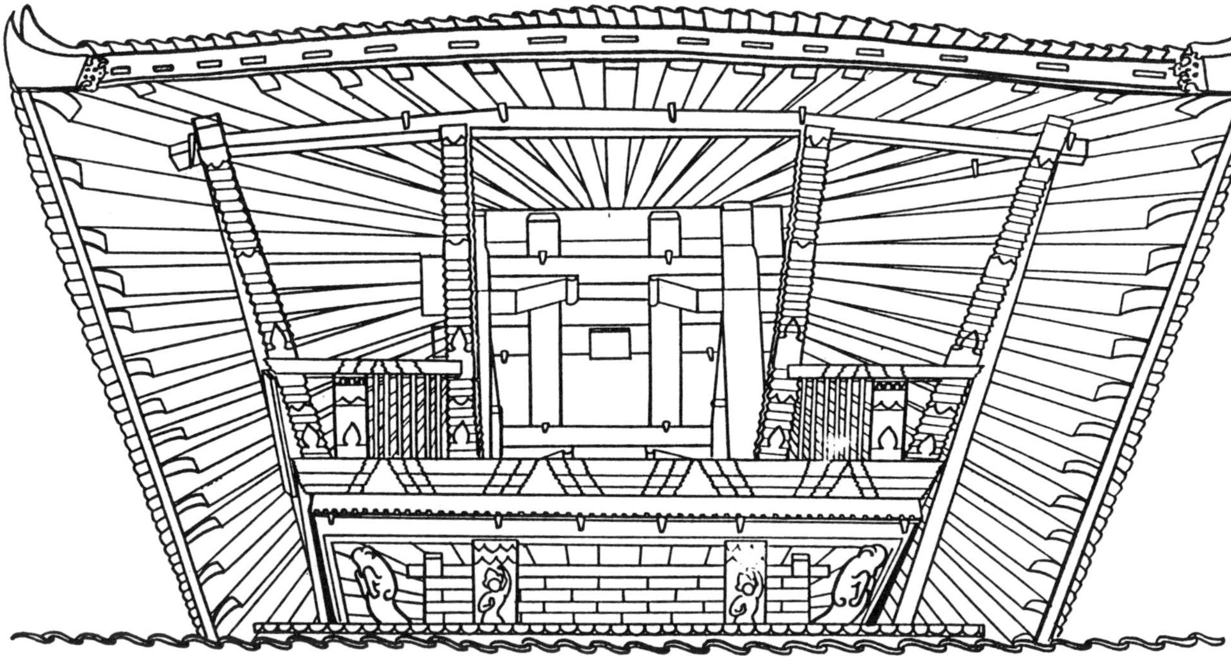

Fanning roof beams with supporting struts of an unusually open temple structure in the palace square of Kathmandu.

present writer's experience of visiting temples and palaces throughout Kerala—the same is not true of Tibetan art. Kerala temples are made of stone—usually laterite—topped with umbrella roofs made of wood and covered with baked tiles of interlocking "Dutch" type, and they often have nine-part planetary ceilings made of wood as well as wooden screens and wooden bracket figures that superficially resemble such images in Nepal. But their setting in unique courtyards, the identity of Hindu gods worshipped, and building methods themselves are quite different from those in Nepal and the Himalaya. Tibet offers more to build on here. Elements of both classical Nepalese carving and classical Tibetan carving include the *padma* or lotus border and the *chos brtsegs* or "dharma stack" that is also called a thunderbolt pattern. There are similarities in the way wooden screens and other objects are put together. The palace of Bhadgaon (Bhaktapur) in Nepal is recorded to once have had ninety-nine courtyards. Any one of them would likely have had the kind of grill windows with tympanum tops that still exist on the buildings that remain, along with shallow projecting balconies. An unfortunate mid-twentieth–century effort to "brighten" and decorate the Bhaktapur palace windows led to their being painted black and daubed with white paint and simple flowers, but that disfigurement has been removed. One can imagine the original Newari artists and craftspeople at work here, and we note their tools, methods, and materials.

Shantaram Bhalchandra Deo is thorough in his records of the kinds of wood that are traditionally used by the Newars—*dhumsi* and *shasi* in Newari language, the former meaning "strong as a tiger" with the botanical names of *Michaelia excelsea* and *Michaelia champaca* and possibly *Shorea robusta*. He adds that today's Newars use *sal, agrat,* and *chapa* woods, that the wood from the village of Sankhu found fifteen miles northeast of Kathmandu is considered to be the best of all, and that repairs are usually made with *chapa* wood. The tools that are used by the Newars include *balasa* (adze of iron), *batan* (right angle), *batra han* (various chisels with wooden handles), *burma* (drill), *buskha* (medium wood shaver or scraper), *hakhi* (a string dipped in black color and with a small plumb attached at one end), *kati* (saw), *khal buskha* (small wood scraper), *namuga* (hammer with iron head), and more. The reader may integrate the universal use of the *maṇḍala* with small pointed pokers for deep cutting and corner dressing.[19]

The above list alone is enough to show that there is nothing "primitive" or basic about the kind of workmanship that appears in Kathmandu Valley, and the same could be said regarding techniques of wood joinery that are used in seemingly endless variety. The temple serves as a house of one or more gods—Michell refers to the very

Carved Nepalese cornice with extending beam ends of clay on a temple in Kathmandu Valley.

Multiple pinnacle of Bhagavatī Maṇḍir beside Taleju temple, Kathmandu, Nepal.

terms used to designate a temple as *prasada* (set or platform of a god), *devagṛha* (house of a god), *devalaya* (residence of a god), and *mandiram* (waiting and abiding place)[20]—and so it must be perfectly built, perfectly proportioned, and perfectly finished. Since the use of both windows and doors in Nepal is truly additive, as they are anchored in the structure without really helping to support it, their role may be termed a "finish."

Wood joinery or *sandhi-karma,* a term that goes back at least as far as medieval times and which has been traced to Manasara as the source of the medieval *Vāstuśāstras* as written guide for artists and artisans, is prescribed in very specific ways. Different procedures are appropriate to different parts of a building. The importance of the grid in South Asian art comes to mind as a carpenter prepares a grilled pattern by using a *hakhi* or string dusted with black color with a plumb attached at the end. When this string is tight along a plank and parallel to its border, as checked with a right angle, the carpenter dabs along the length of the string to leave a black line on the surface of the wood. This is repeated until the entire plank is marked with parallel lines and the workman then saws along these lines to make strips of wood. The parts of a decorative pattern are then drawn on the plank in such a way that the strips will become interlocking parts of an integrated whole that is both practical and beautiful. The strips meet precisely at 45-degree angles, pressed together and interlocking so that no nails or glue are needed.[21] Attachments may be added over such grillwork

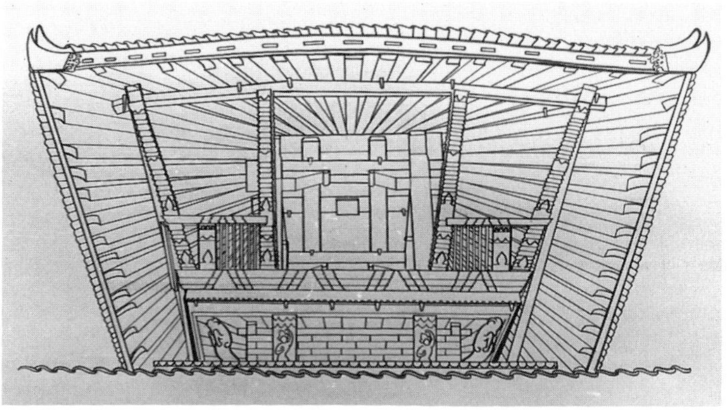

Typical roof construction (with open balcony), Nepal.

Guardian leogryph at Woku Bahāl, Patan, Nepal.

(the famous peacock window on the Pujārī Maṭh in Bhaktapur is an example), and the window itself may have various shapes beside rectangular. Round and octagonal windows are just two examples.

Doors are categorized as being rectangular, trilobed or trefoil, foliated, and arched. Of these four varieties, the second is useful to prove connections to Islamic art, especially Mughal art of the sixteenth to nineteenth centuries. The comparison goes back further to early medieval art of Kashmir and to Greek-influenced art of the Gandhara tradition in northwestern India that has its beginnings with the coming of Alexander the Great in the third century B.C. Foliated doors may show Islamic or European influence, the latter being especially likely for late buildings that were patronized by the large families of *mahārājas* around the rulers. Arched doors have still broader fields of reference, including to the Mediterranean world. Deo provides a selection of possible "decorations" on the lavishly carved doors and their frames, from receding doorjambs *(kaksas)* to the *chowry* or flywhisk, to the *pūrṇa kalaśa* as vase of plenty, rows of lizards, and much more. Doors may be divided into four, each panel having a different pattern from such choices as *machikan* (square grill) and *ichikan* (diamond grill). A special feature of Nepalese design consists of extended "wings" of wood at the top of the doorframe where they reach out to be surrounded by and anchored in the brick walls. They may act as brackets to support a lintel above them, or they may be nonfunctional. These are to be expected in monastery or temple art, and they normally have a standing female in *tribhaṅga* or hip-shot pose on top of a supporting *makara* as esteemed water monster and sign of plenty. Any other figures carved here might well belong to the family of divinities or *parivara-devata* of the god to whom the temple is dedicated.[22]

The covered statue of Sveta Matsyendranātha, a Buddhist protector Godhisattva *is brought out of its temple in Kathmandu, Nepal.*

The combination of materials that are found on the exterior of a temple or palace—stone, brick, metal, wood—being meticulously carved, molded, and pounded into three-dimensional form, makes Nepalese buildings the most tactile in the mountain region. An extreme example of this impact that is largely due to an additive approach to building and honoring a sacred or royal place is found in the temple of Sveta ("White") Matsyendranātha in Kathmandu. Its entry side appears almost spongelike because of an accumulation of additive materials, mainly floral and vegetal elements made of brass *repoussé* sheeting. Matsyendranātha is a Nepalese incarnation of the benevolent bodhisattva Avalokiteśvara, and he is worshipped in white emanation in Kathmandu and in Red *(Rāto)* form in Patan. The temple concerned is part of a *vihāra* or monastery compound, one of the eighteen chief *vihāras* of the city, and Mary Shepherd Slusser attributes the origin of the important image inside to the time of the reign of King Yakṣamalla (1428–82). The accretions on the surface of the temple, including "Grecian" statuary of an attendent female and framed paintings of Avalokiteśvara in his almost countless forms are all

The temple of Bagh Bhairava in Bhaktapur, Nepal.

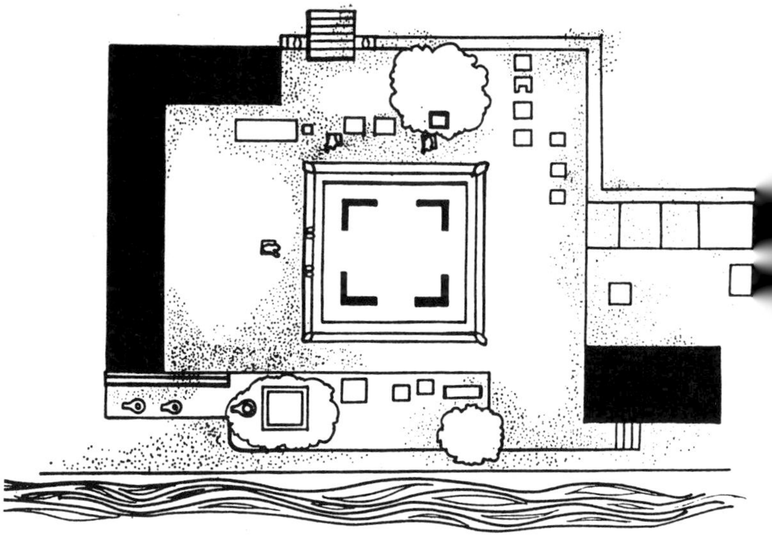

Plan and compound of Kaṅkeśvarī temple on the Bagmati River in Kathmandu. Note three Śiva liṅga *forms in* yoni *bases at the lower left corner. The temple interior is semisubterranean.*

Nārāyaṇa temple with patuka *banner, Bhaktapur (copyright His Majesty's Government of Nepal Department of Archaeology).*

Interior of semi-subterranean temple of Kankeśvarī, Kathmandu, Nepal.

much later. They serve as a reminder that in the additive tradition of Himalayan architecture—the animal horns mounted on the façade of the Hidimba Devī temple in Kulu Valley, the crowd of metal pots and pans that adorn the front of Chobar's Ādinātha temple as another monument honoring Avalokiteśvara, and the aforementioned photographs of soldiers that are placed on the temple of Kālī in Gorkha all come to mind. It is an aesthetic that is foreign to western eyes but one that suits the Himalaya as the offerings of devotion outweigh any concern for visual clarity.

When temple or shrine doors of any style mentioned above are opened, they provide access to a small and dark space that is normally occupied only by the symbol or image of the deity concerned and the priest or (rarely) priestess who attends that symbol or image. This room is the *garbha gṛha* or womb house. It is, however, quite common to find that a passage also exists inside of such a building, a circumambulatory passage that allows for *pradakṣiṇā* or pilgrimage around the inner sanctum and the sacred focus that it contains. This movement is always clockwise and, in Nepal, it is usually restricted to priests on those rare occasions when the passage is used. Anyone may circumambulate the building from outside, however. It is useful to recall that the great pilgrimage path that goes all around Kathmandu Valley, with stops at specific shrines and miraculous sites, is itself a *pradakṣiṇā patha* that defines a huge *maṇḍala*.

Double-wall construction allows for the passage that goes around the outside walls of the inner room. This double-wall pattern also allows the inner walls to project upward and form the outer enclosure of the next higher story of a Nepalese pagoda. It is a building method that Ulrich Weisner traces to early Indian prototypes in his *Nepalese Temple Architecture,* a fine study that is most useful in drawing exact correspondences between Nepalese architectural plans and structural/ornamental details and their often lost prototypes in India. It is, of course, true that Himalayan borrowing from India and other foreign cultures is always selective, but Weisner is very exact as he refers to origins. Architectural patterns of Gupta

Collapsing small temple in compound of Indreśvara Mahādeva in Panauti, Nepal, showing double-wall construction.

Bhagavatī temple, Dhulikhel, Kathmandu, Nepal.

and earlier beginnings are frequent in Nepalese building arts, so that Nepal and Himachal Pradesh may be judged to be the most important states in terms of showing both preservation of and variation upon the arts of the Gupta Dynasty, so often called India's Golden Age. Weisner states that,

> It is now assumed that there was once a style of timber construction now lost in India, traces of which can still be found in the temples surviving in Kashmir, Kathiawar, South Kanara and in Orissa too. This view, advocated with qualifications by Coomaraswamy and Rowland, renders superfluous any assumption of a coherent architectural complex extending from China to Nepal and Burma, as argued by [James] Fergusson. Instead, the expedient of a lost style of timber construction is used to fit the Nepalese temples into the overall development of Indian architecture.

But he points out problems with this assumption because,

> As early as 1883, [W.] Simpson pointed out . . . that this style of timber construction, defined by the criterion of a straight sloping roof, is to be found in none of the innumerable reliefs of Indian architecture.

As he notes,

> No attempt has been made till now to investigate and identify the characteristic features of the postulated Indian style of timber construction. Hence, no precise definition or demarcation from the architecture of other countries will hardly suffice as a criterion . . . Anyhow, as far as Nepalese architecture is concerned, one aspect has been overlooked, viz. that this is not primarily a style of timber construction. Nepalese temples are built rather of brick, with only the roof structure, false ceilings and frames of doors and windows consisting of wood. The roof shape too as

Wood carvings of Tripureśvara temple, Kathmandu, Nepal.

Roof-supporting struts of Tripureśvara temple, Kathmandu, Nepal.

> defined hitherto (straight sloping roof) is a completely inadequate criterion.[23]

The above quotations are lengthy because basic questions of relationships to other Asian buildings still comes up frequently, and because the term "pagoda" has been so broadly applied that a temple like the seventh-century tower at Horyu-ji in Nara, Japan, is assumed to be a close relative of a temple like Nyātapola in Bhaktapur, dated 1708. Weisner notes that Sylvain Levi wrote in his influential study *Le Nepal* (3 vols.) of 1905–8 that,

> Le kondo et le pagode du temple d'Horiuji au Japan, eleves sous la rene de Shotoko Taishi (593–621), attestent que des la fin du VI siecle le type consacre de la pagode en bois, tel qu'il existe encore au Nepal, s'etait propage par l'intermeditaire du bouddhisme chinois, jusqu'a la Coree, l'initiatrice des artistes japonais.

> [The Kondo and the pagoda of the temple of Horyu-ji in Japan, built during the reign of Shotoku Taishi (593–621), shows that the type of wooden pagoda consecrated at the end of the 6th century is like that which also exists in Nepal, spread by the intermediary of Chinese Buddhism as far as Korea, to be introduced to Japanese artists.]

But grouping Nepal, Korea, and Japan according to architectural similarities based on Indian beginnings does not entirely work. For one thing, puzzling arts of southwestern India, including Kerala, are not specifically considered in Levi's proposal.

Weisner advises looking closely at the two earliest sacred sites in Kathmandu Valley: Paśupatinātha and Changu Nārāyaṇa. Paśupatinātha is the best-known temple in Nepal, visited by great crowds at festival time and by a constant stream of believers every day and every night. It is a type site that may function as a criterion for measuring the quality and degree of adherence to type and tradition for almost any other sacred structure in Nepal . . . or even outside. The temple has many renovations and additions but it remains classical in almost every detail. Also often noted is a temple of brick and wood in Nepalese design that stands among all of the Indian-style *śikhara* temples of stone along the Ganges River in Varanasi (Benares). It is a structure of Paśupati temple type. Weisner credits the patronage of Gorkha (Śah) Dynasty kings in having the "imported" temple built among its native neighbors as he notes that Varanasi was [and is] popular with Nepalese royalty both for pilgrimage and for plots involving the future of Nepal. The deity honored there is Paśupatinātha, Śiva as Lord of Animals. He is also the supreme god of the Paśupata sect that may be traced to times as early as the second century B.C., and his primacy was stressed in Nepal in such early times that even in India he is often considered to be a Nepali god.

The temple of Paśupatinātha at Deopatan on the Bagmati River within Kathmandu Valley is the country's outstanding and most frequented dedication to Śiva Mahādeva, Śiva as "Great God." The Bagmati is honored here as the Ganges is respected in India, and its banks are the perfect place for Hindus to die and to be burned for entrance into the next cycle of existence. The temple has been rebuilt many times in its 1,500-year history. It began with two roofs, which were probably increased to a height of three roofs by King Mahendramalla and then brought back to two-roof size in renovation that was sponsored by Queen Gaṅgā Rānī in 1585 A.D. King Jyotirmalla (1409–28) endowed the monument with a golden *kalaśa* (water vase, vase of plenty) and a golden flag, and King Pratāpamalla (1641–74) had the temple precincts repaired and added a new finial to the building. Major repairs were carried out by King Parthivendramalla (1680–87) and others, but no event stands out more than the destruction of the golden *liṅga* as phallic symbol symbolic of Śiva and bearing his four faces that was smashed into three parts by the invading troops of the Bengali Muslim Sultan Shams ud-din Ilyas of Bengal in 1349 A.D. By 1360 the *liṅga* was replaced by order of King Jayasiṃharama of Nepal. The temple itself was probably burned when the *liṅga* was desecrated, and Weisner refers to little-known records that indicate that every town in the valley was burned to the ground at that time.

The temple's present size and its situation within a walled courtyard at the top of very steep stairs that lead down to the water at Ārya Ghat are recorded from at least as early as the fourteenth century. A moving river of worshippers cover the stairs and crowd the courtyard at the annual Paśupatinātha festival and its full moon. Other Paśupatinātha temples have been built elsewhere in the valley, including as parts of palace compounds in all three royal cities. The earliest of these is the monument first known as Yakṣeśvara in Bhadgaon (Bhaktapur) that was built by King Yakṣamalla in 1460 A.D., now generally called Paśupatinātha. Weisner suggests that any ruler needed the legitimacy of having the supreme deity of the country near the seat of his reign.[24]

So important was devotion to the protector god that King Yakṣamalla was required to make a daily pilgrimage to the distant temple on the Bagmati before his own temple was built. It was after Yakṣamalla's death in 1482 that the "country" of Nepal divided itself into three autonomous kingdoms.[26] King Mahendramalla (1560–74) built Mahendreśvara temple dedicated to Paśupatinātha as part of his palace in Kathmandu, basing it upon the aforementioned Yakṣeśvara temple in Bhaktapur. Considerably later, in the mainly Buddhist royal town of Patan, King Śrinivāsamalla oversaw the association of Paśupatinātha with the existing site of Kumbheśvara temple, dated 1392 A.D., and installation of an appropriate cult image there in 1672. The image is a *mukhaliṅga* (*liṅga* with faces) made of gold with four faces of Śiva that look to the cardinal directions.

Once each year the *mukhaliṅga* of Kumbheśvara temple is placed on top of a special pedestal that is approached by narrow wooden walkways in the center of a large and temporarily flooded fountain depression in front of the temple. Women scale the wooden walks with offerings to Śiva and the *liṅga* while boys swim to the center juncture in the deep pool. The attention paid by common people is as essential to the well-being of the kingdom as is the attention paid by kings. At other than festival times the fountain depression is drained and the metal *liṅga* rests in the exact center of its five-roof temple, one of only two such surviving towers, with the other being the dramatic temple of a secret Tantric deity that is Nyātapola in Bhadgaon.

To return to Paśupatinātha temple on the Bagmati, it is perfectly square with directional orientation and the expansion of sacred power that is always implied by a cosmic axis or *axis muṇḍi* of vertical thrust. The same may be said of Kathmandu's impressive temple of Taleju, protective mother goddess and royal matriarch, that is found in one of the many courts of the palace in the Darbar (Palace) Square, raised as it is on multiple plinth levels to soar skyward in an additional way. It is one of a group of temples that were and are believed to be in constant touch with each other as they house the spirit of the awesome Taleju, protectress of kings. Legend records that this tutelary goddess of royalty was first introduced to Nepal by King Harisiṃha in 1324 A.D. This is one more illustration of the importance of the interaction of Hindu or Buddhist gods with pious rulers and god-protected kings in Nepal and, by extension, all of the Himalaya. Taleju towers stand above the palaces of both Patan and Kathmandu, and the two-story temple of the goddess is off limits to foreigners as it rests at ground level within the palace complex in Bhadgaon just as it is restricted in the other two cities.

A very rare glimpse of the outstanding but restricted frescoes on the outside of the Bhadgaon

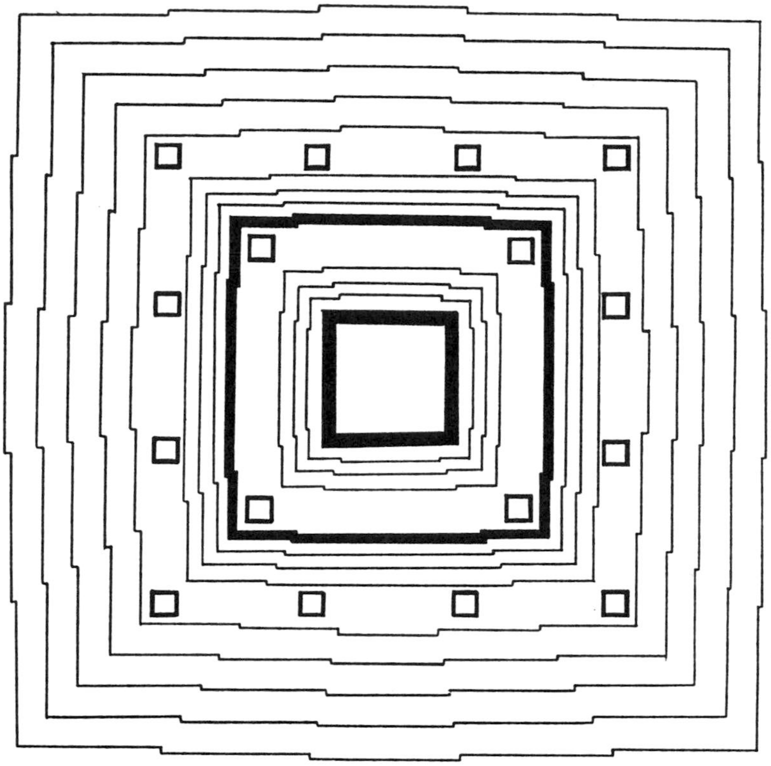

Maṇḍala-*derived foundation of eight steps at the temple of the goddess Taleju in Kathmandu Palace Square. The dark lines represent the upper wall around the temple and the walls of the temple tower itself.*

home of the goddess Taleju is provided by Madanjeet Singh in his *Himalayan Art,* pages 192–93. "Sumbha and Nisumbha" are identified as riding in a chariot pulled by seven horses as they advance toward an aggressive Devī Bhairavī in beautiful and also horrific form in paintings that are attributed to the seventeenth century. They show little or nothing in common with the usually flat-colored and intensely contrasting paintings that are seen in the northeastern Himalaya, Sikkim, and Bhutan. Instead, the murals show delicate line of brown-black with touches of orange-red and white as the superhuman and sometimes grotesque figures are presented with a kind of clean-lined clarity and dignity that recalls Pahāri painting of the Rājput tradition rather than Tibet. Mewar painting may be the most direct comparison, according to Gautam Vajracharya of the University of Wisconsin in Madison. Legend has it that such arts of Taleju and her major temples were once connected by ropes that were strung across the valley to facilitate communication between the three incarnations of the great goddess. The Malla rulers followed a custom of passing on from dying father to his eldest son the *mantra* or spoken invocation that would make the goddess Taleju obey his wishes, as noted by Weisner and based upon Wright.

In summary, the power that the goddess Taleju was believed to have is illustrated by the actions of King Jayaprakāśamalla as he hid in the Taleju temple of Kathmandu while the forces of Pṛthvī Nārāyaṇa Śah attacked Kathmandu. When the Malla king realized that he had lost his throne, he attempted to blow up the temple, but the damage was incomplete and the invading Hindu leader took the city and the monument. He did not, however, have the secret *mantra* that would make the goddess serve him. He performed human sacrifices to Taleju in order to control her, but the goddess is said to have appeared to him in a dream to express her dissatisfaction, so he ceased his efforts. Today the Kathmandu structure stands tall on a stone and brick base in stepped-pyramid pattern with twelve levels, and its doors on all four sides are almost always kept locked. While the first structure here was built by King Ratnamalla in 1501 A.D., the present building was put up during the reign of King Mahendramalla in 1564. The shining copper roofing, along with portal frames and gilt doors of the temple, was added by King Pratāpamalla (1641–74), and other additions followed. Of special interest is that in the 1560s, as Weisner points out, three temples were built in various parts of the valley in the perfect and most prominent pagoda style. They are Mahendreśvara or Paśupatinātha itself, the huge Taleju Maṇḍir in Kathmandu that has an additional third roof and very high base, and the two-story temple of Nārāyaṇa that stands in front of the Patan palace of King Puramdarasiṃha.

The temple of Taleju escaped serious damage in the three major earthquakes that struck the valley in 1810, 1833, and 1934, and it still stands tall in a way that reduces human importance in the overall setting of the heart of Kathmandu. It is one of the most impressive elements of the Darbar Square, and it is best seen together with its neighbors. Indeed, Nepalese structures, more than any other Himalayan buildings, should be seen in combination. The intersection and repetition of angled roofs that extend from relatively narrow substructures are dynamic and ever changing as one walks through the palace squares of any royal city in the valley. The interaction of sharply angled positive and negative areas is exciting and dynamic. It should be noted that the tight presentation of colorful and interactive monuments is itself set aside from the ordinary world of farmland outside, for the three capitals of Kathmandu, Patan, and Bhadgaon were each walled for protection, and moats were even used for further separation from possible assailants. In her maps for *Nepal Mandala,* Mary Shepherd Slusser reconstructs the entire walled enclosures for Kathmandu and Patan and a major section of wall for Bhadgaon. Like the ongoing work of George Michell and John Fritz at South India's Vijayanagar, her reconstructions are an excellent product of surface archaeology.

A selection of other temple and palace buildings in Kathmandu Valley represents the varied placements and styles of building art in Nepal. The reader is urged to look for the details, for the "finish" of the wood-carved structures and the veil of

Courtyard of Palace, Patan, Nepal.

Personified Yamunā River as female guardian in the Palace, Patan, Nepal.

Circular tower in the Palace complex, Kathmandu, Nepal.

ornament that almost seems to have been "hung" over them. These and other touches of refinement remain in one's memory. It should also be remembered that there is no division between temple/monastery, palace, and domestic buildings in terms of the wooden arts that may be attached to them, except that major deities will not be represented on houses. There is much more connection between secular and sacred buildings than in Sikkim, Bhutan, Ladakh, or Tibet. Palaces and palace temples are merged in Kathmandu, Patan, and Bhaktapur, as witnessed not only by the Taleju temples but by shrine towers of Hanuman, the monkey god who protects Rāma and Sīta in the *Rāmāyaṇa,* Kriṣṇa of *Bhagavad Gīta* fame in medieval devotional poetry, and other towers that are integrated into palace compounds.

An important combination of house and temple that is essential to the orientation of any ruler, whether or not it is beside the palace itself as in Kathmandu, is the dwelling-temple of the living goddess, Kumārī. The Kathmandu dwelling is built around a courtyard with a small door that opens to the street outside, and all four inner walls in here have lavishly carved balconies. Through a window in one of the balconies it is often possible to see the exotically made-up child who is the sym-

Decorative motifs taken from the carved wood in the courtyard of the temple of Kumārī the living goddess in the palace square of Kathmandu.

bol of female goodness and strength as she is the virgin expression of Durgā as goddess incarnation of Śiva and omnipotent destroyer of evil. Art abounds with dynamic representations of Durgā, whether in seventeenth-century miniature paintings from Basohli in India's Pahārī Hills or in the imposing cave temples that were carved of granite at Mahabalipuram in South India during the seventh century. But no visual expression of the goddess is more memorable than this child in a goddess-woman's make-up who glances casually down at the visitors who come to her court hoping for a glimpse of something both mysteriously otherworldly and, sadly, part of this earth.

Kumārī is another character who brings Nepalese art to life. As everyone in the valley knows, Kumārī is a virgin goddess who is part of the Hindu-Buddhist family and who takes living form by becoming incarnate in the body of a prepubescent girl. After being chosen as a small child by undergoing an ordeal of terror, a living Kumārī will remain in her temple house under constant care until she has her first menstrual period. At that time she can no longer personify Kumārī and she is set "free," but to a lonely life since she is considered to be too dangerous to marry and must often survive by living as a prostitute. At least this is a general explanation that is given regarding her strange existence, a subject that merits more serious study. Kumārī is found in all three major cities of the valley, and in some villages besides. Mary Shepherd Slusser numbers four Kumārīs in Kathmandu, three in Bhaktapur, two in Patan, and at least one in each of numerous villages including Tokha, Bungamati, Kirtipur, and Cha Bahil.[25] The temple and the goddess found just beside the original palace in Kathmandu are the most important, the structure that is popularly called Kumārī Bahāl being properly called Rājalakṣmīkula-vihāra.[26]

A second architectural variety of basically domestic design belongs to the *sattal* or resthouse for holy men that is sometimes built near an especially important temple to which visitors come from far away, needing shelter when they arrive. The best known of these is Kaṣṭhamaṇḍapa in Kathmandu, a structure that gave its name to the town and dates from 1143 A.D., with the first use of its name to designate the place being found in a colophon that also has a date equal to 1143 A.D. It is a very large enclosure with two stories, although the usable space is nearly all on the ground floor. Four massive columns are visible from the interior as they support the heavy superstructure, and a narrow log with cuts for footsteps climbs to the second level, which has its own balconies. The ground floor has balconies on all four sides, with the four huge columns instead of the kind of wall-within-wall construction that is typical of temples. A related kind of building is the *maṭh* or priestly dwelling.

Pujārī Maṭh beside the temple of Viṣṇu temple of Daṭṭātreya in Bhadgaon has been totally renovated by traditional artisans under German direction who used traditional materials, and it is an excellent example of what can be done to rescue important structures from ravages of climate and time. The building also represents crucial interest that has been shown by foreign countries to preserve Nepalese cultural history—support that is sadly missing in Himachal Pradesh, Ladakh, and northern Pakistan. The inner courtyards of Pujārī Maṭh are small but the wealth of woodcarving that is lavished on all three floors around each court, with tripled windows in complex frames on the upper two levels and intricately cut columns on the open ground floor, is as finely rendered as the wooden art of any temple or palace.

Freestanding temples have already been described, including the Taleju structure in Kathmandu, as they are often the most prominent in any part of the valley and in the few places where they exist elsewhere—Muktinath, Varanasi, and Pokhara among them. A banner painting from Guita Bahīl in Patan (Slusser, plate 186) shows a nine-roof temple that was recorded to have existed at the center of a Buddhist *bahīl* there. Kumbheśvara temple and Nyātapola temple have been mentioned as the only five-roof structures that remain, with four-roof pagodas being found in Harasiddhi and Chapagaon. It should be mentioned that Nepal's *śikhara* temples made of stone or brick, like Patan's Mahābouddha temple that was built in the sixteenth century as a replica in terra cotta of India's Bodh Gayā temple, are themselves powerful representations of *maṇḍala*-borne centering and cosmic axis symbolism.

Three-roof temples are numerous, with the twelfth-century temple of Indreśvara Mahādeva honoring Śiva with some of the country's finest carved brackets in the village of Panauti, while a

Kankeśvarī temple, Kathmandu, Nepal.

Wedding preparations at the temple of Indreśvara Mahādeva in Panauti, Nepal.

related temple of Brāhmanī stands across a small river from it. Nearby Panauti's Indreśvara Mahādeva temple is another "family" member in the form of a collapsing Śivadeva temple with exposed double-wall construction. Single-roof temples are frequently found as well, generally having special uses and varying plans, like the Navadurgā temple as a rectangular shrine of multiple mother goddesses that is found just downriver from the main Paśupatinātha temple, or the low temple of attendant gods that shares the courtyard of Changu Nārāyaṇa.

Changu Nārāyaṇa has the oldest known foundation date among the temples of Kathmandu Valley, and it deserves special attention here. If only one

Changu Nārāyaṇa temple, Kathmandu Valley, Nepal.

Entrance to Changu Nārāyaṇa temple, Kathmandu Valley.

Attendant stone elephants at Changu Nārāyaṇa temple. Department of Archaeology, His Majesty's Government of Nepal, used with permission.

monument were chosen to represent each Himalayan area—the Barpeta *satra* for Assam, Ghoom Monastery for the Darjeeling area, Pemayangtse for Sikkim, Thimpu Dzong for Bhutan, Bhima Kālī temple for Himachal Pradesh, the palace of Leh in Ladakh, Shah Hamadan mosque for Kashmir, and a mosque in Swat for Pakistan—then Changu Nārāyaṇa would stand for Nepalese color and carving and preciousness along with combination of materials, all as projected in the three-dimensional *maṇḍala* of Nepal. The building, dedicated to Viṣṇu, rests on its own steep hill that is itself a kind of marker. Taken together with its courtyard full of some of Nepal's earliest stone carving, its pillar with dated inscription that is equivalent to 464 A.D. and the stone Garuḍa man/bird that rests on the ground beside it, the metal-covered doors and doorframes, and the brilliantly colored bracket figures that support both of its roofs, the sanctuary is breathtaking.

Changu Nārāyaṇa temple may be the best possible example of classical architecture in Nepal. Its size, though large, is not overwhelming; its only base is the natural hill upon which it rests; there is more painted wood than precious materials to evoke the attention of gods as well as the adoration of humans; its courtyard compound is open and available to all. Like any Himalayan temple, it must be understood within the total setting of its realm—an agricultural world of *jyapu* farmers who toil hard in their rice fields while the pinnacle of the temple of Viṣṇu glitters in the sun as a sign of the universal cosmic axis.

Mary Shepherd Slusser likens the Nārāyaṇa of this place to Viṣṇu worship in the way that Paśupatinātha relates to Śiva worship as most prominent, most sacred incarnation of the god.[27] The Viṣṇu temple with its two roofs and numerous attendant images in stone as some of Nepal's most important sculptures are found in a small Newar village on top of a steeply sloping hill. Here Changu Nārāyaṇa is Dolaśikhara-svamin as he is placed in the temple at the top of its Hill of the Palanquin (Cangum), we are told. Surrounding the temple are *dharmaśālās* as resthouses for holy men. They have open porches that face the centrally placed building. Slusser refers to the structure as the largest of all sacred structures in the purely Newar style, and this might surprise a visitor who is impressed by the quiet intimacy of the site and the very approachable temple. There is much to see—including subsidiary shrines to Kṛṣṇa, Śiva, *matṛkas* as mother goddesses. An unusual presence is the beheaded goddess Chinnamastā, an incarnation of the Hindu goddess Durgā, who accepts blood offerings out of Viṣṇu's sight, in the southeast corner of the courtyard. Such a presence serves to illustrate the fact that Vajrayāna or Tantric themes are as much part of late Hinduism as they are of late Buddhism and that their development is prominent during the transitional period between the fading of the Licchavi period and the beginnings of Malla times.

The Buddhists who worship here consider the main deity to be a form of the bodhisattva Avalokiteśvara. While the present building is an eighteenth-century reconstruction that was accomplished in 1702, it has an associated date of 464 A.D., as inscribed as dedication of a pillar by King Mānadeva, a pillar that still stands before the temple entrance and may once have supported the large stone Garuḍa that is beside it. The inscription has long been recognized as the earliest such record known in Kathmandu Valley. It praises Viṣṇu as Hari, the Remover of Suffering. Yet Mānadeva is not necessarily recognized as the builder of the temple, a distinction that some say belongs to Haridaṭṭavarman who is listed in the *Gopālarāja-vaṃśāvalī* as the ninth predecessor of Mānadeva and perhaps the first ruler of the Licchavi Dynasty around 300 A.D. A recent discovery of a second inspiration, this one of a date equivalent to 607 A.D., is mentioned by Slusser, who quotes the *Gopālarāja-vaṃśāvalī* and records that the gilt sheath over the main image of Viṣṇu, a covering that was given by the famous King Aṃśuvarman, was a replacement for an earlier sheath that had "become dilapidated with the passage of time" and thus suggests that a very long period of use preceded Aṃśuvarman's time.[28]

Associated by identity with the concealed image of Viṣṇu in Changu Nārāyaṇa is another important sculpture, the Jalaśayana Nārāyaṇa, better known by the name of its small village, Budhanilkantha. This is a more than life-size stone image of Viṣṇu lying on his back on a cushion of entwined *nāga* snakes, representing the god at rest as he waits to perform acts of preservation, like the lifting of the world from premordial waters as shown in the Varāha image mentioned above. The reclining Viṣṇu is surrounded by actual waters in its tank setting, a reminder of the image of Viṣṇu that is washed by ocean tides at the Shore Temple of 700 A.D. in Mahabalipuram, South India. The style of the full-volumed figure and especially its perfect face with lotus-petal eyes, hawk-bill nose, and full mango lips is classically Gupta, showing Nepal's debt to Indian art. The image was consecrated by King Viṣṇugupta in about 641 A.D.[29]

The statue that is inside of Changu Nārāyaṇa temple is not shown to non-Hindus. Its design has remained an intriguing mystery at one of the country's foremost monuments, at least until a recent study that is noted below. Formal analysis and historical reconstruction are useful tools that aid the art historian's efforts toward making art come alive in logical ways, but there are other approaches that are equally useful. At this point, therefore, this study turns to very recent research that has been done by a young and resourceful scholar in the field of religious and cultural studies: Mr. Jeffrey Lidke. His soon-to-be published work entitled *Vishvarupa Mandir—A Study of Changu Narayan, Nepal's Most Ancient Temple* is an example of the kind of "living architecture" analysis that involves immersion in many aspects of context, belief in, and *use* of important monuments. It represents developments of architectural anthropology that remain all too rare in the study of Asia. He treats the mythic origins of the monument, its architecture as "divine," its sculpture as multiple forms in one, and its worship patterns that are the true animation of the temple. These subjects incorporate historical study and interpretation of symbolic meaning, but with a welcome freshness that seems to result from affectionate sympathy with the values of believers. It is apparent here that people live *with* the temple.

Lidke quotes a well-known but still puzzling statement by the Chinese traveler Wang Hiuen-T'se, written in the seventh century and published by Perceval Landon in *Nepal* (vol. 2, p. 25):

> In the capital of Nepal there is a construction of stories which is above 200 tch'eu in height and 80 pou (400 feet) in circuit. Ten thousand men can find room underneath it. It is divided into three terraces, and each terrace is divided into seven stories. In the four pavilions, there are works of sculpture to astonish you. Stones and pearls decorate them.

The location and the materials of the great tower are among its mysteries, but analysis of Changu Nārāyaṇa in terms of a temple as Viśvarūpa is a worthy effort toward solving its own puzzles.

Lidke reports that the inner image of Changu Nārāyaṇa has two gilded pillars beneath a gold canopy engraved with a cow suckling her calf called a *kamadohini* as it relates to yielding desires, and he theorizes that the first structure of Changu Nārāyaṇa was smaller and may have been built as early as the second century A.D. The present author saw a silver canopy held high above the central spot within but did not glimpse the image itself in 1995. His drawing illustrates the "central image of Garudasana (Changu) Narayana" that he proposes to date to the first or second century. It is reported to be made of gilded stone, and Lidke states that it may first have been made without a head, in harmony with the myth of the beheading of Viṣṇu by "Mura" as king of demons, an act that freed Lakṣmī as Viṣṇu's female counterpart so that she emerged from Viṣṇu's form in her own beheaded condition and slew Mura. Lakṣmī thereby takes the form of Chinnamasta-Devī, the Beheaded Goddess, and her temple is beside that of Viṣṇu. [We are told that her beheading and the coming forth of her life-blood bring forth Viṣvarūpa or Universal Form] and that the temple of Changu Nārāyaṇa is far more than a *devagṛha* or house of the god—it is his Viśvarūpa or Universal Form. Such emphasis upon architectural form as magical and sacred *in itself* is not known among other temples in the Himalaya. The sketch of the small Viṣṇu image inside presumably shows a figure of the god wearing a crown as he rests on the back of Garuḍa with outstretched wings. The god has four arms and holds a club and a *chakra* wheel against a background of a halo and a larger enclosure of swirling clouds. An additional point is especially useful, for the investigator states that the seventh century Garuḍāsana Nārāyaṇa made of stone that rests in the temple courtyard is a copy of the interior image.

Another essential fact that involves the importance of this hilltop expression of Viṣṇu is detailed by Mary Shepherd Slusser as she describes the twice-yearly visits of Changu Nārāyaṇa to Kathmandu at the time of the winter solstice and again in summer. We learn that for certain travels the god leaves behind his anthropomorphic image and the Garuḍa that supports him and invisibly moves his spirit into a large silver water pot as sacred vase or *kalaśa*. We also learn that he is accompanied by his consorts Sarasvatī as goddess of learning and Lakṣmī as goddess of wealth in smaller silver vessels. Something of the living reality of fantastic spirits is captured as Slusser continues:

> Arriving at the outskirts of Old Kathmandu at dusk, the deities are formally welcomed by a palace honor guard at the modest *dharmaśālā* beside the Rani Pokhari, just outside of the former city gates. Then with pipe and drum and the crack of musket shots, the platoon escorts Nārāyaṇa in a rush through the crowded bazaar. Today few persons take much notice of his passage, but the elderly greet him with devotion and toss coins into the outspread aprons on his bearer priests. Making directly for Hanuman Dhoka, the cortege stops at the palace gates for a short welcome ceremony presided over by Durgā as the living Kumārī. Nārāyaṇa then formally enters the palace for a rendezvous with Taleju and, traditionally, the king. After the appropriate ceremonies, Nārāyaṇa and his company leave the palace and hurry headlong out of the sleeping city to make their way up the winding paths to Dolādri before dawn.[30]

Lidke's study proceeds to examine the "mountain-*maṇḍala*" as "nature's blueprint" while it relates to trees, actual mountains, and lakes, while coordinating with concepts of the Divine Body, the Vāstupuruṣa. His hermeneutical or interpretive stance is reinforced by the broadest references to past and present symbols and beliefs. The temple functions as Viṣvarūpa because of the symbols of tree-axis, cosmic mountain, and supreme person. He concludes that universal form is sustained through sacrifice and that the Beheaded One is the supreme symbol of sacrifice.

Lastly, geometry is part of an additional conclusion that is relevant to all the regions that are under study in this volume. The eighty-four squares of the ground plan of any Vāstupuruṣa *maṇḍala* make up the body of the Cosmic Man, we are told, and the equation is: *mandala* = the Purusha = the Totality = Vishvarupa = Mandir.[31] Thus the term Viśvarūpa may be defined as that which Arjuna, the Paṇdava brother in the ancient *Mahābhārata* begs Kṛṣṇa as incarnation of Viṣṇu to show him as all-encompassing divinity, the god revealed in universal form.

From considering the major temples of Paśupatinātha, Taleju, and Changu Nārāyaṇa this overview of Nepalese architecture broadens to a selection of buildings that represent the variety of pagodas that are found in Kathmandu Valley. Detailed reference to the important temples of the three main towns is available elsewhere, and this selective study points mainly to structural variations upon universal themes of structure and orna-

Vajra Yoginī temple, Sanku, Nepal (copyright His Majesty's Government of Nepal Department of Archaeology).

ment and placement that are continual throughout this extraordinary and physically limited area. Stone temples that are of basically Indian design (Kāla Mocana domed temple dated 1874 on the Bagmati River shore in Kathmandu is an example) will be bypassed in favor of proper pagodas that are made of brick, wood, and tile on bases made of stone or brick.[32]

Open-air shrines are those that have no real structure or have only a simple back wall and so they are not detailed here, even though they may have great symbolic significance. One example among many is a shrine to Gaṇeśa who is worshipped in the form of an uncut rock in the hillside location of Kvena Gaṇeśa above Bhaktapur. Some temples are placed in open settings beside rivers because of their need to attend burning *ghats* as sacred places of the dead. These include temples to the *matṛkas* or mother goddesses such as Kankeśvarī. Some of them, including Kankeśvarī Maṇḍir, appear to have been built over earlier hypaethral or roofless shrines, and the interiors are likely to be subterranean. The temple itself represents the symmetrical and four-sided pagoda with multiple roofs in reduced sizes as they ascend and may be categorized as a *freestanding pagoda tower*.

These towers are the most numerous temple forms in the valley. Most often square in plan, they rise along with palace towers to give Kathmandu Valley towns their unique and bristling skylines. The Darbar Square of each of the three major towns has examples of such freestanding towers, including Śiva Maṇḍir in Kathmandu. Some of the most notable examples of the square and freestanding temples are outside of royal precincts like Kumbheśvara Maṇḍir built in 1392 in Patan and Nyātapola Maṇḍir built in (1708) Bhaktapur. The main aesthetic statement beyond the impressive verticality is found in the animated figures of deities and leogryphs that are carved as part of bracket supports *(tona)* on all sides of the structures, braced against the cornice of a building's core as they angle up to support the heavy roofs.

The marvelous strut figures of Indreśvara Mahādeva temple in Panauti display characters in the very extended family of Śiva, including an emaciated and frightful Kālī as his darkest female form. Less expected is a charming smiling image of Hanuman the monkey god who is part of the *Rāmāyaṇa* story. The figures here are elongated and remarkably rhythmic in their movements within the confining frame of a very elongated rectangle. The thirds into which most such struts are divided, with foliage or other framing material at the top and a secondary scene, often erotic, at the bottom, are here integrated by the sinuous movement of the linear bodies of gods. The sculptures recall Buddhist figures at the little-known temple of Itum Bahāl, one of the oldest Buddhist sites in Kathmandu. Returning to Changu Nārāyaṇa temple, it is useful to note that Jeffrey Lidke lists 40 gods and attendants within the bracket placement, and to this we must add eight figures of leogryph protectors that stand under all four corners of each roof. He also shows that the placement of the figures is far from random, for their progression reveals specific stories, including those of Vedic gods and multiple (with some nontraditional) incarnations of Viṣṇu. Color is crucial not only to the drama of their expression but also to the iconography that makes the figures identifiable even from a distance. As for the lion-dragons, Lidke quotes his main informant, Makunda Aryal, who begins with a reference to the violent man/lion *avatar* or incarnation of Viṣṇu as destroyer of evil. Aryal explains:

> After the Narasinha *avatar* had killed the demon he was filled with such anger that he began to shake the entire universe. To protect the world, Lord Shiva assumed the form of a man-headed, flying beast, grabbed the enraged avatar, carried him out into space and killed him. Thereafter Shiva tore off the man-lion's skin and draped it around himself.[33]

Without doubt, the sculptural statement that is made by roof-supporting struts in Nepal is the strongest expression of exterior sculptural imagery that exists in all of Himalayan architecture.

Freestanding pagodas of rectangular plan also exist in the valley, and these come closer to domestic design in terms of spatial organization, balcony windows, and the use of levels above the ground floor. Examples include Bhīmasena temple in the Palace Square of Kathmandu, Bagh Bhairava temple in Kirtipur, Bhairavanātha temple in Bhaktapur, and the temple of Daṭṭatreya in that same town. Such buildings give a much stronger orientation to a facade that is true of square towers, and access to the inner chambers is sometimes more freely available than at Changu Nārāyaṇa, for example.

Rectangular temples attached to other buildings is a variation that is at least as likely to be Buddhist as Hindu, and these are often part of a monastery, called in Nepali a *bahāl* (Sanskrit *vihāra*) or in Nepali a *bahīl*. The Newari terms are *bahā* and *bahī*.[37] Either type of *vihāra* or monastery will single out the "temple" that is part of its two-story courtyard enclosure by having a more elaborate façade with sacred symbols on that part of the compound that is across the court and opposite the entrance from the street. An especially fine example is Chusya Bahāl in Kathmandu, with its remarkably beautiful wooden *toraṇa* of the sixteenth century that highlighted it on the street until its recent removal for safekeeping. But it should also be noted that many such buildings are secular apartment complexes today, with no resident priest or priestess.

Patan might be called the most Buddhist town among the three former capitals of Kathmandu Valley, and it still contains about 150 functioning *vihāra* buildings along with four (possibly five) early *stūpas* that are associated with India's Emperor Aśoka and the third century B.C. These *stūpas* with their cousins at Svayambhūnatha and Bodhnātha are great markers upon the land, but the reader is advised that signs of sacred presence are literally *everywhere* in Nepal. A small stone in the middle of a road, a grove of bamboo, a pond with fishes, a large boulder, the confluence of two streams—any and all of these are honored and blessed for they are part of an all-encompassing sphere of existence that is animated by spirit forces. Everywhere is the "spirit consonance" that is one definition of the Chinese term *ch'i* and that can bring a work of art to life. In their own way the Nepalese make their way through a world that is imbued with Tao.

An exception to all of the above building types is created when a small pagoda structure is integrated into a domestic structure for use as a *family shrine*. One such compound building opens into the Darbar Square of Kathmandu at the back of the high Śiva temple there. It may be said that such a private shrine, usually marked in no way on the outside of a house, is the most important of all. Most Newar houses have three stories plus an attic, and each level has assigned functions. Storage of farm equipment and shelter for animals are two uses for the lowest floor, and it may open to the street to function as a shop. The middle floor is usually divided into rooms that are used for sleeping, and the third floor is used for all kinds of activities, including entertaining. But the top level, a kind of half-story, is most important to any family because it is the place of the kitchen and eating area, thus subject to many rules of religious etiquette, and also the place of the family shrine or *āgama*. This special alcove is opened only to family members, and it may have a physical representation of a family god as a representative and guardian of the line of descent. Palaces of the Mallas and the Śahs are essentially Newar-style houses brought to great size and maximum height. A *maṭh* or house for priests is also based on Newar domestic design.

Single roof temples or shrines are not frequent in Nepal except as votive markers that are given as miniature temples by the devout, but there are a few exceptional examples. Bhairavanātha in Bhaktapur is a very large example that is unique in many ways, as is the temple of Śiva and Pārvatī in Kathmandu from whose window the two gods, carved of wood, look down nonchalantly upon the changing street scene below them. Navadurgā Maṇḍir on the Bagmati River downstream from Paśupatinātha is typical in being fairly low in spite of its gilt-copper roof and being quite open so that the nine goddesses who occupy the temple's inner room may be seen. The "nine" incarnations of Durgā are a variation upon the Aṣṭamatṛka sets of eight mother goddesses that are very widespread in India, with a ninth female whose identity varies. It is useful to remember that the concept of mother goddesses turns up throughout the Himalaya and that, as in Nepal, they are often worshipped in the form of rocks. The temple of Hiḍimba Devī in Manali at the head of the Kulu Valley gives us India's most remarkable instance of such earth worship. Outside of the village of Lubhu there is a "mother" shrine of the goddess Mahālakṣmī who is honored by a larger structure in the town, and this shrine is almost as simple as a *sattal* or rest-house. It looms large, however, as it represents the great family of Nepalese gods and humans.

Octagonal temples may be freestanding like the Chyasimdeval ("eight-sided") temple of Kṛṣṇa in Kathmandu's Durbār Square, or that may be attached to a palace building like the Kṛṣṇa temple in the Mulchok courtyard of Patan's Darbar Square that is also called Chyasimdeval. The eight-sided design is associated only with Kṛṣṇa. Only two *round temple towers* are known in Nepal, the tower of Hanuman the monkey god and attendant to Rāma that is found inside of the gate of the Hanuman Dhoka entrance to Kathmandu's old palace and the round tower of Śiva that is within the compound at Paśupatinātha temple on the river in Deopatan.

Temples attached to living rock show accommodation to natural landscape and topography that is somewhat like that which allows Tiger's Nest monastery of Bhutan to cling to its cliff. There some simple cave shrines are inside of natural hollows, but more relevant to this broad study is Gorakhanātha at Pharping because structure is added to the natural cave there—Bisanku Nārāyaṇa temple with a brick buttress fronting a twisted cave entry through which believers crawl, and the well-known Sekhara Nārāyaṇa temple on the main road from Pharping to Kathmandu where a kind of single-roof half-temple has been constructed tightly against a cliff in order to stand as directly as possible below a natural rock projection that is said to miraculously reveal the udder of a cow, the animal so dear to Kṛṣṇa as a herdsman.

Temples on river sides are to be expected in any Asian country where water is considered to be a blessing, even to be descended from heaven. Paśupatinātha and Kankeśvarī temples, both already mentioned, are just two that are placed in harmony with *ghats* that are used both for bathing and for burning bodies after death. *Forest temples,* often associated with dark and dangerous forces including those of Śiva as he lurks in burning grounds as the God of Destruction, may include quite standard pagoda buildings like Vajra Vārāhī, dedicated to a horrific and blood-thirsty goddess who is associated as *śakti* with Hevajra/Sambara, an extremely violent protector of the faith who is also known in the Tibetan world.

Hilltop shrines are a well-known category here, and one that is shared with all of Asia. The lofty and timeless setting of such placement makes them especially memorable, the earliest such example being the temple that is named for Śaṅkarācharya in Kashmir. Ādinātha with its surface of gifted pots and pans is a hilltop temple in Chobar town, Bhagavatī Maṇḍir occupies a high placement in Dhulikhel, Umā-Maheśvara temple of Śiva and Pārvatī stands high atop the ridge of Kirtipur as the town that long resisted the invasion of Pṛthvī Nārāyaṇa Śah, and there is the temple of Santaneśvara Mahādeva west of Thaibo. None of these, however, approaches the significance of Changu Nārāyaṇa Temple on top of Dolagiri Hill.

Most temples are set in the midst of village or town landscapes and do not fall into the more unusual categories noted above. But a very rare placement, for *temples in the middle of a lake,* is illustrated by a small temple of Śiva that is found at the end of a long causeway in the large Rani Pokhari or Queen's Tank in Kathmandu and by the temple of Macche Nārāyaṇa—Viṣṇu incarnate as a fish—that is approached in its tank by a narrow footpath in Macchagaon. As noteworthy as these, however, is a small pagoda that honors Varāhī as the female equivalent of Varāha, the boar *avatar* of Viṣṇu the Preservor who lifts the world from premordial waters. The temple is sheltered in a thick forest

Eyes of Śiva painted on the door of a Palace area shrine, Kathmandu, Nepal.

near the village of Chapagaon, a suitably mysterious place for a goddess who is said to have a very strong will. These examples are a hint of the rich architectural variety that Nepal preserves and of the beings who build them and are honored within.

The great tower of the Darbar or Palace in Kathmandu—simply trabeate in construction and recently restored to its full size and textural plus symbolic fullness—stands a full twelve-stories tall. It is a hallmark of the Nepalese and the Newari tradition. Yet even there the broader references of Himalayan tradition are again evident, for one of the tallest towers of the palace, covered over with brass roofing, has the curved bamboo-like pattern of temple roofs in Bengal. It is also a link from Nepal to Assam with its own history of royal patronage. Recently it was restored, and its main tower no longer tilts disastrously, and woodcarvings—even "seven-metal" bells—have been re-

Indreśvara Mahādeva temple, Panauti, Nepal.

stored by traditional craftspeople. It is one of the most positive examples of art and culture being saved in the twentieth century that can be found anywhere. It is not only Venice that is sinking.

Of all the mountain structures that have been encountered so far, Nepalese temples and palaces are the most "pagoda"-like, and we have used that antique term to describe them. It is important to realize that they are not especially related to the temples and palace towers of China, nor of Japan or Korea, except through a general emphasis upon axiality and height. If there is a common ancestor for all of these, it is much more likely to have been part of a now almost completely lost tradition of early India, as proposed by Ulrich Weisner. It is a mistake to think of Nepal's tower designs as growing up in isolation. Perhaps it is more useful to compare them to buildings in Himachal Pradesh than to any other Himalayan tradition. There we find wooden architecture (and perhaps the link that Weisner looked for) in the form of temple buildings with steeply sloping roofs that date from as early as the seventh century and the end of the Gupta period. The difference is that they survive not on the Gangetic plain but in a high Himalayan setting. The exploration continues.

6

Building Arts of Himachal Pradesh

THE DYNAMICS OF HIMALAYAN TEMPLE DESIGN have been hinted at in preceding sections, along with animation of the landscape by sacred, axis-oriented structures and integration of palace and temple buildings that have been noted to be continuous with structures in the northwest Indian state of Himachal Pradesh. While absolutely integral with other mountain traditions, this state is exciting for its special accomplishments and its beautiful geography. The frame-and-fill structural methods that have been encountered in every mountain country, sometimes with additive wooden cornices, *nāga*-strips, and metal punctuations, like those found in Sikkim and Bhutan, are found here as well. Still, Himachal Pradesh is a state that felt the brunt of invasions from Nepal without, it seems, ever accepting direct artistic inspiration from those particular outsiders. This is a place where animistic concerns—especially respect for unseen forces in the earth as best explained by James Fergusson in his *Tree and Serpent Worship*—still live on. Local gods and goddesses are paraded through village lanes in the form of *devata* masks made of metal. They ride in special palanquins that are carried on the shoulders of men, as in Kulu Valley, or they are even carried doll-like and one at a time door-to-door by a temple priest, as in the village of Nirmand. Ancient beliefs blend with ongoing artistry.

With its varied topography and its proximity to prominent Rājput culture and to the political boundaries of the Mughal Dynasty, Himachal Pradesh is a challenge to the student of architecture. The palace fortress at Arki in the lower elevations of the state is essentially Rājput with mixed Mughal inspiration, although its interior paintings are sometimes in European style and certainly unique. While village shrines will be examined in these pages for their variations upon western Himalayan norms, most attention will be given here to the arts of Chamba, Brahmor, and Nirmand along with the village sites of the most imposing *bhandars* or temple storage towers as structures unique to this region. One site that is unlike any other is that of the remarkable temple complex of Bhima Kālī that is found above the clouds in Sarahan. In addition, this analysis will cross over the forbidding Rohtang Pass at the head of the Kulu Valley in order to briefly examine two impressive buildings in Lahaul.

As Nepal illustrated long-term development of proper kingdoms in Kathmandu Valley and stratified society with royal families at the top and outcasts at the bottom (including foreign investigators, at least in early times), Himachal Pradesh shows dominance of the folk population with their interpretations of sacred architecture even when powerful kings and queens were in of-

Four-roof temple of Ādi Brahmā in the Kulu Valley of Himachal Pradesh. Drawing by Charles Benson.

Four-roof pagoda of Ādi-Brahmā at Khokhan, Kulu Valley, Himachal Pradesh.

fice. The art of this large and varied northwestern state of India is rich, yet this was never a center of international trade in the way of Kathmandu Valley. It provides no major valley that was a crossroads of trade. Himachal Pradesh does provide, above all, village art. The only royal towns of any size were Brahmor and Chamba, both at the edge of precipitous river valleys, and some of the finest architecture, such as the temple of Chatrarhi on the road from Chamba to Brahmor, is very remote. Neither Tibet nor the northern plains of India had revolutionary effect in Himachal Pradesh. More than in Kathmandu Valley or Solo Khumbu, more than in Assam with that state's remarkable *satra* tradition, more than in Tibet-oriented Bhutan, Sikkim, Ladakh, and the Darjeeling area—Himachal Pradesh presents the gods and goddesses of the hills and mountains in absolute combination with the major deities of the so-called great traditions. While referring readers to his work *Himalayan Towers—Temples and Palaces of Himachal Pradesh* for detailed overview, the author will focus here on monuments that represent major types of buildings that are differentiated from each other but that also reveal a consistent and identifiable northwestern aesthetic.

Once more it is appropriate to mention early scholars whose work in the Himalaya is pioneering. Marco Polo reached China in 1292, with his father and his uncle, and his accounts of the far north, of cannibals on Sumatra, of luxury trade goods, and of Kubilai Khan himself became, as is well known, the inspiration for further ventures to the East, both commercial and religious, both practical and romantic. The French traveler François Bernier moved from Europe to Syria and Egypt before traveling on to the Mughal court of Shah Jahan in the seventeenth century, and then on to Kashmir as personal physician to Emperor Aurangzeb, who succeeded his father Shah Jahan on the throne of India. Bernier stayed in India for twelve years and then returned to Paris to publish his *Work of Travels* in 1670. He had been preceded by another adventurer, a Portuguese layman named Diogo d'Almeria who reached Ladakh during the sixteenth century. Much earlier, the very first European to reach Ladakh was the Franciscan named Oderico of Pordenone (1286–1331) who left Italy to find Tibet but did not live to return home. Most notable about these travelers from the point of view of studying Himachal Pradesh is that there is no record of any of them passing through this land. Perhaps the rugged terrain that kept the Rājputs from colonizing their northern neighbors, and discouraged the Mughals from much movement beyond the relatively accessible Kulu Valley, has always served to dispel outsiders. To find works of architecture that show strong outside influence, one need only look to the lower elevations, the foothills of the mountain state.

As introduction to the state in terms of its constituent parts and its recent history, it is useful to turn to *Eternal Himalaya* by Major H. P. S. Ahluwalia, published in 1982. The author states that,

> During the re-organization of the Punjab in 1966 on linguistic basis the State of Himachal Pradesh was formed by joining a number of princely states, namely, Chamba, Mandi Suket, Sirmur, Bashahr, and 20 other smaller states as well as the hill areas of Punjab like Kangra, Lahaul and Spiti, and Simla. The state of Himachal Pradesh is rugged and mountainous. The northern border of Himachal Pradesh is bounded by Tibet, in the north-west it has a common border with Kashmir, and in the south lie the plains of Punjab. The eastern border of the state is common with the hills of Uttar Pradesh.[1]

The separate smaller states that the author mentions still maintain their own identity to a considerable degree. Because the Rohtang Pass between Kulu and Lahaul is closed by snow for half of each year, communication and trade suffer major interruptions. Garhwal and the Kumaon region, including Almorah and Nainital, are neighbors with less dramatic topography and somewhat less dramatic art. Himachal Pradesh covers 22,269 square miles, with a population (1984) of 4,288,000 people. Its capital city of Simla had 60,000 inhabitants in 1984 and, although it is very near some of the finest folk architecture in the state, it has always seemed to retain its colonial separateness, even long after independence was achieved in 1947. For a time, now seeming to be very long ago, Simla was the official summer capital of India under the British Raj, as has been mentioned previously. It is dominated by the former Residency of the British Viceroy and Vicerine, a great pile of stone that is filled with beautiful woodwork.

Himachal Pradesh, Kashmir, and the northern part of Uttar Pradesh share three mountain chains that are almost parallel in the Himalaya and the Karakorum ranges. As has been mentioned, the base of these mountains hold the fertile farming region that is known as the Doabs and the steamy jungle Terai that extends into the plains. The lowlands are dependent upon the Indus River and the Ganges River for their life and their crops. The lands far above were once heavily forested, although it is now hard to imagine that the mass of huge trees that has been preserved in the center of the tourist town of Manali in Kulu Valley was once the rule and not the exception in these lofty parts of northwestern India.

While Assam has almost constant rainfall, even through the winter, and claims to hold the world's wettest spot, and while Nepal with the central Himalaya depends upon abundant rain in the summer months, such is not the case in the northwest. The western Himalaya including Kashmir receives meager rainfall, and further north there is even less. Much of present-day Pakistan and Azad or "Free" Kashmir is steppeland and desert. The western Himalaya including today's inhospitable parts is likely to have been settled in the Old Stone Age, archaeologists tell us, perhaps first in the caves of the Swat region to the west of the Indus. The petroglyphs of northern Pakistan are vexing hints of the distant past. From Baltistan in Kashmir across to Ladakh, Spiti, and Lahaul, the physical type and the cultural orientation of people is Tibetan. But that region only touches upon Himachal Pradesh and its Lahauli sector.

Himachal Pradesh and the architecture of this still largely unfamiliar land present a challenge to outsiders, for many of the most important buildings here are defensive and, for that reason, erected in the security of very forbidding and remote terrain. Penelope Chetwode, author of *Kulu—The End of the Habitable World,* was dauntless in her perusal of Hindu folk art and castles in the hills, however. At an advanced age, she traced the places that she had known as a girl in India. She succeeded and more. Her publications on wooden arts of Himachal Pradesh are among the first records of a rich northwestern tradition that most westerners never had encountered. She is an inspiration for the present author, even though he failed to reach some of the more difficult sites that the lady and her mule named Bhalu (Bear) had already conquered.

Penelope Chetwode devised four major categories for the sacred architecture of Himachal Pradesh: the *Classical Style* that consists of *śikhara* temples of the type that she traces to northern Indian plains, like the small stone temple of Gauri Śaṅkara at Jagatsukh in Kulu Valley; the indigenous *Timber-bonded Style* of the Western Himalaya such as the temple treasury *(bhandar)* of Sarahan in Outer Sarai; the *Chalet Style* that is used for temples all over the region including the temple of a famous Rishi outside of Sarahan near the Bashleo Pass in Outer Saraj; and the *Pagoda Style* with superimposed roofs like the temple of Tripura Sundari at Nagar in Kulu Valley. To some degree, her classification is used in the following pages as these monuments are compared to those of other regions under study. The last category of pagodas offers the closest comparisons.

Himachal Pradesh is rich in timber of types that are especially strong and long-lasting as building materials. The finest wood is deodar, which takes its name from Devidar meaning "the tree of divinities." Its botanical name is *Cedrus deodara,* and it is a species related to the Sal wood of Nepal. A well-known folk saying is that this Himalayan wood will last for 1,000 years in water and five or ten times that long in air.[2] The system of construction is, once again, trabeate with basic post-and-lintel elements and a piling up of frame and fill. Rock and earth are the usual fillers, and there is some use of *terra pise* or pounded earth. Pent roofs have substantial overhangs and are normally covered over with slate shingles. These reflect the sun, making villages seem to glow on the mountainsides in daylight. Stone foundations are usual and, as throughout the Himalaya, they are not set into the ground but "ride" on top of it in the western earthquake zone that still shudders with the force of two tectonic plates that impacted each other in fairly recent geological time.

Some of the world's rawest and most interesting features of geology are found here, matching the kind of folding of layers in marine sediments that are a record of the former Tethyan Ocean in Dolpo, northwestern Nepal. Here engravings on four hundred million year old slate are themselves one hundred or more years old. As geography is considered, it is useful to return briefly to Bhutan, for we are told that,

> In the Buddhist search for suitable locations for temples and monasteries, it is not only the sacred lakes that play a role. Geological factors are considered,

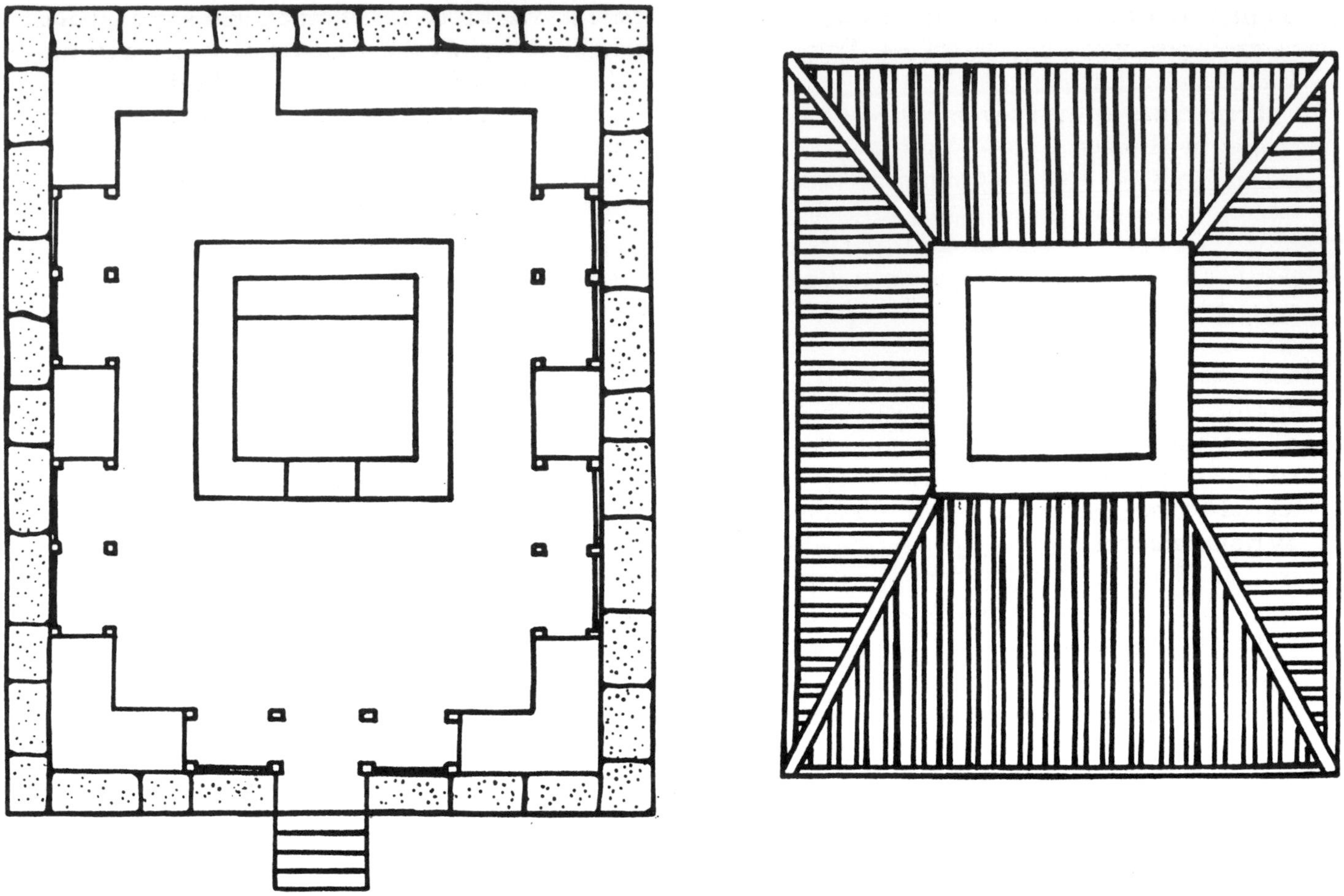

Plan and ceiling pattern of Śivalaya temple in lower Chamba town, Himachal Pradesh.

too: the famous Sakya [Tibet] monastery was founded near the "great white spot" which consists of volcanic ash. In many of the monasteries of Bhutan the footprints of the famous Padmasambhava, the Lotus-born, here mostly worshipped as Guru Rinpoche, are preserved. These were decisive in choosing the site of the monastery. It is a fact that in the cliff monastery of Taktshang [Tiger's Nest] and in other monasteries of eastern Bhutan, one can see round concretions in the cliffs that do indeed look like footprints.[3]

There is a timelessness about landscape that appears to be almost untouched by its human occupants. A recent conference at the East-West Center in Honolulu on "Arts of the Land" showed the profound relationship between art and geography from the Taoist harmony of China to the Christian landscape of Europe to the realm of Pacific gods of Samoa and Fiji to the mother goddesses born of rock and fire in South Asia to Shinto deities of Japan and to the forces of the goddess Pele who lives in Hawaiian volcanoes.

In Himachal Pradesh, the color of a village is the color of the land. Similarly, the color of the houses of Gilgit in northern Pakistan, not far from the shining peaks of the mountain range locally called the "crystal cathedral," is the same as the color of the land—dusty brown and tan. Villages in many parts of the great mountain range look almost ecologically planned, since their impact on the environment appears to be very slight. Deforestation is always a danger, however, and in the dry western regions the dangerous rivers are especially crucial to survival. This is not to imply that there is no change. As in Kashmir and Ladakh, the rivers and streams are gradually being harnessed, not only for irrigation but to provide hydroelectric power to the mountains and, more importantly, to the teeming populations on the plains below.

Some temples have been destroyed in the process as great reservoirs are created and farms and villages flooded forever.

Legend has it that Padmasambhava traveled and taught in Himachal Pradesh on his way to other Asian lands, and one wonders whether he saw castle watchtowers like the tower at Gondhla in Lahaul. If so, he would have been reminded of northwest mountain architecture and perhaps of the Yumbu Lhakhang with its graceful watchtower in the Yarlung Valley of Tibet. That tower and the temple of Tara Dolma to which it is attached is attributed to Nyathitsenpo as founder of the Yarlung Dynasty. Legend gives the latter complex an age of two thousand years (like the legendary beginnings of Nepal's Bodhnātha and Svayambhūnātha *stūpas*). It was completely destroyed during China's Cultural Revolution of 1966–76, then rebuilt as exactly as possible in 1985. It is especially photogenic, a draw for tourists.

As stories of Guru Rinpoche/Padmasambhava are familiar from east to west in the mountains, so are high towers that view the vistas of hills and mountains for protection and, sometimes, as symbol of removal to higher realms of existence. Drugyel Dzong in Bhutan is cousin to Sikkim's hilltop temples of Pemayangste and Rumtek, while Darjeeling's Bhutia Bustee has a cliffside location to compare to Nepal's cliff-hugging *gompa* at Thami on the way to Mr. Everest. Himachal Pradesh provides some of the most impressive towers of all.

It may be useful at this point to review the fact that this analysis has moved from the foothills of the eastern Himalaya and Assam through the central regions and toward the west, where the Himalayan range meets the Karakoram. The 2,200-kilometer length of the Himalaya from west to east may be subdivided as done by H. P. S. Ahluwalia:

1. Punjab, Ladakh Himalaya, and Himachal Pradesh
2. Garhwal Himalaya
3. Kailas Range
4. Nepal Himalaya
5. Sikkim Himalaya
6. Bhutan and Assam Himalaya[4]

These categories are not the most useful for defining areas with identifiable architectural styles, for there is overlap of classification and some unique developments. At the same time, shared qualities of buildings and their uses should begin to reveal a definable regional preference in art. If so, the shared qualities will show consistency and unity in the mountain arts so that the large and varied entity may be recognized for its special contribution to the history of world art. In the following pages, selected works of art will build upon one another until a special tradition is defined, and Indian Kashmir with Pakistan will be added to the divisions suggested by Ahluwalia.

Arki is a suitable place to begin investigation of individual monuments of Himachal Pradesh, for the palace fort that is found there is typical of hill efforts to absorb but not totally accept Rājput and Mughal customs in art. Arki is the capital of the early Beghal state and is located about twenty miles from Simla at a much lower elevation. It preserves some elements of the art of Kangra, which has probably received more scholarly attention than any other part of these northwestern hills, mainly for its famous style of miniature painting. Mural painting in the Diwankhana or hall of public audience in the Arki palace relates in part to the painting traditions of Kangra, Garhwal, Guler, and Nurpur, yet the art inside the palace and on the walls of its spacious verandah reveals a certain twist of perspective and a directness of silhouette shapes and intense, unvaried colors that suggest folk art impact. The most important patron of the arts in the region is Rāja Sansar Chand (r. 1794–1808) whose taste for and support of the arts are as important as those of any other ruler of the hills. He governed the Simla hills from Sujanpur Tira, itself an art center. While M. S. Randhawa finds the Diwankhana paintings of Arki to show "decadent Kangra style,"[5] they also display powerful directness in a way that is native to the hills.

As for the architecture itself in Arki, no mountain elements contribute to the essentially Mughal/Rājput design of the art with its multifoil arches and curved architraves along with false domes. The flat ceiling of the Arki palace verandah is a textbook example of all-over floral design that can be traced to Islamic settings from Delhi to Kashmir to Lahore. The frieze of the entablature within the verandah is filled by European scenes that include a view of Venice, drawn in Renaissance perspective, and Rome with Trajan's column. It also is filled with Gaddi shepherds who are indigenous to the hills and some strangely animalistic soldiers. Uniformed British soldiers march in tight formation, possibly in recognition of the British act of freeing Arki of Gurkha occupation that had come from Nepal. J. C. French writes in his early *Himalayan Art* that,

> Under the Gurkhas the Western Himalaya, from Nepal to the Sutlej, became a desert. Gurkha reputation for revenge was such that if he cut his foot on a stone, he would not go on until he smashed it to pieces.[6]

Arki palace is a pastiche of art forms from many sources, and it may be contrasted to much more indigenous buildings that are found at higher elevations. At the same time, art of the monolithic stone-carved temple of Masrur at 2,500 feet with its attention to Śiva and Viṇu, attacked by the iconoclast Mahmud of Ghazni, retains clear evidence of its inspiration in art of the Gupta Empire (320–650 A.D.). The figures at the doorframes, male and female *dharmapālas* as voluptuous guardians, are fine examples of the Gangetic plain type. Historical records are incomplete but it has been suggested that the fifteen-shrine compound was carved with patronage by rulers of Jalandhara on the Punjab plain but near the foothills, and that this would have happened during times of Kashmiri expansion under King Lalitāditya (725–756 A.D.)

The famous Kangra temple of Vajreśvarī, also called Mata Devī, was demolished by Mahmud of Ghazni as he invaded India in the eleventh century from the direction of Afghanistan, and it was last rebuilt after the disastrous earthquake that shook the western Himalaya in 1905. It has little if any evidence of hill art. The same cannot really be said of the impressive stone ruins of Kangra Fort, origi-

Village of Jenog with bhandar *tower, Sarahan, Himachal Pradesh.*

nally known as Bhimkot or Bhimnagar with roots in the word for "tower." It contains the base of a now destroyed temple that measures 117 feet long by 50 feet wide. Like the ramparts of the fort, this base is covered with relief carvings that are sharper and bolder than the softer Gupta-style stone carvings of Masrur, and perhaps hill tastes have something to do with the directness of these reliefs. The patron, once again, is assumed to be Sansar Chand.

It is perhaps apparent that this survey seeks those monuments that are more characteristic of mountain traditions than of borrowing from India's flatland dynasties, and so our next goal takes this study to higher elevations of the Simla hills: the small village of Jenog. This settlement is only a few kilometers by road from Simla and one wonders how many tourists, both Indian and foreign, would slow down on their circuit of mountain "sights" if they knew that only a few hundred feet downhill from the paved road rested a hamlet with a small but exquisite temple to Śiva and a substantial wooden tower to attend it. The tower, with projecting top floor on all sides and a steep notched log as ladder of entrance to the highest floor, is called a *bhandar*.

The *bhandar* and the small compound beside it are sometimes used as a school today, but its prime purpose is to provide protection and storage for ritual implements and other materials associated with a small temple that is located on its own hill just a short walk away. The *bhandar* as temple storehouse is related to all of the towers that have been seen in the mountains, even the pagodas of Nepal. It is as vertical as the tower of the Thakur's Castle in Gondla across the Rohtang Pass from Kulu Valley to Lahaul. It is built by the same methods used anywhere in the region and it is a kind of stone structure that artists lavish woodcarved

Bhandar *or temple storehouse in Jenog, Himachal Pradesh that is associated with the small temple of Trigareśvara Śiva. Drawing by Charles Benson.*

Bhandar *storage tower, Jenog village, Sarahan, Himachal Pradesh.*

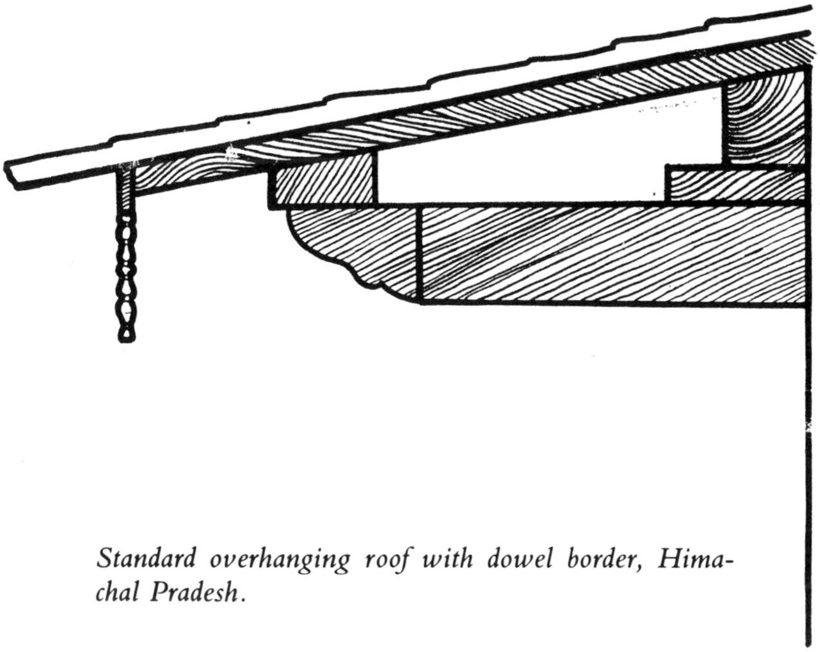

Standard overhanging roof with dowel border, Himachal Pradesh.

ornament and symbolism upon, as in the Tibetan sphere and in Pakistan. It may have considerable exterior color, like the *gompas* of Solo Khumbu, Bhutan, Nepal, or Sikkim, and it is protected by its height, physical setting, and by trapdoors that can be closed from within. It is an observation post, and its windows are not so large as to make the watchers vulnerable. In other words, the *bhandar* of Jenog or any other settlement in Himachal Pradesh is built to suit the traditions of Himalayan art in general; thus it is hung with fringe as a finishing touch.

Fringe made from wooden dowels is hung all the way around the projecting top level of the tower, and their making was witnessed by Penelope Chetwode. She writes that producing the wooden ornaments is a family project, for a woman will turn the dowels of wood with a rope while her husband applies metal tools to cut them evenly. They are mounted at their tops in a double course of wood as their frame so they will move in any wind. The fringe pieces are called *khururu,* and the lady explains that it is important for a woman to learn to "set her hand" in order to apply just the right pressure to the hand-powered lathe as it turns. As many as one hundred of the pieces, each usually about eighteen inches long, can be made in a day. A surprising and disturbing point that Chetwode makes is that the craftspeople who make such art in Himachal Pradesh belong to the *misri* subcaste and that, because this group has very low status and is considered "unclean," it is possible that workers who are employed to finish the interior of a temple or shrine may never be allowed to return to it once the main image inside has been consecrated.

Fringe is not the only adornment that may grace a *bhandar*. The structure in Jenog has pierced designs that go right through the outer boards to provide spots of patterned illumination inside which resemble certain Celtic patterns to some degree. There is an elaborate door-pull of cast and pierced metal on the tower that calls for comparison to Chinese, Tibetan, and Nepalese metalwork. It is inscribed with the date 1946 along with a message that it was made by the Lohar (smith) Nardass Sadhram. Penelope Chetwode found him on her return to Jenog and he proved to be mainly involved in making scissors.

Although such additions as fringes and metalwork are impressive and the tower itself can be seen from great distances, the true orientation of the town is toward its temple of Śiva. When people make the short walk up to Jenog's wooden temple and onto the truncated earth and stone platform upon which it rests, they must remove their shoes before walking on the ground that leads up to its small gate and into a humble courtyard that stands before the shrine. Red flags blow in the wind here at the highest point in the village landscape, but the temple itself is smaller than any house in Jenog. Trigareśvara Śiva is the major local god here, the main *devata* in a large family that extends throughout the hill state. His house is his temple, respected by all who live around it.

The temple has a *maṇḍapa* porch before the main doorway, and the porch has a floor that is about four feet higher than the courtyard and gate. Chetwode would call the building a "chalet," but it might be more appropriate to call it alpine style, since that term can be used to refer simply to art in high elevations. The *maṇḍapa* has its own covering of pent-roof type with extending ridge beam (a mark of Himachal design) with a protective face beneath the projection. In his early study of the region, *Antiquities of Indian Tibet,* A. H. Francke observed that "Many of the roofs or gable beams end in dragon heads with open mouths."[7] The floor measures about eight by twelve feet. In the center of the floor is a small mound of earth as a place to receive offerings, including those that are burned. In every way this is a humble assemblage, very different from the multiplicity of Nepal in terms of the parts of the building. Rather than shimmering with repeated cornices and doorframes, this building is absolutely basic in its structural parts, perhaps the simplest structure that this study has yet encountered. But the lantern ceiling of the porch is carved, and there is a tiny but elaborate window above the lintel of the doorway. The door itself is magnificently carved by wood chipping to reveal a circular design with expanding animal and vegetal patterns. It is earthy, direct, and very fine. Himachal Pradesh stands for folk arts of the heights in their fullest and freshest expression.

Returning to the ceiling, one finds relief sculpture that is not yet much weathered by exposure to the elements. Besides an accordion-like succession of borders there are crowds of figures carved

Entrance to a small Śiva shrine above the village of Jenog, Sarahan, Himachal Pradesh.

into every beam end. These include Durgā, Narisiṃha as lion/man expression of Viṣṇu, and Varāha along with other *avatars* of the god of preservation. Durgā is shown, as seen earlier, having vanquished the buffalo-headed Mahiṣa. Lakṣmī is present, in a typical pose of being bathed by two elephants. There are serpents, more serpents than one expects without having read Fergusson's *Tree and Serpent Worship*. There are entire figures of snakes or *nāga* spirits, and the *Punjab Gazetteers* recorded in Fergusson's time that in the Saraj area of today's Himachal Pradesh *nāga* spirits dominated religious practices. The carved door also has serpent motifs amid the four successive borders that lead out from the sunburst at the center, along with meandering vines and active figures of Hindu gods, including Śiva, Gaṇeśa, Lakṣmī, Narasiṃha, and Durgā. If attitudes toward sacred snakes or *nāgas* have changed since the nineteenth century, it would be interesting to know how so and why.

The *garbha gṛha* as sanctum is very small in this temple, and it holds a simple *liṅga* of Śiva as potent and destructive lord. A second *liṅga* is found in a small building outside and to the right of the temple. A short distance away there is a hillock with a platform for visitors to rest upon, this with a square pillar that is carved with a simple face. It would be tempting to associate this abbreviated art with ancestor boards that are carved in some tribal areas of Nepal, or even with rare representational carvings that come from remote parts of Pakistan. But it might also be called another phallic symbol, this one as *mukhaliṅga* or *liṅga* with the face of Śiva on it. Whatever its meaning, it is best examined in context not only of Hinduism but of the ever-present animism of the hills. The same is true of all northwestern arts, for indigenous gods do survive.

Manan is another village in the Simla Hills, located seventeen kilometers from Thyog and near Jenog, but 1,200 feet lower. Once again the village is dominated by the vertical accent of a *bhandar* tower that relates to a small temple nearby. The tower is dedicated to Mananeśvar as another local form of Śiva, and the temple belongs to a harmonizing incarnation of Bhagavatī as Durgā Mahiṣāsuramardinī. The *bhandar* is both more open and a bit more colorful than the example in Jenog, for it has repeated arched openings in the high balcony that goes around it with much colored painting of floral designs and more along with almost playful variations of *jhali* windows as they exist in many parts of lowland India. Its sharply angular roof has three golden pinnacles, and around its courtyard are buildings that probably function as either the *maṭh* or *sattal* in Kathmandu Valley. The tower is timber-bonded throughout; the balconies are entirely wood, and the base is painted white in contrast to the dark brown wood and the slate-gray roof shingles. It is a "classic" *bhandar* and very much like the tower in Jenog. Observation must be one of the reasons for its existence, a reminder once again of military threats in the mountains.

The small temple of Manan is a rectangular building with a single small tower at the entrance end. It cannot be called a pagoda because its design is long and low rather than vertical and axis-oriented. There is beauty in the combination of circular tower on square base with large and shiny "scales" of slate covering roofs of both the tower and the rectangular hall. The building is most memorable for its colors, for it is brilliantly painted with reds and yellows and silvers on its railings, its border boards, and the underside of the roof. Chetwode notes that J. B. Fraser illustrated the temple in *Views of the Himalaya Mountains* (London 1820) but she despairs at the effect of new paints that were applied in 1967, colors that appear to be modern enamels. She refers to the temple as having been "sadly restored" and describes the carvings of Durgā and other characters as "crudely painted in strident colors."[7] Perhaps stridency is in the eye of the beholder, but then it is making a value judgment just to include some arts in this volume while omitting others. The color does help to pick out certain features of a very crowded exterior full of carving and painting. In 1820 Fraser wrote:

> The whole of the interior is sculptured over with wood, with infinite labour and probably forms a detail of the exploits of the deity, with these I am totally unacquainted, but she seems to have been frequently engaged with monsters of very uninviting shapes. The portion of the carving, however, which neither represents the human nor animal figure, is by far the most beautiful.[8]

The temple is unusual in its openness, with two balconies below its round tower covering. Here silver dots of paint have been given to the wooden fringe pieces, making them seem all the more weightless, almost like an illusion, as they sway in the breeze.

None of the abovementioned buildings of Himachal Pradesh is likely to be more than two or three centuries old, at least in their present state. But Hat Koti is a place holding stone structures—with wooden additions—that are attributed to the seventh or eighth century, partly on the basis of Gupta stylistic comparisons and partly because of two inscriptions of those same centuries that are explained by V. C. Ohri of the Himachal State Museum as being in Sankha and Siddha-matṛka scripts as they suggest that "the tradition of sculpture at Hat Koti was being refreshed by new influences" at that time.[9] The *maṇḍapa* porch plus *garbha gṛha* inner room are the classical plan of Hat Koti temples, but the square structure of stone is covered by unusual wooden roofs as pyramids with concave contours and fringe. The design is quite unique to this place. The temple of Durgā has a splendid image of golden bronze to represent the mighty goddess. She is surrounded by an elaborate frame or mandorla halo that is inscribed in Siddhamatrika script of a type attributable to the eighth or ninth century, while Mian Goverdhan Singh suggests the seventh century an approximate date for the figure itself.[10] It shows an eight-armed image of Durgā in the act, once again, of destroying Mahiṣa. The beautiful image has a sister in Sarahan, as will be discussed.

Besides the temple of Hat Koti Durgā (Hateśvarī) and the Śiva temple next to it, there is a stone *śikhara* temple, also dedicated to Śiva, that was probably re-roofed with the addition of a pagoda type covering of wood in the seventh or eighth century. If so, the additive wood combination predates the same happening in Chamba, where stone *śikharas* are crowned with wooden tops. All of the Hat Koti temples make a strong impact of solid form in space, and they are both more solid and

Hateśvarī Durgā temple, Hatkoti, Himachal Pradesh.

more secretive than an "open" structure with balconies like the temple of Bhagavatī in Manan.

One more monument remains to complete this brief look at temples in the hills near Simla. It is found in the small village of Sarahan (not to be confused with the royal town of Sarahan that holds the great Bhima Kālī temple) in this fairly limited geographical area that has many accessible temples. Sarahan village near Simla is a place strewn with fragments of very early stone architecture, including many *āmalaka* sun-discs from *śikharas* that have long since disappeared. Sometimes the fragments are piled on top of each other to form a kind of *axis muṇḍi,* with or without a temple below it. An unusual variety of temple form is found here—and it should be stressed that more experimentation with the designs of sacred architecture is found in the Himachal area than any other Himalayan state—showing two separate

Gilt-bronze and silver image of Durgā Mahiṣāsuramardinī inside Hateśvarī Durgā temple, Hatkoti, Himachal Pradesh.

pent roofs with concave form with a circular tower topped by a golden pinnacle between them. The nearby *bhandar* is perhaps the finest in the region because it has perfect proportion of extending top floor on tall, narrower base to convey poise and balance, because it is painted neatly in many colors, including yellow and green vertical stripes that belie the great weight of the structure and invite the viewer's eye to come closer to the delicate carving and brilliant painting of fringes, bargeboards, running vines, and much more. Truly this is the mountain version of the "necklace of the gods." One wonders whether the shadows of Tibet and the Indian plain, both of which seem more distant in Himachal country, explain the freedom to try new things in art.

Experimentation means that a temple like Guru Ghantal Lhakhang in Lahaul shows two slate-covered roofs with a gable at the front and door-frame borders of interwoven snakes, as illustrated in Romi Khosla, *Buddhist Monasteries in the Western Himalaya* (plates 153 and 154). It means that the proportions of door and window openings may vary and that column capitals take on new and baroque designs of flowing volutes that are in tune with florid designs at Nirmand in the Sutlej River area and Bhima Kālī temple near the peaks of the Shirikund Range above Rampur. A cantilever bridge like that at Bhurkote, illustrated by George Francis White in 1825, has its counterparts in Bhutan and Kashmir and thus serves as a link to distant Himalayan cultures, while a small alpine style temple of Durgā at Gushaini, with its open frame pent-roof and wide encircling verandah that has almost cartoon-like folk images, belongs completely to its area quite near the Kulu Valley. Hanuman is shown with a spiral tail that is as large as the monkey himself, and confronting peacocks along with a kind of atlante figure appear over repeated spirals that Chetwode calls "Celtic scrollwork." There are miniature shrines like one made of wood that honors Hiḍimba Devī in a private garden not far from Manali's sixteenth-century pagoda of that same goddess.

The village of Koghera in its setting of deodar forest utilized that particular wood, along with earth and rock, to erect a tower near Choor mountain that measured 160 feet in height. This information is drawn from George Francis White and his publication of 1825. He adds that there were reports of towers standing as tall as 180 feet. In repeating this intriguing information, the present-day researcher is once again indebted to those who have gone before.

Folk-style carving on a temple in Kulu Valley, Himachal Pradesh.

The temple of Jagatsukh, found on the busy main road of Kulu ten kilometers from Naggar on the floor of the valley and beside a *śikhara* temple of late Gupta style that may be attributed to the seventh or eighth century, is a large and partly open structure that dates from 1428. It is dedicated to Sandhya Devī as goddess of this special place and is much more local than imported in its design. A large *śikhara* of Jagannathi Devī, yet another local goddess, dated 1728, is nearby, and all three temples are government protected, a status that is lacking for so many northern monuments. Their coexistence is a key to understanding Himalayan

A domestic carved window at the village of Dashal, Kulu Valley, Himachal Pradesh.

choices, for the spirit force within is much more important than the exterior form of any temple. Yet for this study the rectangular Sandhva Devī temple with its slate-covered pent-roof, open verandah, wood carved railings, arcuate colonnade, *khururu* fringes, and substantial stone base is most noteworthy. Its walls and especially its broad corner columns present absolute combination of stone and wood in a layering from bottom to top that uses the materials as if they were brick. Tensile strength is not a consideration as the columns stand by virtue of their own mass and weight.

The structure is certainly solid, but it could hardly be called sophisticated. Domestic organization is part of its open porch plan. Its main virtue, perhaps, is found in the lovely carvings that combine half-lotus flowers with silhouetted soldiers carrying rifles and lush vegetation with scallopped and squared woodchipping on adorned pillars. The pent roof that runs the length of the building with a projecting ridge beam at the front is a link to distant arts in the Simla hills while prominent volute capitals above slender pillars around the porch are most like capitals in Pakistan. Yet it is essentially local.

The development of style over time, as crucial as it is to the discipline of art history, is not often the main subject in understanding Himalayan art. Between the earliest and latest monuments there may be centuries without datable arts. This is partly due to the ephemeral quality of some of the materials used in hill-style structures, as opposed to established Indian monuments of stone that are found usually at lower elevations. In Kulu Valley the disparity can be shown between two important works. First there is the stone temple of Viśveśvara Mahādeva at Bajaura near the lower end of the valley. It is attributed to the eighth century and is a well-proportioned *śikhara* tower with four arms as entrance and three large niches around the center enclosure. The total form has the kind of facetted surface of many buildings in Nepal, although on a larger scale, the result is a seemingly endless repetition of small angular projections that are part of ancient geometric and mathematical ideals. These derive, once more, from the Vāstupuruṣa Maṇḍala as the first perfect and, thus, holy form. The gradually curving silhouette of the structure leads one's eyes up to the *āmalaka* as radiating sun-disc. This crescendo is an impressive accomplishment of the design, as are the sculptures that are found here at Bajaura, but it is an import.

Most instructive and most refined is a large stone image of Durgā Mahisāsuramardinī that is close to post-Gupta types of the Pāla-Sena and Pratihāra traditions of early medieval India, with no evidence at all of Himalayan preferences. The temple relates to countless sanctuaries on the plains below, and even to Bhutan and Tibet in terms of symbolism because of its auspicious placement at the confluence of two rivers, the Beas and the Parbatti. Bajaura presents one aesthetic pole, the "classic" expression, that makes the interpretations of the imaginative hill artists all the more intriguing.

There are several buildings in Kulu Valley that could stand for the opposite pole, the one that favors folk art, including the fine but heavily restored triple-roofed temple of Durgā called Tripura Sundarī in Naggar, a pagoda that is attributed to the fifteenth century. But a more elaborate and less reconstructed temple tower is found further upstream along the river valley. Khokhan or Khokhana is a walkable distance from the Kulu/Manali road, and its temple of Ādi-Brahmā is one of the few four-roof temples in the state. Its lower floor is unusually wide, but the axis effect of the multiple roof tower is still one of lightness and grace. The tower is about thirty meters high and its topmost roof is square like the ones below it, more like a Nepalese pagoda than like some other Himachal structures that end with circular roof coverings. The three top levels are very open, with scallop-shaped brackets to support their roofs. Together the struts create a kind of basket or cage of braces for the heavy burden of roofing slate and wooden frames. The walls are unlike the double-wall construction of Nepal, and probably less practical, but this design makes for an especially dramatic silhouette. More than in other hill areas, this building evokes forceful geometry. A rare comparison might be to cone-shaped temple roofs in Kerala, but it belongs to the family of Himalayan pagodas.

Simple animal heads, possibly of horses, project from the corners of the second and third roofs, a rare occurrence in Kulu, although Mian Goverdhan Singh illustrates (plate 90) the *maṇḍapa* of Ajodhyanātha temple in Rampur-Bashahr near Simla with its carved heads of antelope and bear. There is an inscription with a date equal to 1753 A.D. found on a portable *devata* mask of metal in the *garbha gṛha* of the temple, but this cannot be taken for the temple as a whole. Interlocking snakes are found on the doorway here, and there are many floral patterns that are simplified and geometric. Wooden dowels hang from all four roof edges, and their flat border boards are carved with scallop-curves that match the unusual struts. Three wooden pinnacles and a trident spear of Śiva that doubles as a lightning rod draw the visitor's view skyward. The overall design is linear, somewhat "metallic" or brittle, and it is tempting to look for Central Asian connections; for example, to the wood chipping tradition of the Uygur people. This temple stands for northern arts as much as Bajaura belongs to the great Indian tradition to the south.

Madanjeet Singh's beautifully illustrated *Himalayan Art* briefly touches upon Himachal Pradesh in a section entitled "The Siwalik Ranges." A rugged stone image of Śiva Mahādeva from the private temple of the Rāja of Mandi is shown, making a somewhat negative impression that would seem to support the view that "peripheral" arts are underdeveloped. But a second illustration showing Triloknāth temples on the shore of the Beas River in Mandi proves that pan-Indian patterns made their way into the foothills. A third and very damaged work of art that shows "Shulapani-Shiva and Parvati" from Chamba, dated to the fifth century, calls for an imaginative eye if comparison to Gupta art is to be made. Two bronze images—"Shulapani-Shiva and Parvati, Sitting on Nandi" from Chatrarhi village of the eighth to ninth century and "Vishnu and Lakshmi" from Chamba and the tenth century—show mastery of lost-wax metal casting while they call for comparison to Kashmiri artistry. Two masks of Devī from Bhakli and the sixteenth to seventeenth centuries represent more local tastes, while murals from Chamba's Rang Mahal Palace are late eighteenth to early nineteenth century records, like those in the paintings of Arki Palace. They show shared painting traditions that come from Garhwal, Kangra, and Guler, among other small kingdoms. The assemblage is impressive, but the author illustrates no temple art in Himachal style, and that decision is a serious error, for it largely dismisses the region's creativity. Fortunately there are several recent studies that deserve attention here.

V. C. Ohri rectifies that omission with his thoroughly researched *Arts of Himachal* (1975) as do

House in Dalas village near Jagatsukh, Kulu Valley, Himachal Pradesh.

Window of a house in Dalas village near Jagatsukh, Kulu Valley, Himachal Pradesh.

Postal, Neven, and Mankodi with *Antiquities of Himachal* (1985) and Shanti Lal Nagar with *The Temples of Himachal Pradesh* (1990). Perhaps the words of Reginald Rankin after his Himalayan tour of 1930, quoted by Mian Goverdhan Singh, will now be widely understood. Speaking of the woodwork of Mandi and Kulu, Rankin writes that, "these Indians are an artistic race. Their houses are wonderfully designed and carved. Even the poorest has an eye to aesthetic effect." Shanti Lal Nagar quotes another early source who visited Kinnaur and observed that:

> Every house, as well as principal temple, is adorned with notable carvings in which, unlike the woodwork observed in the Ganges valley, Mughal influence is hardly apparent. The style and design is based on square forms, and seemed to us to have a connection with that of the older Jain temples of Northern India. The temple was a masterpiece of the wood workers [sic] craft, with rich floral devices, elegant verandahs and pierced panels. Round it hung a fringe of wooden drops, which produced a soft jingling in the wind, like the ghost of a xylophone.[11]

Shanti Lal Nagar classifies the temples with more subdivisions than does Chetwode. His divisions are listed as:

1. *Nāgara* or *Śikhara* type subdivided into
   (a) Pyramidal Type
   Śikhara temples of pyramidal appearance with *āmalaka* at the top crowned by *chhatra* or *kalaśa* with the addition of an umbrella-shaped covering of wood or zinc sheets placed over the *āmalaka,* probably as protection from heavy rain and snowfall.
   (b) *Latika* Type
   Similar to the above but with projecting stones arranged in the tier system resembling temples.
2. Wooden Temples
   Early wooden temples in the state resemble Gupta style, and structural features of many early stone temples are derived from wooden prototypes. There is rich carving of which James Baille Fraser notes has "an ease that does honour to the mountain artist, and considering his tools, is truly wonderful."
   (i) Pent-roof-Hill Type Temples
   Rectangular stone and wood temples with pent-roof made of stone tiles that are the oldest in the state.
   (ii) Pagoda Type Temples
   Rectangular stone and wood structures with successive roofs, placed one over the other, which in some cases makes them multistory edifices.
3. Dome-Shaped Temples
   Belonging to comparatively later periods, these show Muslim influence.
4. Rock-cut Cave Temples
   The rock-cut sanctuaries of Masrur are most notable, and there are remote caves

with *Śivalinga* installed inside. The most famous *linga* in a cave is that at Gomukh, the "cow's mouth" cave with natural *linga* of ice at the place said to be the source of the Ganges.

5. Other Miscellaneous Types

   Temples like the square column type and those that appear like ordinary flat-roofed dwellings.

6. Buddhist Monasteries

   The establishment of hill monasteries in Himachal Pradesh is thought to have begun as early as the time of Emperor Aśoka in the third century B.C.

The above categories are useful, with the exception of 2.ii. For that grouping the author "explains" that, "These temples are believed to have Chinese or Tibetan influence in their architecture."[12] As regarding Nepal and, by extension, the rest of the mountain region, the statement can be proven to be false, especially with regard to China.

The authors of *Antiquities of Himachal* are most concerned with cast metal sculpture in their well-researched volume, especially with *mohras* or *devata* masks. One hopes that they are now familiar with Chandra Reedy's scientific procedures of determining provenance of bronzes through X-ray and analysis of core materials as they deal with large quantities of metal objects from throughout the hills.[13] John Mosteller's development of measures of stylistic consistency through computer analysis might also be of use. But the study is important here for its coverage of temple architecture in both stone and wood. The authors treat such important structures as the temple of Śiva Vaidyanātha in Baijnath of Kangra District that was renovated in 1204 A.D. and a miniature stone shrine in Nirmand that may date from about the eleventh century. More relevant to this work, they also discuss wooden monuments like the remote temple of Parāśara Ṛṣi beside its lake in Parashar, Mandi District, where it dates from about the fourteenth century. They term the wooden temples to be "classic" and, in terms of what is classically native here, they certainly are.

The wooden temple of Markula-Devī in Udaipur, Lahual-Spiti District, is noted as having interior wood carvings that date from the tenth to eleventh centuries, and the innermost door and frame of the Parashar Temple are perhaps later—seventeenth or eighteenth century—but they are illustrated as the most delicately carved to be found anywhere in Himachal Pradesh. The authors correctly emphasize the importance of the temples found in Chatrarhi and Brahmor, upriver through narrow canyons from Chamba, former capital of the district having that name. Both places are enriched by the survival of their refined and priceless inner images, and the same may be said of the *śikhara* towers with wooden *chhatra* (umbrella) caps that are found with inner sculptures intact in Chamba's temple square. The present author has visited all of these sites, with a hostile reception only in Udaipur.

Chamba, former capital of the small state that

Temple of Hari Rai, Chowgan Maidan, Chamba, Himachal Pradesh (copyright Archaeological Survey of India).

View of Chamba town with palaces, Himachal Pradesh (copyright Archaeological Survey of India).

still bears its name as a district in Himachal state, is an extraordinary place. Chamba was one of eleven hill states of pre-Independence India, joined together with Nurpur, Guler, Datapur, Siba, Jaswan, Kangra, Kutlehr, Mandi, Suket, and Kulu. In its way, today's Chamba town is as unexpected as a cultural center of considerable size, with its great open *maidan* or parade ground at the edge of its steeply banked hill, as Thimpu is unexpected in the quiet green space of its surroundings in Bhutan. After Nepal and Bhutan, Himachal Pradesh holds the grandest palaces in the Himalaya. There are two main palaces surviving in Chamba, both of "mixed" design that includes European elements, and temples of borrowed and local type are found throughout the town.

All of the houses in Chamba are Himalayan timber-bonded, but the palaces are not. As in Arki, and as among the late *maharajas* of Nepal, the taste in palaces ran to European reproductions. Thus the nineteenth-century Akhand-Chandi palace, long a center of political power in a state that preserved a mixture of Victorian/Rajput/Mughal styles, is a white-painted building that is imposing and reflective of the Indo-Saracenic aesthetic that Thomas Metcalf investigates in his effective study of British ambitions as reflected in colonial art of the empire.[14] The large complex now serves as a government college; most of its splendid furnishings are gone, but the spaces and walls still come alive. One progresses from the main entry at the garden level to a sitting room with balcony that offers a splendid view of the town and river valley. Further on, one sees a doorway that is attended by two painted soldiers on the walls beside it as it leads into a dark audience room. On its wall is a dazzling painting of Kṛṣṇa and Rādhā in riding costumes in a picture that is framed by flowers. The image is suggestive of Kangra, Guler, and other "refined" versions of miniature painting. But it is a dry fresco painting of pan-Indian technique combined with local colors, with some violent action as severed heads of enemies fly through the air.

Adjoining this room is a private audience hall, the place of some of the most action-filled and exciting of all Himalayan paintings. In this modest hallway Śiva is shown seated on an animal skin with his "holy family" around him and Durgā is shown in the midst of adoring devotees. Paintings in painted frames in the lowest horizontal row of the wall complex show monkeys, Himalayan bears, and many other animals, while the entryway has an image of blessing Gaṇeśa above it. But the real story here is found in the large compositions that cover most of the walls. The art is cosmopolitan, royal, refined, and very Hindu, like the town and former kingdom themselves. The paintings are historical, devotional, and to some extent decorative. There is an intensity here that is not found in those areas, like Kangra, that show a "cool" world view with pastel colors and shaded illusionism that is borrowed from Islamic Persia and from Europe. Once more, it is the directness of the art that is most memorable. The use of color is so strong and so unrelated to rendering the natural world that the paintings could almost be called expressionistic. The background field of crimson against which stories unfold is the main ingredient in this powerful mix. The colors are more vibrant than those in the paintings on plaster walls that the Archaeological Survey of India removed so carefully from the interior of the Rang Mahal (Red Palace) in Chamba and mounted in the national India Museum in New Delhi. Its asymmetrical composition is more dramatic than the more ordered and segmented pictures of Hindu gods that the Rang Mahal palace surrendered.

The earliest palace, Rang Mahal, is generally thought to have been founded by Rāja Umed Singh after he lost his earlier fortress in wars with the kingdom of Basohli in 1771–75. In his *Himalayan Art,* J. C. French attributes the building to the eighteenth century or earlier. One might wonder if the experience with ghosts that French faced while lodging in the castle of Naggar, above Kulu Valley, came before or after he viewed the battle scenes in the Akhand-Chaṇḍi Palace. Things are "quieter" in the Rang Mahal, mainly in the form of larger scale versions of intimate album paintings that include love scenes from the *Kṛṣṇa Līla* and action scenes from the *Rāmāyaṇa* along with stories of the *Mahābhārata*. But to become immersed in the endless tale of evil and righteousness that is the *Mahābhārata,* it is better to return to Akhand-Chaṇḍi.

Sweeping compositions and intense, saturated colors are found in the battle scenes in the Akhand-Chaṇḍi Palace hall of private audience. This so-called "new palace" was built around 1860, as noted by French. He states that, "Its most striking feature is the frescoes of its Picture Room. They were painted by Kangra artists and are varnished and difficult to photograph." He goes on to link the practice of varnishing frescoes to European influence that dates from the nineteenth century, without mentioning the disastrous discoloration that resulted from British application of varnishes to dry frescoes in the Ajaṇṭā caves. He describes the paintings as:

1. A scene of two opposing armies from the *Mahābhārata*. This occupies the whole of one wall.

   and

2. Some curious old sporting scenes, showing Englishmen in top-hats pig sticking [a less-than charming spectacle], shooting wild buffaloes with pistols from horseback, and hunting bears with hounds. All three are famous old Indian sports, but only the first survives nowadays. The frescoes were painted when the palace was built (1860).[15]

Returning to the temple square in Chamba, it is noted that the *śikhara* towers with wooden *chhatra* attachments as protective roofs are odd combinations that simply "paste" Himalayan parts onto forms that belong to the plains. The sanctified images inside require detailed consideration. This state provides the most direct links to late Gupta and early medieval arts in metal while showing that new directions are added to them. Because of this factor the Chamba figures are of crucial importance. Rather than folk simplification, the sculptures show their own refinements upon "classic" North Indian patterns, including elongation of divine bodies and perfection of aquiline features that suggest medieval Nepal in divine faces. In these aspects, the sculptures of Chamba are closer to the victorious Durgā made of stone in Visveśvara Mahādeva temple in Bajaura, dating from the mid-eighth century, than to "heavier" images like those of the Śiva Vaidyanātha temple at Baijnath that was reconstructed in 1786.

The compound image of Lakṣmī-Nārāyaṇa is found inside of Chamba's temple of the same name, a *śikhara* that has two shingled pent-roofs attached to its projecting porch sections that are made of stone while its top has a three-part wooden umbrella with tiles that sandwich the usual stone *āmalaka* between its two lower sections. The sculpture is made of marble, but its high base and *mandorla* frame show fine metal casting and *repoussé*. They date from the early tenth century and possibly from the reign of King Sahilavarman, although Mian Goverdhan Singh provides a date of 940 A. D. and attributes patronage to Sahilavarman's son Yugakaravarman.[16] The image has the wide staring eyes that are often associated with Jain art, and stories of the origin of the marble itself suggest ties to Mt. Abu, most famous site of Jain temple art.

Marble and metal image of Viṣṇu with attendants inside Lakṣmī-Nārāyaṇa temple, Chamba, Himachal Pradesh (copyright Archaeological Survey of India).

More impressive for their originality are the figures of Śiva and Pārvatī with Naṇḍi the bull, from about 1025 A.D., that are found in the same temple complex. They are the central images of Gauri-Śaṅkara temple at this place. The figures are very "full," with the exaggerated *tribhaṅga* or hip-shot pose of Pārvatī and the baroque drapery worn by Śiva giving action to their weighty appearance. The relatively late date of the sculpture is shown by the unnatural way of putting the breasts high on the chest of Pārvatī and their stiff, hemispherical design.[17] The inlaid silver eyes of the gods are one element that shows possible ties to Kashmir. The sequence of historical art periods that is proposed for the region in the recently published *Antiquities of Himachal* is:

1. The Early Classical Period (500–800 A.D.)
2. The Kashmiri Period (eighth to early tenth century)
3. The Pratihāra Renewal (tenth to twelfth century)
4. The Post-Classical Period (thirteenth to twentieth century)

The Kashmiri connection is assumed to have involved conquest of Chamba by King Lalitāditya in the eighth century, after the reign of Chamba's King Meruvarman, probably extending to southern Lahaul and the valleys of Kulu and Kangra by rulers of Kashmir's Karkota Dynasty. The foundation of Chamba as a new capital around 1025 A.D. shows fresh artistic products that increasingly mix Pratihāra features with Kashmiri style.

As regards Himachal wooden architecture, Chamba presents the temple of Chamuṇḍa Devī overlooking the town itself and high above the

Ravi River. The porch ceiling and the entrance of the small structure present eight-pointed stars and carved flowers with images of Śiva and Pārvatī, Kṛṣṇa and Rādhā, Kārttikeya, Viṣṇu and Lakṣmī, and Durgā herself. A well-preserved, late medieval painting shows Hari-Hara as Śiva and Viṣṇu in one. The circumambulatory porch is filled with multiple lantern-roofs filled with attendant figures carved in relief around the interior as they show Rajput/Mughal style.

The most prominent art for this area study, however, are the bronze images and their wooden temples that are found at Chatrarhi and Brahmor. Wall paintings are also important. In Chamba itself the dry fresco paintings on wooden buildings like the Chamuṇḍa Devī temple are in the subdued colors and shapes of Kangra/Garhwal/Guler once again, and they relate to the riverside temple of Śivalaya that is also made largely of wood with plastered walls within its porch passage.

The jeep trip from Chamba to the earlier settlement and former capital of Brahmor is breathtaking. It also leads to the earliest wooden and sculptural arts to be considered in this Himalayan study, works of art that have survived almost miraculously in their high and beautiful setting. The river gorge is narrow, and at one point it is crossed by a bridge made of cable and wood that swings in the wind. One leaves the main road temporarily between Chamba and Brahmor in order to visit Chatrarhi, a tiny settlement below Brahmor, where Musinavarman established a kingdom and where Meruvarman was king in the late seventh or early eighth century. The hamlet of Chatrarhi is twenty-five kilometers west of Brahmor, and like Brahmor it is a treasure-trove of early Himalayan art. Chatrarhi holds the temple of Śakti Devī, also called Chaṇḍeśvarī Maṇḍir, on a dramatic ridgetop.

The temple of Chatrarhi dates from the late sev-

Temple of Śakti Devī (Candeśvarī Devī), Chatrarhi, Himachal Pradesh.

enth or early eighth century and the time of Meruvarman and, like its sister temple in Brahmor itself, it is an exceedingly rare survival of wooden arts from such early times. In terms of structure it shows the usual timber-bonding of stones placed between horizontally laid timbers, and the wood is deodar. Like Jagatsukh temple in Kulu Valley, it has a domestic form with a colonnade porch. There are small images of Gaṇeśa and Naṇḍi inside, and several females including Tārā, that are illustrated in *Antiquities of Himachal,* figures 91–95. The astounding work of sculpture is a bronze (more precisely brass) image of Śakti Devī. Hermann Goetz is not an author of rapturous or poetic nature, but he did express wonderment at these three images that he calls the "finest examples of late classic Hindu art of the age of Harshavardhana of Thanesar." He also states that only Chatrarhi and Brahmor exhibit early remnants of the late "Rococo" Gupta style as he credits Meruvarman with its introduction.[18] There are problems regarding the exact dates of Meruvarman's reign, with J. Ph. Vogel dating the reign and the associated images to the mid-eighth century, while Goetz proposes a mid-seventh century date. One important question is whether Meruvarman was a contemporary of King Lalitāditva Muktapida who reigned in Kashmir ca. 724–760. Vogel reports that

Durgā Mahiṣāsuramardinī and other deities carved on the inner doorframe of Śakti Devī temple, Chatrarhi, Himachal Pradesh (copyright Archaeological Survey of India).

Candeśvarī Devī (Śakti Devī) inside of her temple, Chatrarhi, Himachal Pradesh.

Detail of a column and capital in Śakti Devī temple, Chatrarhi, Himachal Pradesh.

Meruvarman conquered his enemies in their fortresses with the help of this goddess, and one is reminded, perhaps, of the Gurkha belief that Kālī will fight beside her soldiers when she is needed.

Śakti Devī is found within a single-roof temple that is a long rectangle covered by slate pieces. It has what may be called semidomestic design, or what may be termed alpine style, and its overhanging roof has protected exterior woodcarving that is among the finest to be found anywhere in the mountains. The inner doorjambs of the entry are especially florid, with an overall porousness that serves as foil to the figures of guardians, atlantes, and deities that also are part of this enclosing complex. Some woodchipping is used, but on the whole the reliefs are more polished and more finished that those of the temple, like the small shrine in Jenog, for example. Although the figures on the doorframe have been said to "bend their bodies with self-consciousness,"[19] the present author did not find that to be true upon personal inspection, for the bands of the frame alternate active figure sections with calming foliage that gives the rest to the eye and a rest to the figures. Ulrich Weisner is one who would be able to draw specific structural comparisons between this art and the buildings of Nepal. He could use the same references as for Nepal, with art of Gupta and earlier times at Ajaṇṭā and elsewhere to compare to columns, capitals, and lantern ceilings in the Chamba area. Columns in the small *mukha maṇḍapa* ("face" porch or the most forward) that opens into a continuous interior passage all around the temple at Chatrarhi, like the *pradakṣiṇa patha* passages inside Nepalese pagodas, are quite broad. Each column culminates in lotiform and vine motifs that support an overflowing *pūrṇa kalaśa* upon which rests an extended capital that supports a ceiling beam, itself being carved into the images of birds, foliage, and seated bulls. From this entry it is easy to see the contents of the small womb house within. The metal figure of the goddess herself is, of course, at the center of the center. She stands where two diagonals drawn from the corners of her square enclosure intersect.

The statue of Śakti Devī stands four feet six inches tall, including the open lotus flower that is its base. She is almost shrouded in offerings of costume, but a photograph in the collection of the Archaeological Survey of India reveals her underlying form. The *aṣṭadhātu* material of "eight metals" makes for a splendid reflective surface that captures the overall fluidity of the slim female who rests on her right leg as she holds a spear and lotus flower in two of her four hands. A long metal scarf crosses her back and flows down over the bend of her forward arms to knee height, and sculpted cloth reaches to the floor behind her as a kind of train. The goddess wears a kind of metal veil at the back of her head and this is topped by a large crown with jewel and flower ornaments. But her face is the center of attention with its perfect arched eyebrows, heavy-lidded eyes, finely bridged nose,

Durgā rides her tiger as Mahiṣāsuramardinī, Candeśvarī temple, Chatrarhi, Himachal Pradesh (copyright Archaeological Survey of India).

and full lips above her neck with three perfect rings. The visage is clearly a descendant of Gupta models, but it is not a copy. In fact it is a key to any suggestion that Himalayan arts are inventive and not merely reflective. Like Nepal, Chamba gives new grace and narrower, fine-boned physiognomy to gods and goddesses. Above Lakṣaṇā Devī is a lantern ceiling of carved wood with four *gandharvas* or flying celestial spirits in its corners. It is possibly the finest carving in all of Himachal Pradesh, and it relates to other refined works in Nepal, Lahaul, and elsewhere. Wood relief work in Chamba is as fine as any in Asia.

The narrow, unpaved road to Brahmor is a passage to a colorful past that is hardly remembered in the rest of South Asia. The town is visible from a long distance in its high placement on a ridge far above the Ravi River. A five-minute walk leads to the main town square and temples of stone and wood. Most prominent is the tall stone tower of its most important Śiva temple—once again a *śikhara,* with three umbrellas added to it. It stands beside an enormous deodar tree that is itself honored for its age and strength. Overall this is the most remarkable temple site in Himachal Pradesh—for the tower and associated wooden temples as well as for its metal sculpture.

Often above the clouds and with a view of snow peaks, Brahmor is still a unified world of Hindu art and Hindu belief and a stronghold of early post-Gupta art. Other elements that survive have sources as early as Kushan art of the first through

Temple of Manimaheśa Śiva and the temple square, Brahmor, Himachal Pradesh.

fourth centuries, and there are signs of Pratihāra dynastic art of ca. 750–1030 A.D. The Bhuri Singh Museum in Chamba displays a brick platform that is the earliest Gupta remains from Chamba, dating from the sixth century as remnant of a temple that once stood in the town. The Indian Museum in Calcutta has a squatting figure of Sūrya in Sassanian dress that was found in the region, while other arts show traces of Palā-Sena and Pratihāra borrowings. Brahmor is itself most notable for works that precede the reign of Sahilavarman and the shift of the capital from Brahmor to Chamba town in the tenth century. This settlement in the hills near the Budhal Valley has always been and still is secure. Vehicles cannot enter the town.

The *śikhara* in Brahmor is dedicated to Maṇimaheśa Śiva, a simple stone tower without *maṇḍapa* attachments. It is structurally plain except for *bhadramukha* faces that are carved high above the simple doorway. Dark shadows form in the deep indentations that rise from bottom to top, emphasizing the temple's verticality. In the center of the inner room a stone *liṅga* is carved in middle Pratihāra style. The monument is dated to the tenth-century reign of Sahilavarman. Its wooden roofs are sometimes said to belong to the "Sutlej Valley style" because such additions are most numerous in that area. A second *śikhara* nearby, this one smaller and devoted to Narasiṁha, is recorded in a copperplate inscription published by Vogel to document its tenth-century foundation and its patronage by Queen Tribhuvanarekha. A striking bronze representation of Narasiṁha as lion-man incarnation of Viṣṇu is inside, made of *aṣṭadhātu* metals or brass. It is undated but may not be as old as other bronzes in Brahmor, even though it does appear to be older than the stone temple that contains it. Narasiṁha comes on strong—he is frontal, ferociously grimacing, luxuriously finished, and threatening, yet he stands only about three feet tall.

The next notable image in the square has lost its original temple enclosure and is housed in a simple wooden shelter. It is Gaṇeśa, Śiva's elephant-headed son, who is still imposing even though it has lost both of its legs. A snake wraps itself around the rotund Defeator of Obstacles, god of wisdom and prudence, and there is an animal skin knotted over his waist while he wears the sacred thread of the Brahman caste across his torso. He has one tusk only, as iconography requires him to illustrate a battle that once occurred between Gaṇeśa and Paraśurāma, sixth incarnation of Viṣṇu. The broken figure is three feet tall, without its fourteen-inch pedestal. It is inscribed with the name of Meruvarman, but—and this a very rare happening—it also has a record of the artist's name, Gugga. This surprising exception to the general rule of anonymity, based in part upon the inappropriateness of any individual taking credit for god-given talent, may reflect especially high regard for the artist during his lifetime. Vogel states that, "we cannot but admire the skill with which he has succeeded in imparting majesty to the grotesque features of the elephant-faced god."[20]

Gaṇeṣa image in temple square, Brahmor, Himachal Pradesh.

Brass statue of Nandi before the Manimaheśa Śiva temple, Brahmor, Himachal Pradesh.

The image of Gaṇeśa has a strong impact that is quite different from that of a smiling, almost comic Naṇḍi, about half life-size, that stands in an open pavilion not far from the simple Gaṇeśa shrine. It faces toward the *śikhara* of Śiva, and its different mood has been attributed to "barbarian" influence as it stands in front of the Maṇimaheśa Śiva tower. Thus, three major metal images that Goetz believes were cast at the site itself are associated with King Meruvarman who assumed the title *rājdhirāja,* "king of kings." This attribution is also proposed for a fourth, and most important, sculpture of the patron goddess Lakṣanā Devī. Her sculptural image is worth attention because it is, once again, the best evidence for the antiquity and stylistic context of Himachal arts, and because she is the protector-goddess of Brahmor.

The temple of Lakṣanā Devī stands for the strong foundation upon which the art and architecture of Himachal Pradesh developed, and it antici-

Temple of Lakṣana Devī in Brahmor, Himachal Pradesh (copyright Archaeological Survey of India).

Entrance pediment of Lakṣana Devī temple, Brahmor, Himachal Pradesh (copyright Archaeological Survey of India).

pates the temple of Hiḍimba Devī in Manali, one of the last two temples to be considered in this chapter as it stands for the full flower of Himachal tradition. Lakṣanā Devī is encountered near the southern and entry edge of the village and some distance from the temple square. From outside it looks so humble that one might almost miss it in favor of walking to the square proper. It now bears a roof of corrugated metal and its exterior is whitewashed over plaster. The plan is a simple rectangle, but the entrance side of the building is very obviously not ordinary.

The entire wooden façade of the original temple survives, and the peak of its contour line shows that the first temple was smaller and had a more steeply pitched roof than the present, slightly enlarged building. In fact, its original form may very well have been similar to that of the forward section of the temple of Markula Devī in Udaipur, Lahaul, a structure that has been added to and changed since its foundation in the tenth or eleventh century.[21] The Brahmor temple surely dates from the early years of the town's status as capital of Chamba. The authors of *Antiquities of Himachal* expand its list of patrons to include Ādityavarman, Balavarman, Divakarman, and Divakaravarman as ancestors of Meruvarman back to his great-great grandfather, and a likely sixth-century beginning for Brahmor arts and government.

The compound doorframe and the pediment of Lakṣanā Devī temple are extremely significant to the history of Himalayan art. It presents the most elaborate carving in the town and it can, indeed, be interpreted in terms of comparison to Ajaṇṭā, the Viṣṇu temple at Deogarh, Nālandā's monastery complex, the key early temples at Aihole, and other monuments of the Guptas' golden age. The overall texture of the façade is organic and inviting to the touch, even as it allows for focus upon such expected figures as the river goddesses Gaṅgā and Yamunā with their usual vehicles the crocodile and the tortoise as they stand at the base of the doorframe. A triple-faced Viṣṇu rides on Garuḍa, fly-whisk bearers stand as attendants, some damaged figures may represent the *navagraha* or nine planets, and there are flying celestials in the upper reaches of the compound relief.

Lithe females in less forceful and therefore perhaps less "self-conscious" poses than the women at Chatrarhi lend their luscious forms to the total. Below these, and very near the lintel of the door itself, are loving *mithuna* couples of the type that becomes more and more common in medieval Indian art. At the same time the very large trefoil arch that is set within the triangular top of the entry wall relates to the Mediterranean world by way of "colonial" art of Gandhara in the early centuries A.D., holding onto patterns that were introduced with the coming to India of a class of artists who were perhaps first trained in the service of Alexander the Great. Since this pattern is frequent in Kashmir, perhaps its appearances in Himachal country increased as King Lalitāditya expanded his empire to include lands from Bengal to the border of the Arab caliphate and from Central Asia to China, so that Kashmiri art came to include "the most heterogeneous style elements side by side of Gandhara, Gupta, Chinese, and even Syrian-Byzantine."[22]

The entry door of the dwelling of the goddess is small and the interior of the temple is quite dark. The first rectangular space inside proves to hold an antechamber with four elaborate pillars and crossing capital extensions with lush carving. This space is the *namaskāra maṇḍapa* as first full porch and a place of preparation for and anticipation of the inner room. The room is continuous with the circumambulatory space that goes all around the *sanctum* enclosure. That inner space is the *garbha gṛha,* small but impressive. Its richly carved lantern ceiling is very similar to the one in Chatrarhi, with a large lotus flower at the center and *gandharva* celestials in the corners. The lantern form itself is so ancient and so widespread as to be of little use in determining origins and relationships, but this example is very noteworthy. All of the symbols that are found at the sister temple in Chatrarhi are here as well, including the outer doorframe which has additional flying angels in two registers. Once again a progressively more mysterious enclosure has been built for the powerful female deity.

The goddess herself, only three feet four inches tall and standing directly at the center of the *maṇḍala*-derived room and ceiling, dates from about 700 A.D. Lakṣanā Devī is a form of Durgā, and so the goddess stands with her right foot resting on the head of Mahiṣa, the evil buffalo-demon, while she holds her trident spear in one hand as its points jab the skull of the vanquished one. The form and face of the goddess seem less linear and crisp than those of the Chatrarhi image, and this sculpture is not as highly polished. Yet both are masterworks, and both sculptures bear the inscribed names of Meruvarman and the artist Gugga. If there is further information on this intriguing artist, hopefully it will be found and published soon.

Carved lotus in the ceiling of Lakṣana Devī temple, Brahmor, Himachal Pradesh (copyright Archaeological Survey of India).

The authors of *The Antiquities of Himachal* ascribe a date for the temple that I believe is too late. But they provide good references to help establish the context of the works of art. They say, for example, that,

> No other complete temple of [such] early date exists in Chamba or H.P., even in the more durable stone medium. But throughout history Chamba was in close cultural contact with Kashmir. Therefore, the Lakṣanā temple can be compared with Kashmiri temples, such as those at Payar or the small Śiva shrine at Pāndreṭhan. There, the triangular gables and trefoil windows mark the four faces; perhaps, when the Bharmaur shrine was entire, it too had a similar form? With Pāndreṭhan, even the ceiling of the Lakṣanā shrine is comparable, in fact it shows more ornamentation, which may argue for a date later than the Pāndreṭhan temple. But if the frontage bespeaks Kashmiri influence, the doorway and the *ghatapallava* pillars are pan-Indian. On consideration of the architecture of the temple, a date of circa eighth or ninth century may be ascribed to our shrine.[23]

This explanation underlines the problem of the relative lack of epigraphy when this part of the northwestern Himalaya is treated, as opposed to Kathmandu Valley, for example.

Lakṣanā Devī, who is also known as Bhadrakālī or, more precisely, Bhagavātī, is both fierce and beautiful. Her form is normally quite hidden by the offered costumes and jewelry that are lavished upon her in Brahmor. A colorburst of red and orange gifts is likely to obscure her appearance on any given day. Beside Śakti Devī in Chatrarhi, she may well be compared to the sparkling image of Durgā Mahisāsuramardinī that was previously discussed at Hatkoti. Both are very early and made of "eight metals" and are dressed in and showered by offerings. They anticipate the lovely sculptures of Durgā that will be discussed at Bhima Kālī temple as this chapter comes to a close. It is useful to remember that whatever the nonbeliever's interests in style, history, and materials may be, these goddesses are "alive," and they call for in-depth anthropological study. It is not that they are idols worshipped for themselves (even though Asians will sometimes use the English term "idol" instead of "image" or "icon" to identify them) but, rather, that they are honored as symbols of higher ideals.

Arts of the hills, mountains, and valleys of Himachal Pradesh have been presented from the Kulu Valley, Mandi, Chamba, and Brahmor as they show indigenous choices, accept foreign patterns, seek to glorify Hindu and animistic forces, house rulers in grandeur, and honor the supreme mother goddess. Two final examples of temple architecture will tie these reasons for art and architecture together as this process of selection moves on to monuments in Manali, the last town on the Beas River before the Rohtang Pass, and in Sarahan above Rampur in the Sutlej Valley region. Both are great towers, with the temple of Hiḍimba Devī in the forests of Manali being a proper pagoda of four roofs and basic construction, while the double monument of Bhima Kālī, in the winter capital of the former *rājas* of Rampur on the Sutlej River, is a composite of temple and *bhandar* in the form of two of the most impressive towers in the Himalaya.

Temple of Hiḍimba Devī, Manali, Kulu Valley, Himachal Pradesh.

Hiḍimba Devī temple was constructed in 1553 A.D., according to an inscription of Mahārāja Bahadur Singh, and the heavy coats of red and green paint that once obscured the excellence of its woodcarving have recently been removed as part of renovation sponsored by the Archaeological Department of India. This happening raises the hope that perhaps the crumbling castle in Leh will receive protected monument status and be similarly "saved," and that Alchi's wall paintings of the eleventh century, also in Ladakh, will not be completely painted over if some government supervision comes into being. The pagoda of three roofs and plain timber-bonded exterior that is whitewashed and covered on the entry side with excellent carvings stands in the deep shade of a deodar forest. Its top roof is covered by brass sheeting. While Manali town itself takes on a carnival atmosphere during the summer, when crowds of Indian and foreign tourists flock to its cool climate, the temple remains enough removed that it can preserve an atmosphere of quiet sanctity. It is an appropriate home for another incarnation of the hill mother—Hiḍimba Devī.

The icon, the symbol, and the center of concentrated power that represents the goddess at this temple is a rock. Not a pebble, as can sometimes be suddenly honored with gifts in the middle of a road in Nepal regardless of traffic (to the consternation of an American bicyclist like the present author). Not a stone that happens to suggest an anthropomorphic subject. Not a sculpted stone that takes on representational meaning. Just a huge boulder, at least two stories high, around which the temple was built because it shows the power of the earth mother as it surges upward from the earth. The only close architectural comparison for this large building is the temple of Tripura Sundari in Naggar, probably datable to the seventeenth or eighteenth century, also in the Kulu Valley region. Both structures are strongly vertical yet wide at the lowest level, and both enclose a large space with no functioning floors above the base. They are part of the axis theme that this study has sought to define, and both have accepted additive offerings—a metal bird that stands as a kind of guardian on the lower roof of the Naggar temple and animal horns as sign of sacrifices that traditionally were mounted on the façade of the temple above Manali, just as they were and are at the Kālī temple in Gorkha, Nepal. Neither of the pagodas has the odd mix of well-separated square and circular roof patterns that are found in the fourteenth-century temple of Parāśara Ṛṣi high in the hills of Mandi district. These are, instead, simple pyramids with overlapping roofs.

Doorframe detail, Hiḍimba Devī temple, Manali, Himachal Pradesh.

The setting of the Manali temple above the town proper is called Dhoongri. Early visitors like A. P. F. Harcourt (*The Himalayan Districts of Kuloo, Lahaul and Spiti* [reprint], Delhi, 1962) were impressed by its setting, and perhaps by its unusual dedication to Hiḍimba of the epic *Mahābhārata*. A mask of the goddess that is kept here is dated to 1418 A.D. and the reign of Udhran Pal, possibly being the earliest such *mohra* or *devata* mask found. It is known that the temple was built after a promise by Rāja Bahadur Singh that he would do so for this deity who is the patron of Kulu Valley. The façade is rich in carving that is traditional in terms of its pan-Indian Hindu stories that center upon Durgā even as it preserves woodchipped folk art designs that are indigenous to the hills. A kind of staccato dance unfolds as one moves along the walls, doorframes, miniature windows, and cornice level beneath suspended *khururu* fringes. The nine planets are present, as are Gaṇeśa and Śiva, and many *burka* or boxlike signs of the thunderbolt that have been borrowed from Tibet. These many features do something to soften the first impres-

Bifurcated window frame, Hiḍimba Devī temple, Manali, Himachal Pradesh.

sion of this very large but powerfully simple statement of geometry amidst the trees. There is some truth in Harcourt's statement that, "The Doongee temple is of most massive construction, but is clumsily put together, and is quite out of the perpendicular." He continues by saying that the goddess "Hurimba," to whom the building is dedicated, and who lived in Purus Ram's time, is shown in the form of a small brass image only three inches high, contrasting "most ludicrously" in terms of size with the temple that towers at least eighty feet above the ground.

Harcourt is surprised as he notes that the interior is occupied by large rocks, with a rope hanging from the roof, a rope from which legend records human victims were hung, suspended by their hands and bleeding as they swung to and fro over the rock that is the presence of the goddess. Harcourt seems to have missed the meaning of the huge boulder inside of the shrine but he does refer to human sacrifice that occurred at the temple, just as it did at the last place to be considered in this chapter. Before moving on, however, it is useful to preserve Harcourt's words that relate to the carving:

> On three sides of the verandah, and the doorway, which is to the east, in wood, of elephants, birds, tigers, and Buddhistical wheels,—the story being that the then reigning monarch, to prevent the artist ever making a duplicate of such a masterpiece, cut off the carver's right hand. But, not to be baffled, the man taught his left hand to take the place of the lost member, and at Triloknath, in Chumba, executed an even finer piece of carving than at Doongree. Here, again, however, adverse fortune followed him; for the Triloknath people, determined that no such workmanship should ever be exhibited elsewhere, now cut off his head!

By touching upon a number of buildings in varied Himachal locations, this chapter is intended to paint a convincing picture of architecture that is local and foreign, simple and elaborate. The choices are especially varied in the region, and there is almost amoeba-like growth of Hindu aesthetics that pick and choose in terms of what to digest and reinterpret. Some of the people and places that produce the arts remain quite unknown, and the Himachal State Museum in Simla has a collection that is both strange and familiar. One may be reminded of Rabindranath Tagore's comment upon his first visit to Indonesia: "I see India all around me, but I don't recognize it." Himachal Pradesh is a place of dynamic arts that are the natural outgrowth of living traditions in which the classic works of Hindu literature are as alive as the *nāga* spirits that entwine on temple doors or the mother goddess who thirsts for blood.

The last architectural work to be considered here is located within sight of the Shirikund Range with its peaks that rise as high as 18,626 feet. Bhima Kālī temple complex in Sarahan is thrilling because of its great size, with two major temple towers and many subsidiary buildings and a procession of enclosed courtyards that lead to the platform of the towers, and also because of its combination of very delicate carved finishing with the strongest possible statements of volume. Forty kilometers above Rampur and reachable only by rough dirt roads, Sarahan is almost like Dhoongri in its feeling of "removal." Yet at the same time it is part of an active town that holds many enthusiastic believers. Their pride when they allow a foreign visitor to see the beautiful images of their goddess is touching. Photography is firmly not allowed.

Sarahan is not a forgotten place known only to wandering shepherds. Surface archaeology is fruitful here, but most monuments remain under worship in an environment quite different from Kashmir where the meaning of truly antique arts is no longer viable. Sarahan is perched on the

Trilokinātha temple in Mandi, Himachal Pradesh (copyright Archaeological Survey of India).

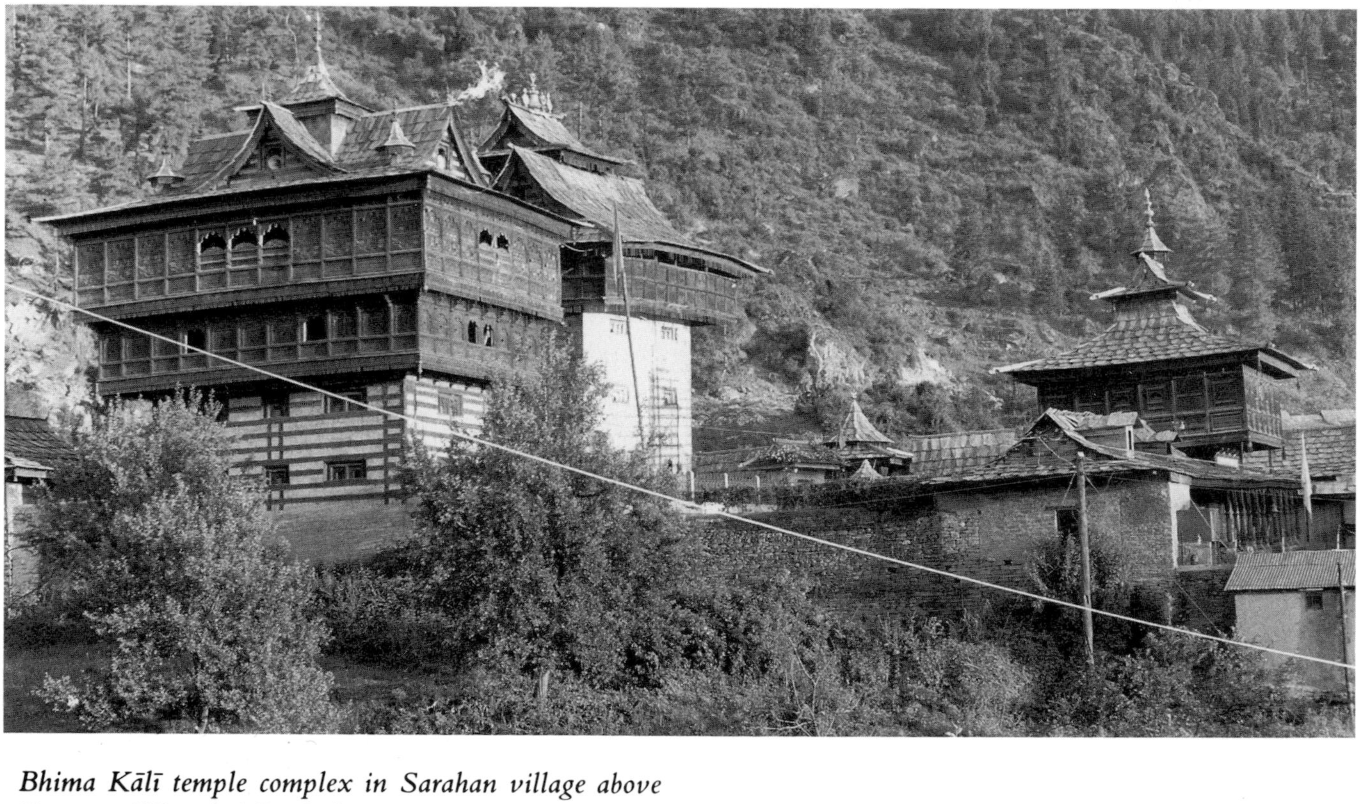

Bhima Kālī temple complex in Sarahan village above Rampur, Himachal Pradesh.

mountainside two thousand meters above the Sutlej River valley, and local belief is that a stone image of Śiva rests on top of the highest visible peak where he is known as Shirikund Mahādeva. Word is that the god is worshipped by having a cup of *charas* presented before his image, and when this is burned to ashes it is placed, along with any other offerings, under a rock at the summit. The peak looks down upon the undated Bhima Kālī complex, called Bijata Devata temple by Shanti Lal Nagar in his *The Temples of Himachal Pradesh* (New Delhi, 1990). Located 184 kilometers from Simla, it is on the route to Kinnaur's tribal district, as are both the palace of Gondhla and the still surviving and very vertical hilltop palace of Chaini. There is nothing "primitive" about Bhima Kālī temple unless it be its deep cavern that emits a groaning voice that is said to be a cry for blood as part of premordial animism.

According to A. H. Francke, this temple complex is best viewed from the mountainside "where it showed all of its symmetrical beauty" as he judged it to be "one of the finest examples of hill architecture" that he had ever seen.[24] The door on the street side access to the compound is covered with plates of brass that have fairly high relief sculptures of Hindu deities including Śiva and Durgā, the seemingly ever-present gods of the mountains. A *śikhara* temple dedicated to Viṣṇu as Narasiṁha opens into this first court where some ordinary activities, like cutting wood for repair work, is done. The temple is attended by folk characters that are stocky, frontal, and smiling. A *pujārī* gate named for priestly attendants is also found here, and is reached by a short stairway. This leads to the first fully paved courtyard; an important place of transformation in which shoes are not worn and a local "Kulu cap" must be worn by men. While surrendering your camera here, you may remember hearing the story of some for-

Back side of Bhima Kālī temple in Sarahan above Rampur with original tower on the left.

eigners who took pictures here without permission and had both of their legs broken for their transgression.

Leading forward from the second court and on to the second paved enclosure is another set of stairs that is attended by two large tigers painted orange and black over plaster. The double doors that are between them are covered over completely with *repoussé* silver panels. They are inscribed with the message that, "These three gates were made during the peaceful reign of H. H. Raja Sahib Padam Singh, 1927."

The silver doors open by way of a vestibule with scalloped arches, topped by a three-roof covering of its own. The tower that is so formed is actually a small temple called Raghunāthji. Inside is a small upstairs shrine that holds a miniature treasure—a sculptural grouping made up of Kṛṣṇa and Rādhā with attendants. They are made of gold, silver, and bronze, and they rest on a little palanquin made of silver. This upstairs room which looks out toward the third courtyard is both peaceful and precious. Another set of doors, also covered with silver and inscribed with the name of Padam Singh, lies ahead. Through this gateway, the last set of double doors can be seen, painted bright red and blue with the lintel marked with the words "Long Live Mother Sri Bhima Kali."

One walks across the last separate court to rise a few more steps, passing through the painted doors, to reach the level of the terrace upon which the two towers actually rest. There are two structures here: an open structure that holds a benign-looking image of Gaṇeśa and a blue-painted one that is frightful because it shelters the deep dark hole that was mentioned above for its dark presence. The blue structure is painted with the name "Sri Lankara Birji," the local *devata* whose full name is Lankara Baro. A local believer reports that the steps that descend into the dark may "lead to water." But A. H. Francke, who was not allowed to enter the premises, reports that, "an ancient Kali temple . . . is said to contain a deep pit. There are rumors that human sacrifices were offered here every tenth year, and that they are still continued secretly."[25] The tower on the right of the terrace has the finest silver doors in Sarahan (with one exception still to be considered) showing Durgā, Kālī, Śiva and others along with elephants, vines, and ring handles like those seen earlier on the *bhandar* in Jenog. Several images show the pan-Indian *kīrti mukha* of "face of glory," and Gaṇeśa is a protective symbol at the top of the door.

Both buildings bear abundant woodcarving of fairly late date, perhaps nineteenth century or later, in very baroque patterns that reveal inspiration both from Europe and from Mughal art. In spite of its fine silverwork the tower on the right is no longer used, perhaps because it is unsound. It tilts toward the second and presumably younger tower, possibly the result of an earthquake. The gently concave silhouette of both towers' roofs reminded Francke of Chinese buildings, but such curved roofs have also been noted on the *bhandar* in Manan village of this state. These Sarahan towers actually combine the functions of temple and *bhandar*.

The tower that remains in use as a shrine has five floors, although visitors are not allowed to climb to the top. The proper shrine of Bhima Kālī is on the third floor, in her "wedding chamber." This raised sanctum can be completely circumambulated, and within its intimate space stands a sparkling image of Bhima Kālī, about three and one-half feet tall and hung with a profusion of ornaments including a nose ring. The goddess has not been published and probably has never been photographed. Her lovely expression is calm and gentle. Her image rests on a silver carpeted dais with four pillars at the sides. This platform is evidently not carried with the goddess in procession, but a simple wooden palanquin on the lowest floor is available for such use. Bhima Kālī is attended by priests in celebration of her wedding in a pattern that recalls treatment of Mīnākṣī as bride of Śiva in the Mīnākṣī Temple of Madurai, South India. On her right side are about fifteen *mohra* masks of local *devatas*. If there is any difficulty in accepting the appealing sculpture of Bhima Kālī, it may derive from Kālī's normal bloodthirsty demeanor as the most dangerous female incarnation of Śiva. Could the voice in the pit be hers?

7

Survival Arts of Ladakh

DEFORESTATION IS, UNFORTUNATELY, A SHARED fact of life in nearly all Himalayan regions, and forests of deodar, fir, and silver fir have been seriously depleted in most lands to the south of the Himalaya's main ridge. Ladakh has never been forested, and it is the driest area to be considered in these pages, making it all the more amazing that a rich and lasting civilization was created and survives there. Perhaps it presents a preview of what may come to be the geography of other Himalayan areas that are subject to incipient desertification and the removal of growing cover that exposes soil to accelerated wind and water erosion, the increased injection of dust and aerosols into the atmosphere and, as Anna Mani continues in "The Climate of the Himalaya" in *The Himalaya—Aspects of Change,* an increased reflection of solar energy from the denuded surface.

Ladakh's mean temperature is 6 degrees C. for the year, with its January lowest temperature reaching −13 degrees C. Rainfall is normally limited to three or four inches annually. The state consists of 97,872 square kilometers with a dispersed population that numbered 120,000 in the 1979 census. The main city of Ladakh is Leh, with only 6,200 inhabitants in 1979 but an estimated 10,000 in 1981, and the technical status of the area is as an Indian administrative union at the district level within the state of Jammu and Kashmir, of which it comprises seventy percent of the land area. It lies between 32.15 to 36 degrees latitude and 75.15 degrees to 80.15 degrees longitude, being bordered by China on the north and east, Gilgit and Skardu on the northwest, Burumulla with Srinigar and Anantnag and Doda districts on the west, and Himachal Pradesh and Doda districts lying to the south. The northern border consists largely of the Karakoram range with passes at elevations of 17,000 and 18,000 feet. It shares this orientation to the range with Pakistan.

Zanskar lies to the southwest of Ladakh's capital and was long part of the kingdom of Leh, with its villages and important monasteries built along the Zanskar River. Remote villages on the south side of the Zanskar range have anthropomorphic images, spirals, intertwined serpents, and abstract woodchipped patterns like the "Celtic" circles seen at the tiny northwestern village of Jenog. All of these call for study and comparison to Himachal Pradesh, Kashmir, and more. The same may be said of the arts of Dolpo and Mustang in Nepal, of Chitral and Azad Kashmir in Pakistan, and other important parts of the mountains. In winter the rivers of the little-studied area of Zanskar freeze and are used as roads that are said to be superior to the artificial ones.

The main town in the long and narrow Zanskar valley is Padum, a place that looks very rough in its setting on top of a glacial rock deposit, while the king of Zanskar has his castle in Zangla. The monastery of Zangla consists of six or seven buildings that climb a mountainside some distance from the town. However, the most important *gompa* is Karsha monastery which overlooks the plains of Zanskar, with the *gompas* of Sani and Zonkhul also well worth study. The most impressive setting belongs to Phygtal Monastery, which consists of about twenty-five small buildings that cling to a steep rock face that has a cave shrine near its top. The adventurer Michel Peissel calls it the most incredible monastery he has ever seen, and he reveals in *Zanskar—The Hidden Kingdom* that there are several large, red buildings inside of the gigantic cavern. While any of these monuments relates more to Tibet than to the pan-Himalayan pagoda tradition, they are also to be noted for their regional inventions.

Ladakh was a separate kingdom until recent time, and the Queen Mother is said to still occupy her formerly royal residence on the banks of the Indus across the river from Leh. While the foregoing information includes some nuts-and-bolts facts, it does nothing to convey the wonder of this land of absolutely clear air and bluest skies that are set off by the yellow sand color of the earth. Nor does it touch upon the breathtaking beauty of monasteries and temples that seem to grow up from the earth and "bloom." Structures here at first appear to be ecological—blending into their beige, yellow, or brown surroundings and having the kind of softened geometry that Georgia O'Keeffe so admired in the adobe church of Ranchos de Taos in New Mexico. But when one goes inside these Buddhist markers upon the endless horizons of sands and raw mountain peaks, one is almost floored by the impact of color, color, and more color. Rather than the heavenly light of Gothic churches, Ladhaki enclosures capture the mysteries of the dark earth's womb and burst with the hardly controlled energy of their own holiness.

Ladakh's climate might be called violent, even as the region is an essential link on the trade routes that reach from northwestern India to Tibet and on to Turkestan along with the more distant destinations of Beijing and Rome. Winter is long and cold, as can be witnessed by the design of houses with narrow windows and very thick walls. Because snow rarely lasts in the populated areas below the high peaks, the roofs may be flat, providing ideal work areas and observation platforms for the industrious and unusually pleasant Ladakhis. The dryness allows for a kind of adobe construction that utilizes sun-dried bricks or pounded earth combined with timbers, which are always costly and rare, to make timber-bonded structures like those already seen in this overview. The closest comparison of Ladakhi buildings is to those of Namche Bazar and other settlements in Solo Khumbu, Nepal. The main Himalayan ridge keeps most snow from reaching Ladakh, and winter is followed by a short, dry summer during which few crops can be grown. Potatoes and barley are the mainstays of Ladakhi diet, supplemented by bracing tea that is mixed with butter. Bread is especially tasty and very nutritious.

The people themselves are a mix, perhaps reminding one of Bhutan or Sikkim or Nepal, since they have both Indo-Arvan and Tibeto-Mongoloid features. The costume of the people sets them apart, however, especially the "top-hat" made of black velvet that mature women wear. The extravagant head and back covering of masses of turquoise, sewn down on a velvet base by Ladakhi women, is seen nowhere else. The garment has competition only among the Kalash women of northern Pakistan. But it is more elaborate and more precious than the headpieces that are worn by Kalash people. Sometimes termed "snake-shaped bonnets," these brilliant headdresses called *perak* often have wide, protruding ear flaps made of black lambskin, and they are covered with large chunks of turquoise and other precious items. These are the most valuable items of costume in all of the Himalaya, and only the royal regalia of old Tibet might equal their beauty.

Leh and the monastic towns around it are so clearly Tibetan and Buddhist that it would be easy to forget that only fifty-two percent of the population is, in fact, Buddhist. Most of the rest—including immigrant Kashmiris, the merchant and farming families in Kargil to the south, and the Dards in their remarkable semisubterranean dwellings that are entered through the roof and remain almost completely closed to the outside world through winter—are Muslim. Recent rioting in Leh was partly due to tensions between the native

Ladakhi Buddhists and the immigrant Muslim merchants from the southern part of the state. It is hoped that accommodation will be reached on both sides.

Legend traces the beginnings of a kingdom in Ladakh to one of three brothers who divided Tibet among themselves in 1020 A.D., at the end of the first Tibetan empire. One is said to have moved to Ladakh where he founded the land's first royal dynasty. Buddhism was flourishing at the time, and its successes in the neighboring Tibetan kingdom of Guge were passed on to Ladakh. An accommodation was made with Bonpo religion as the expansion was made, and many early Bon temples are said to have been modified to become Buddhist monasteries and Buddhist temples. Sometimes the required changes were minor, as earlier chapters have indicated, and elements of Bön sorcery and animistic spirits can still be picked out in today's Ladakh. The new kingdom extended its own influence after the eleventh century, with its borders expanding under King Lhachen Utpala (1080–1110 A.D.) to meet the related kingdoms of Purang and Mustang in today's Nepal.

When reforms under the guidance of the sainted teacher Tsongkhapa resulted in formation of the Gelugpa sect and the growth of new monasteries and their arts in the fifteenth century, Ladakh rose to some prominence, even though interior troubles had divided the ruling family and the "empire." One is informed by Blanche Christine Olschak and her coauthors that Lhachen Bhagan unified Ladakh in 1470 and established a new dynasty named Namgyal. His successor withstood an attempted invasion from east Turkestan, but Muslim forces from outside held many successful attacks on Ladakh in later years. The Ladakhi rulers expanded their territories during the seventeenth century, but the fifth Dalai Lama of Tibet (Nawang Lobsang Gyatso, 1617–82), whose incredibly ornate funerary *chorten* may be seen in the Potala in Lhasa, is said to have convinced the newly converted Buddhist Mongolians to attack western Tibet and Ladakh. The Ladakhi king, Delegs Namgyal, requested help from Kashmir and, with the battle of Basgo in about 1685, the Tibetans and Mongolians were turned back. The legacy of the alliance with Kashmir was that Ladakh was ruled by the Mughal dynasty for the rest of the tenure of Muslim rule from Delhi.[1] Still, Lamaism was maintained and great works of Vajrayāna Buddhist art continued to be made. While its isolation and the scarcity of roads has hindered the development of any large-scale industries in Ladakh, arts and handicrafts of high quality continue to be made. They have an economic importance unmatched in any other Himalayan area.

The art and architecture of Ladakh is, like that of Bhutan with Sikkim as well as Solo Khumbu and the Darjeeling area, part of the Tibetan sphere of influence. For that reason, there is no need to examine monuments singly or in terms of the basic function of *gompa* monasteries or *lhakhang* temples, or even to explain the massive solidity of fortified palaces like the crumbling splendor that is the Palace in Leh. With the Karakoram range to the northwest and the Himalaya to the southwest, Ladakh is at the core of the Transhimalaya, a geographic term that is favored by the Olschak scholars as well as by Giuseppe Tucci in the *Trans-Himalaya* volume of the *Archaeologia Mundi* series. In this central position Ladakh offers, as clearly shown by the varied forms of trefoliated windows at the eleventh-century monastery of Alchi, architectural forms that relate to Kashmir, Gandhara, and, once again, the Mediterranean world.

To illustrate the internationalism of which Ladakhi art is a part, Romi Khosla looks to a small monastery measuring just thirty-eight feet by fifty-seven feet at the confluence of the Chandra and Bhaga rivers at Tandi that he calls the oldest in neighboring Lahaul—Guru Ghantal Gompa—in order to point out broad artistic references in woodcarvings. First he notes that the present slate roof is not original but a replacement for a steeply pitched timber roof like the one that survives at Hiḍimba Devī temple in Manali, and then he speaks of a dormer door with highly unusual carving patterns "that are clearly European in origin." He notes intertwined circle motifs that are "surely very close to Celtic patterns" as seen on early Christian manuscripts. There is reduplicated plaitwork of serpents that is associated "more with Celtic, Hellenistic or Byzantine traditions than with anything Indian." Then he notes that "a substantial number of Byzantine craftsmen entered the service of Lalitadidtya Muktapida (725–756 A.D.), and it is very likely that there is some connection between the influx of European and Central Asian craftsmen into North India and the presence of

Ki monastery, Spiti, Ladakh region (copyright Archaeological Survey of India).

these unusual motifs in Lahoul." Such questions are always involved in any consideration of Himalayan arts, whether they are stated or not. But Khosla takes the usual puzzles further and includes Himachal Pradesh as he states,

> Two of the adjoining states, Kishtawar and Chamba had been conquered by the Kashmir monarch Anantadeva (1028–1063) and, if Lahoul too was under his reign, it is certain that a whole tradition of Kashmir wood carving was imported into Chamba and Lahoul during this period. His queen Suryamati was, at any rate, a devout Shiva worshipper and the founder of many temples. It might have been assumed that the carved door at Guru Ganthal could have been brought to the site from another part of India but there was a very rich tradition of wood carving as evidenced in the temples of Lakshana Devi and Markula Devi which surely confirm the presence of a whole tradition of wood carving of Kashmir origin even though it was probably influenced by cultural influx from Central Asia when it was formulating in Kashmir.[2]

His encompassing view of interrelated states is all too rare in the field of Himalayan studies.

The route to Central Asia from Ladakh, as from Lahaul, is reasonably direct. Giuseppe Tucci, Nicholas Roerich, Mrs. A. W. Macdonald, and A. H. Francke are among scholars of the early twentieth century who interpreted the discoveries of archaeological digs and early tombs of Ladakh, including some near the capital. Their investigations included examination of human remains in order to propose that early skulls from the area are dolichocephalic whereas the present-day population of Ladakh is brachycephalic, calling for comparison to different parts of Tibet. But, for this study, surface archaeology is more appropriate, even urgent, for Ladakh holds mammoth Buddhist centers that are increasingly impoverished in the twentieth century and whose arts often appear to be at the edge of collapse. This is another mountain region where preservation of the arts is sorely needed.

The last dispairing statement about the art does not reflect the judgment of the society as a whole as made by Helena Norberg-Hodge as she writes of "Ladakh: Development without Destruction" in *The Himalaya—Aspects of Change* (1981). She notes the strength of Ladakhi identity, saying that the everyday life of the Ladakhi people is not really affected by the presence of a large influx of the Indian army to bases near Leh, since trouble with the Chinese began in 1962, as just one example of how traditional Ladakhi society is firmly established and largely unchanging. She states optimistically but perhaps also cautiously that the success of traditional life in this area results from the most frugal and prudent use of very limited natural resources, and that irrigation is hardly even possible as farmers depend upon snow melt to water their small fields. Water channels called *yura* are up to five kilometers long as they are traced through the desert terrain. For the first time, this study follows along to consider the limited resources of a Himalayan area, an important factor that has always affected the development of mountain art. The author goes on to explain that,

> Altitude and topography determine the choice of every crop but barley, which is roasted and ground to form the staple *ngamphe,* is by far the most important. *Ngamphe* does not require cooking, and is therefore particularly suitable for consumption in winter.[3]

Only in certain parts of Central Asia like Turfan, where annual rainfall is measured by a few milliliters, are there conservative irrigation measures to equal those of Ladakh.

Houses are substantial and long-lasting in Ladakh, being passed on to a family's eldest son upon or even before the death of his father, while younger sons were traditionally sent to the monasteries to become monks. Wealthy and aristocratic Ladakhis might have very large houses with many rooms but it is probably more useful here to consider average houses. A typical house in Leh has its property defined by mud walls over six feet tall, and the grounds are shared by the house and several cattle pens. The walls begin as hand-formed mud bricks that are dried in the sun and, as in southwestern adobe walls in America, the mud is smoothed and whitewashed. Stone rubble that is the norm in Himachal Pradesh and Lahaul is not used for dwellings in Ladakh. The house is rectangular and might measure about thirty-three feet by forty-six feet in land area as it rises to a height of two stories. The ground floor might have as many as six stables for cows and *dzo* (a cross-breed of cow and yak) and small cubicles for sheep and goats.

Romi Khosla further notes that windows are narrow with shutters that open to admit light and air while thick mud walls rest on stone foundations. Entrance to the upper floor is afforded by an exterior staircase, and toilets are at ground level, allowing collection of manure for the fields. An entrance portico or porch precedes the upper door into the house, the heart of which is the kitchen *(chensa),* and utensils kept there are often inherited over generations. The *chensa* serves as a sleeping room for an entire family, and there may be partitioned space set aside as a sleeping area for guests. Seats with low tables *(chok-tse)* are found around the room. A flue through the ceiling, called a *chula,* was introduced to the people of Leh by Moravian missionaries in the nineteenth century so that houses there could have smokeless interiors, unlike those of Solo Khumbu, for example.

Separated from the rest by a passage hall and measuring perhaps nine by eighteen feet is a prayer room or *lhakhang* of the family (*lhakhang* is the same term used for an unfortified temple in Bhutan). It has an altar, possibly with a stucco image of Śākyamuni Buddha, and there might be *tanka* paintings that are commissioned for family ceremonies. This simple room has low seats running lengthwise for monks to sit upon while reciting prayers when invited to do so by the family.

Finally, a *dzod* or storage room measuring about seven by eleven feet is used for many things but mainly for storing sacks of grain and dried meat and fruit. The roof of a house is flat, as in Solo Khumbu and parts of Pakistan, and it is reached by an interior stairway. Door and window frames as well as shutters are prefabricated and brought to a village from carpetry specialists elsewhere, for joinery is considered to be a special skill. Khosla adds that trade caravans into Spiti from Kulu and

Kunawar often carry prefabricated frames and shutters, and that in Lahaul the prefabricated items even include cupboards that are brought to a site before the masonry walls go up. Timber lintels are always used in the northwest.[4]

Ladakh is a place where low stone walls have to be erected beside potato plants to protect them from constant wind and flowers bloom atop stems that are only one or two inches long. Knowing the harshness of the land, Ladakhis are very careful not to overuse it. This can only make its lush art more impressive, for the art does have splendor. Even though the monasteries are no longer centers of political power and administration, and while links to Tibet were cut when the border was closed in 1959, the Buddhist centers are still central to the lives of more than half of the people who live in Ladakh. Trade with some great neighbors has been upset in modern times, however, and the people no longer pay taxes to *gompas*. It appears that monasteries like Shey Gompa, Phyang Gompa, Thikse Gompa, and even Hemis Gompa with its famous yearly festival that draws visitors from very far away may not be able to properly care for their treasures. Yet Ladakh has always accepted the basic requirements of Vajrayāna arts: that they be colossal in size, multiple, and precious.

A large chapel just a short walk up the dry mountainside by the Leh Palace is dedicated to Maitreya as Buddha of the Future. Inside is a huge image of the seated spiritual leader who will come to the world when need is greatest. Its red-painted temple is probably the oldest in Leh, and A. H. Francke suggests that it is identical with the "Red College" that was erected in Leh in the early fourteenth century. Records show that a palace on the very top of the dry hill was erected in about 1520 A.D.

The giant sculpture in the Maitreya temple, more than two stories high, is made of clay and brightly painted along with some application of gilt. Paintings on the walls around it have lengthy inscriptions and, according to Francke, dates that correspond to the second half of the fifteenth century. They are among the very few such works that can be dated even approximately. Further up the hill of Maitreya there is a second red temple, and this one belongs to the "four lords" *(mGon-khang)* who are sculpted here and vary from three to eight feet in height, with an image of Vaiśrāvana (Kubera) that is shown only once each year. Attributed dating to the sixteenth century is suggested here, including for the wall frescoes that include Vaiśrāvana in sexual *yab-yum* union with his *śakti* or female counterpart. Some "Muhammadan portraits" puzzled Francke because of their placement inside a Buddhist temple until they were explained by the lama in charge as being of Ladakhi kings who, Francke suggests, may have dressed in unusual ways to express their "close attachment" to Turkomans, who had invaded Ladakh.[5]

While Ladakh appears to have one of the world's most isolated civilizations, it once again reveals international contacts, including political and commercial relations to the western world, that in fact exist for all Himalayan peoples. Descending from the temples and the high palace ruins, one passes by the majestic Great Palace of Leh that was erected in about 1620 A.D. as the stronghold, it is said, of King Senge Namgyal, although there is some confusion regarding his regnal dates. Francke puts them at ca. 1590–1620 but S. S. Gergan and F. M. Hassnain correct them to be 1569–94.

The palace is crumbling, unprotected, and unsafe to enter today, but one can still see the "lion gate" at the entry with two wooden columns that extend and cross capitals below a multilevel porch roof that shelters the main entrance. Lions are carved as part of the projecting supports, and there is a small window above the opening with the protruding head of a guardian. A single element can, in many ways, stand for the whole at this place.

The description of appropriate symbolism for columns in palace chapels or monasteries here should sound familiar to anyone acquainted with buildings in the Tibetan sphere of influence, for the main shaft of a column has petals of the lotus flower that continue outwards along the doorframe. The most common symbol on a column capital is the *makara* water monster or a lotus flower or a *mantra* as invocation written in Tibetan script. The simple column and capital developed into a complex system of "piled" capitals over the column. Some of the columns could be termed facetted or radiating. Since logs large enough to be capitals in very high rooms were always rare, a solution was worked out whereby the internal height was raised by giving an elaborate base to each column along with a double or triple capital.

Additional signs of importance are shallow balconies that are added on the entrance side of a *gompa,* as throughout the Himalaya region. Finally, the external plastering of walls is common, both for monasteries and houses of the wealthy. The mud used for plastering needs to have a rich clay content so as not to crack, and the final smoothing of the mud is done by hand. Chaff of barley stems is often mixed with the mud, while mud with high mica content gives a special luminosity to walls. In addition, mud provides protection from wind erosion and wind-swept snow. Inner walls are covered in the same way, but those to receive paintings require additional surface preparation. As Khosla reminds the reader,

> To discuss the painted symbols and images and their meaning is synonymous with discussing the architecture. The mere representation of a *mandala* in three dimensional form as a *Lhakhang,* is in itself, a powerful link between building, symbolism and the Buddhist philosophy centering on the achievement of *nirvana.*[6]

Paintings cover the walls in Ladakh's monasteries, and they are as dense with iconographical story, as brilliantly colored, and as meticulously drawn as any frescoes found elsewhere in the mountains. Hemis Gompa, for example, has murals outdoors, all around the roofless courtyard where its annual festival and dancing draw throngs in summer. They come to this remarkable complex that was founded in 1620 and completed in 1640 A.D., based on texts found in the *gompa,* and established and given extensive land holdings by King Senge Namgyal (1570–1642). It may be compared to the many other monastery complexes that are briefly described in the following way.

Phyang Gompa on the trade route from the Indus to the Jehlam rivers and in a place that Francke calls "probably the most ancient town of Western Tibet" holds a fine bronze image of the Buddha in Gandhara/Gupta drapery that may date from the ninth century. It has major importance in the complex history of Asian art, partly because of its

Hemis monastery, Ladakh.

closeness to the silver-eyed and broad-shouldered ideal of Kashmir's Buddhist art before the coming of Islam. Can these treasures that convey colossal size, multiplicity, and preciousness survive in the midst of poverty that has even led some monasteries to demand paid admissions?

Thikse monastery, just ten miles from Leh on the road to Hemis, reportedly was founded in the fifteenth century. It may be the most dramatic of all the *gompas* in Ladakh in its appearance because of the way its white pyramidal form soars skyward to be crowned by its main halls that are painted yellow and red. Its shrine of Maitreya as Buddha of the Future is highly regarded, as are the paintings of eighty-four Mahāsiddhas, the great "miracle workers," that appear in frescoes all around its dancing court. Like Lamayuru Monastery, located halfway down from the Photo Pass at 13,432 feet where it belongs to the Kargyupa school of Tibetan Buddhism, Thikse is impressive in its harmony with the dramatic landscape around it. It is a reminder of Tiger's Nest Monastery in Bhutan.

Lamayuru Monastery has an image of Vairocana Buddha on a lion throne as its main image, with a mandorla halo formed by *makaras* and Garuḍa as mythical bird that is most prominent in Hindu rather than Buddhist context as carrier of Viṣṇu. Some details of mural painting here suggest relationships to Alchi and prototypes from as early as the eleventh century, but the date of the *gompa*'s foundation is unknown. It is built on many levels and commands one of the broadest views of the surrounding lands. At its base are the ruins of what may have been a temple of Bön-po.

Basgo is a ruined citadel that is still the most impressive of Ladakhi tower structures as it shows the damaging effects of a three-year siege that it withstood in the seventeenth century. Two temples and one small shrine are within its walls, and each sacred building holds an image of Maitreya Buddha that is proportioned according to its placement. Like any Maitreya in art, all of these recall the important rock wall relief at Mulbek at the entrance to the valley of Ladakh in deep and rounded style that may derive from late Gupta art in the seventh century, when such iconography first appeared according to Snellgrove and Skorupski. The giant rock-cut image at Mulbek in the lower Indus valley has traditionally welcomed pilgrims and traders to Buddhist Ladakh and its iconography is, once more, international.

Shey (from *shel* in Tibetan meaning "crystal") began as a hilltop fortress like all of the early "Tibetan" sites in Ladakh, and there are ruins of several higher levels on the top of today's buildings. An artificial lake that once was a mirror in front of the palace is now a swamp, but its interior still preserves faded glories. Also found on the road from Leh to Hemis, like Thikse, Shey Gompa is just as integral with the natural hill foundation that helps it build a miniature mountain of its own. There is a giant seated image of Śākyamuni inside of the main hall. Snellgrove and Skorupski point out that it is so large that one first circles it at the base, then climbs to the second floor to go around its shoulders and head, and then finishes viewing the head of the figure on the third floor. The statue is constructed of clay and gilded, in keeping with the aesthetic rules of Vajrayāna. It is confidently colossal.

Spituk is another semipyramidal monastery built on a natural hill, a few kilometers from Leh and now close to the large camp of the Indian army. The main temple is approached by a flight of steep stairs, and its interior is dominated by a large throne that awaits the presence of His Holiness the Dalai Lama. To the left of the throne is a sizeable sculpture of Vajra-Bhairava in his threatening glory while being especially protective of the Gelugpa order. On the right is an eleven-headed and many-armed image of Avalokiteśvara. It is stunningly multiple.

Likir Monastery is charged with the crucial task of caring for Alchi Gompa, the greatest jewel of Ladakhi art, and it is also near the army camp. Its hilltop setting is more "regular" in terms of an accumulation of buildings that harmonize in that their many vertical and painted window niches are regular, almost modular. A fresco here shows Mount Meru at the center of the universe in the form of an architectural tower with a body as a high white rectangle that is topped by three arched doors and five mountain peaks. Should such a form be compared to the most vertical buildings of Lahaul, like the "Thakur's Castle" in Gondhla, or to the now-ruined watchtower that guards the entrance to Swat at the Malakand Pass? Touches of gold are frequent. It is appropriately precious.

The humble Sankar Gompa is used by Kusho Bakula, named for one of the Sixteen Arhats and head of Spituk Gompa, as a residence when he is in Leh. Its upper floor contains a silver-painted incarnation of Duk-kar (Ushnishasitatapatra) that is as powerfully evocative of divine strength as any other clay image in the Himalaya. It belongs to the category of Thikse Gompa's gleefully victorious clay statues of Yamāntaka (Vajrabhairava) and his attendants that are wrapped in the skins of animals and snakes. Its subject is instructional horror, and it may be compared to the memorable clay sculptures of Sikkim.

Some impoverished monks of today will open the secret rooms meant only for highest initiates in such grand monasteries for a few rupees, revealing black-painted walls with gold lines that represent the world of Bardo, the after-death plane that is detailed in *The Tibetan Book of the Dead,* and terrors that should not be betrayed. They are meant to be seen and dealt with only by the most elevated seekers of wisdom. The wealth of art and meaning in other settings and for other purposes can only be touched upon, but perhaps a single monument can summarize the great quality and historical significance of art in Ladakh: Alchi Monastery.

Recent work with Alchi by art historians Pratapaditya Pal and Susan and John Huntington, plus the in-depth analysis of David L. Snellgrove and Tadeusz Skorupski, along with *Buddhist Monasteries in the Western Himalaya* by Romi Khosla in the *Bibliotheca Himalayica* series that is published in Kathmandu, are succeeding in exposing and interpreting the importance of Alchi. Additional comments made here are meant to emphasize its early date and its internationalism while conveying something of the experience of visiting this extraordinary place as a Ladakhi treasure trove.

The small village of Alchi is approached over a bridge that crosses a part of the Indus River network and, as Romi Khosla explains, it is actually a grouping of four very small villages, each having ten to fourteen houses. The monastery itself consists of numerous constructions. This complex is surprisingly informal in appearance, partly because lesser buildings of monks' houses, animal pens, and storerooms are scattered around the small compound. Vegetable gardens and apricot orchards are found beside the religious buildings. The grounds do not seem to be set apart as sacred as in most monasteries (an opposite extreme is illustrated by the perfect geometry of blessed earth in the circular *maṇḍala*/cosmic plan of Samye Gompa in Tibet). The presence of three large and two small *chortens* at the entrance to the compound is also unusual, and there is another large one in the ground of the local minister who is known as the Alchi *lon-po*.[7] The logic behind the arrangement of these additions is unclear, but the lay of the land may have something to do with the placement of the main buildings, for they progress from highest to lowest points as:

1. Lha-khang Soma
2. Sum-tsek
3. 'Du-khang
4. Lotsawa Lha-khang
5. Mañjuśrī Lha-khang

The difference in elevation between highest and lowest levels is about sixteen feet, and all the structures are found to the east of the compound village.

Madanjeet Singh prefaces brief comments on the arts of Alchi by pointing out that their well-being is partly due to the efforts of King Lhachen Utpala to consolidate Buddhism in Ladakh during his reign of about 1080–1110 A.D.[8] He emphasizes the great altar that is found in the 'Dukhang at Alchi as an outstanding creation of the post-Lalitāditya style of Kashmir and part of a "natural evolution from later Gupta mannerism and early Indian medieval art, [for] it retains a perfect balance and harmony of the design as a whole." These can be taken only as preliminary comments, and one could say much more, for the marvelously swirling and entwined composition of this altar complex, with undulating *makara* water monsters, flying *gandharva* angels, leaping animals and dragons, cloud and foliate volutes, all curling symmetrically to enclose male and female bodhisattvas who attend the central and calmly unmoving Avalokiteśvara, is unmatched in the Himalaya. Above the wooden altar and with exception of part of the wooden mandorla complex behind the Most Compassionate One with his multiple heads, the open sculpture that is at least fifteen feet high is made entirely of unbaked clay. Its setting against a dark, shadowed background effectively contrasts its brightly painted colors.

The monastery compound, as measured by Snellgrove and Skorupski, is about one hundred meters long from north to south and about forty meters wide at the southern end. Visitors enter from this southern end, coming first to three houses and to the *chortens* that are referred to above. Next is the Kanjur Lhakhang with the slightly smaller Lhakhang Soma behind it. Next, and still to the walker's left, is the Sumtsek meaning "Three Tier" as the most important structure of the group, with red bands painted on the outside of each level and two small *chortens* across from it on the visitor's right. Then comes a large house of irregular plan and the attached structures of the 'Dukhang or Assembly Hall and its courtyard. Last are the Lotsawa Lhakhang dedicated to the "great translator" (Lo-tsa-ba in Tibetan), the small Jampal Lhakhang with a "four-fold image of Manjusri" (Jam-dpal in Tibetan), and the Kanjur Lhakang with volumes of the Tibetan Canon but no wall paintings. These last structures lead to the walled northern end of the compound toward the Indus River.[9] No major chronicles of royal rule over this area have been found, but Romi Khosla gives a concise description of the many buildings at the site in his *Buddhist Monasteries of Western Tibet*.[10]

In the absence of more complete historical evidence, stylistic analysis becomes especially important at Alchi. The present author has had two brief visits to Alchi Monastery (A-lci Chos-'khor in Tibetan) and not the lengthy stays that were experienced by Snellgrove and Skorupski or the Huntingtons, but anyone can see that the complex is most important for its dry fresco paintings that are a textbook example of trans-Himalayan internationalism. Pratapaditya Pal and Ravi Kumar, who date the murals of Alchi to the eleventh century, published excellent color photographs of them with commentary in order of their placement, partly to capture their hues before continual exposure to artificial light fades them further and partly to call attention to the urgent need to preserve and restore them. The second need is especially urgent, we are told, since a team of foreign citizens was allowed not only to photograph the frescoes with flood lighting but to actually make rubbings (tracings) of the murals, thereby inflicting damage that will take years to repair. Kumar calls their action "an act of vandalism."[11] The ephemeral beauty of Himalayan arts is all too apparent to anyone who saw the final destruction of the wing of the royal palace in Kathmandu with its important fresco paintings where it had stood unrepaired for decades after the 1934 earthquake. The future of Alchi is a matter of worldwide concern.

Pal begins his commentary on Alchi by quoting Inscription No. 1 in the 'Dukhang, written by Kalden Sherap:

> In that best of continents, southern Jambudivya, at this spot, the hermitage of Alchi in sPu-rgyal's Tibet, land of pure ground and high mountains, I have built a precious temple with devoted veneration . . .
> Through whatever merit I have obtained in founding a precious temple and composing this "Lamp of Clear Recollection" may I and the infinity of living beings be born in the excellent pure realm which is called the "Great Bliss of the Lord and the blessed one Akshobhya."
>
> Kalden Sherap

Indeed, this is an appropriate preface to any study of Alchi, for in spite of its art historical and iconographical importance it is, firstly and lastly, a product of devotion.

The buildings are plain, whitewashed everywhere but for a narrow band of red-orange ochre between two ridges along the top. They are flat-roofed, have small doors, and blend with the environment. These features are unremarkable but the paintings on the walls—especially of the 'Dukhang, Sum-tsek, Lhakhang Soma, and Lotsawa Lakhang—are unmatched anywhere. Even one of the *chortens* near the entrance has paintings. In comparison to other painted interiors that this volume has treated, Alchi's are the richest and the most precisely detailed. They have an impact like rich brocade, but clearer, more jewel-like, and, once again, so vulnerable. Upon the current author's most recent visit, an entry wall painted with hundreds of Buddhas was being covered with whitewash!

The artistic style of Alchi's murals is attributable to Kashmir overall, but additional influences also are seen. Pal refers to the murals of the 'Dukhang and Sumtsek as the earliest buildings as being in Style 1, a Kashmir style that is now missing there but which still survives in western Tibet, as well as in the paintings of Alchi and of Sumda Gompa not far from Alchi on the road to Zanskar. He judges Style 2, found inside Lhakhang Soma as the New Temple, to be "radically different" while relating directly or indirectly to known styles in India and Tibet. Pal reinforces Tucci's publication by referring to copious literary allusions to Kashmiri artists in western Tibet. He points to the biography of Rinchen Sangpo as showing that he was responsible not only for temples and monasteries in western Tibet but perhaps for Alchi as well. He was a major patron of Kashmiri artists, bringing thirty-two of them to Tibet. So, Pal continues,

> These thirty-two artists from Kashmir with the help of local talent were largely responsible for most of the Kashmiri style murals that today delight the visitors to the eleventh century monasteries in Ladakh and Guge founded either by Rinchen Sangpo or by the local princes and gentry.[12]

The appearance of pearl rondel framing devices at Alchi is an indication of ancient Sassanian contact, while horsemen are shown shooting arrows over their shoulders in the classical pose of the very early "Parthian shot." Intense colors with emphasis on red, blue, and black along with frontal and symmetrical compositions show memories of Central Asia and even Afghanistan while certain *yab-yum* compositions of gods against backgrounds of flaming crimson suggest contact with Vajrayāna art from Nepal. At the same time, a manifestation of the green Tārā or Durgottarini Tārā as Prajñāpāramitā at the entrance of the 'Dukhang calls for comparison to Kashmir because of its elegance of extremely fine line, its presentation of the lovely figure in three-quarter view, and its fluid frame of curling vines. Another Kashmiri element is the shading of human forms, especially females, for illusionistic roundness, as in another treatment of the green Tārā as Prajñāpāramitā in the lefthand alcove of the Sumtsek, in animal images like the "Persian" horses that are painted on the left leg of Avalokiteśvara in that same alcove, and in a representation of Buddha Amitāyus (Amitābha) on the wall opposite the second Tārā mentioned above.

That textiles traded along the Silk Route beginning in the second century B.C. impacted these paintings is readily apparent in the ceiling paintings of the first floor as they present repeated "Central Asian" silhouettes, equestrian hunters and leaping lions, and double rondels with horseback or elephantback hunters. The silk fabrics of Japan's Shoso-in treasure house in Nara, sealed in 756 A.D., are just one source of close comparison. Amitābha, strikingly framed by red, yellow, and blue borders and with rampant leogryphs at either side, floats in a sea of Buddha images that are everywhere in Sumtsek. They are like divine wallpaper in the lefthand wall just before the central alcove as one of the Himalaya's finest examples of international Buddhist ideals. Angels fly above Amitābha, musicians play below, and he is utterly poised. Yet, while so much can be recognized, even from places as far away as Tunhuang in China, the miniature paintings of the life of the historical Buddha and other scenes that cover the drapery on the legs of more than life-size clay sculptures of Maitreya in the central alcove, Avalokiteśvara in the left alcove, the Mañjuśrī in the alcove to the right, are unexpected. The paintings create their own tiny space-cells, one subject at a time, as they literally wrap the *bodhisattvas* in iconographical story.

Maṇḍalas are found in all of the painted buildings at Alchi, and they return this study to its most continual and reliable guide to Himalayan art and architecture. They are fewer in number inside the 'Dukhang and Sumtsek as the earliest buildings, although the very large *maṇḍala* of Vairocana just to the left of the entry of Sumtsek is very impressive as well as equalled by a *maṇḍala* of Five Buddhas represented in female manifestation near the back right corner of Sumtsek's second floor.

In the later halls the paintings are multiplied and seem to help create a celestial totality as they pull the viewer's eye around the interiors. They are more clearly Tibetan in these buildings, including an image of Mahākāla that hovers over the entrance to Lhakhang Soma and Vajrapāṇi trampling on evil ones in the back left corner of the same structure. The visual power of these paintings is equalled in a more abstract way by the multicolumned exterior carvings, with their open entablature holding angular and lobate arches with Buddhas and Buddhas-to-be inside. There is also an upper cornice with projecting lions of the kind that may be found from Kathmandu Valley to Persia and beyond. The triangular surrounds that enclose the Buddha figures on the outside of the Sumtsek reappear inside the temple placed over the heads of the main images.[13] That the temple here is a treasure trove like the others at Alchi is confirmed by the following description of what is to be found on its upper floor:

> Thus going upstairs we see a magnificent mural of Vairocana on the wall above the alcove enshrining

Maitreya's head. Above Avalokiteśvara is shown the triumphant 11-headed 1000-armed form of the same divinity, and above Mañjuśrī is Prajñāpāramitā, the Lady Perfection of Wisdom. These two powerful divinities represent Means (which is Compassion) and Wisdom in late Mahāyāna tradition, and they are coefficients of the Omniscient Buddhahood of Vairocana. Thus all the elements are brought together in this temple in a coherent whole.[14]

There is some loosening of brush control as Akṣobhya touches the earth on the right wall of the Lhakhang Soma, while elongated and lotiform eyes of Pāla-Sena/Nepalese origin are almost caricatured in a scene that shows Buddha preaching to his followers, found on the immediate right beside Lakhang Soma's doorway. Yet the later art is perhaps the most successful in creating harmony between painted sculptures and painted walls. The central image of the historical Buddha Śākyamuni repeats the composition and color of the same subject painted on the wall behind him, and it is satisfying to see the graph or the model become three-dimensional reality. Volume shows power in the form of figures on the Golden, Blue, Red, and White Mañjuśrī that radiate out in four directions from the center of Mañjuśrī Lhakhang. While the structures themselves are among the simplest that Himalayan art produces, every temple should be seen in its entirety. Thus Alchi is unforgettable.

The preceding analysis of art in Ladakh treats only a selection of palace and sacred structures, offering no important variations in religious art from that in other Tibet-influenced areas. But there is a raw grandeur of towering temples, shrines, and palaces (notably Basgo and Leh) that is especially impressive in the windswept plains of the Indus River Valley. This is art at the edge—the edge of survival. Yet this is some of the most international art that this study has encompassed. Ladakh is a devout land, its populace charming and open as it follows timehonored paths toward nirvana. Is this how Christian Europe was during the Middle Ages? Yet the twentieth century is now closing in hard upon Ladakh. The question of survival keeps coming up—survival of monuments and survival of society. The land is poor, but the identity and cohesiveness of society are strong. If ninety-five percent of the religious art in Tibet is truly lost today because of the same political forces that made it necessary to bring Indian troops to Ladakh's borders, then the preservation of Ladakh's heritage is more important than ever.

8

Heritage of Wooden Arts in Kashmir

THE NAME KASHMIR MAY CARRY WITH IT MORE romantic associations than any other Himalayan area as this broad examination of Himalayan arts moves forward. Yet Kashmir, with its capital at Srinigar, is a political powderkeg in many ways, in striking contrast to the cool quiet of its Dal Lake, Wuler Lake, Gulmarg, Sonemarg as the "field of flowers" on the way to Ladakh, and other beauty spots that draw Indians and foreigners alike to its hills and valleys. Jammu and Kashmir are a combined federal state of India that includes Ladakh as its largest but least populated area. The total land area is 400,228 square miles. Olschak, Gansser, and Buhrer are once again helpful as they show that beginning in the seventh century A.D., Kashmir gradually came under the influence of the Tibetan kingdom of Tubo and that, like almost all the lands of the Himalayan chain, it was called part of the Tibetan empire in the eighth century. The latter suggestion ignores the great strength and influence of the land's greatest king, Lalitāditya, however. Kashmir came to hold several principalities of her own within 150 years, and the next major political event caused by outsiders to affect the region of Kashmir was control by Islamic rulers.

By the fourteenth century Srinigar became the summer residence of Muslim kings, and it was an important destination of the Mughals throughout their sixteenth to nineteenth century reign from their capital in Delhi. Mughal rule ended when invading Sikhs from the Punjab, at the height of their strength, conquered Kashmir and united it with Hindu Jammu to the south. After partition of India with independence from the British crown in 1947 and the violent events that followed it, Pakistan incorporated its part of Jammu (Punch) into its state of Azad or "Free" Kashmir (35,522 square miles) with its capital at Muzaffarabad. The question of the allegience of the rest of Kashmir to India remains open and has been the cause of two wars and bitter fighting that continues to the present day. Among disturbing reactions to the redrawn political map of 1947–48 is that Ladakhis have demanded direct incorporation of their state under the Indian central government.[1] There has been serious strain and violence between resident Buddhists and incoming Muslims in the small city of Leh as the capital of Ladakh. In terms of art history there has been serious research in both Kashmir and Ladakh, but many questions remain unanswered. Garhwal and Kumaon to the south of Himachal Pradesh, and Himachal itself, are the only rivals of Kashmir in terms of having early and important stone temples of Hindu dedication. Wooden architecture is essentially medieval and very impressive.

Keddarnāth temple at the source of the Mendakhani River is one of four major pilgrimage shrines in this mountain region of Kashmir, along with Badrinath, Gangotri, and Yamunotri. The rivers here are associated with the miraculous descent of the Ganges from heaven—Mother Gaṅgā—as it flowed down through Śiva's hair to bless all of the world. Kashmir is the goal of Hindu pilgrims who make the annual pilgrimage to Gomukh (Cow's Mouth) cave where a formation of ice is said to miraculously be the *liṅga* of Lord Śiva. The temples themselves are tall *śikhara* towers made of stone with roofed balconies at the top that are made of wood. They are an odd combination of forms, somewhat like the woodtopped temples of Chamba in Himachal Pradesh. In fact, one could say that their closest "cousins" in the Himalaya are the *śikharas* found in Chamba, stone towers that also wear "hats" in the form of wooden umbrellas. The Baijnāth temple of Śiva in Kangra, on the other hand, is a neighbor to Garhwal, which is made entirely of stone, although the square and layered roof of its *maṇḍapa* porch may be based on wooden traditions. Another comparison is the temple of Brijeśvarī Devī in Kangra which, although very famous, has nothing to do with mountain patterns. Besides the multiple verticals of its main tower, painted very white, it has a Mughal-inspired dome and a curved roof over the entrance that owes its smooth contour to faraway Bengal traditions. Kashmir monuments have their own identity.

The valley of Kashmir lies between the Karakoram mountains and the Pir Panjal mountains of the Himalayan chain. Like Kathmandu Valley, Kashmir is proven by geological evidence to have once been a great lake and it, too, is the subject of stories of miraculous origin. In the third century B.C., Emperor Aśoka of the Mauryan Dynasty (322–185 B.C.) encouraged the spread of Buddhism there. The most prominent markers upon the land are the Hari Parbat fort that was built during Pathan times, preceding Mughal occupation, later to be used by Emperor Akbar as it crowns a northern ridge that is visible from Dal Lake, and the intriguing temple of Śaṅkarāchārya high on its rugged hill (now marked by a communications tower) 1,000 feet above the lakeshore. The former complex is a classic defensive structure with Mughal additions while the latter was once a Buddhist temple in Greco-Roman design that must have had quantities of the kind of international details in sculpture and architecture that Pakistan also preserves. Legend has it that the temple was founded by Jaluka, son of Aśoka, around 200 B.C., as a Buddhist sanctuary. It was reconstructed during the reign of King Lalitāditya in the eighth century to become a Hindu temple. Resting on top of a hill that was named Gapadri in Hindu times, the building is dedicated to Śiva today, and it has also taken on the meaning of memorializing the saint and Hindu teacher Śaṅkarāchārya, thus its name. It contains a *liṅga* of Śiva in its center, while the interior once had eighty-four round-headed niches in triangular steps. Its entrance gate is not trefoil, like those of other early stone temples that retain memories of classical European contact, and there is nothing truly Himalayan about its design. One is reminded of broad artistic associations—even Celtic, Hellenistic, and Byzantine.[2] Its visual prominence alone warrants its inclusion in this study.

A relief from Kashmir's temple of Sūrya at Martand shows how early international details *do* persist, even into a Hindu context and after a separation of more than 1,000 years. When looking at its earliest remains, it is useful to quote Robert E. Fisher as he notes that

> Prior to the process of Islamicization that began in the fourteenth century in Kashmir, Hinduism and Buddhism flourished there for almost two thousand years. Today, the remnants of a few Hindu temples survive and Buddhist monuments are so fragmentary that their original forms must be completely reconstructed from other evidence. Even during Kalhana's time in the twelfth century, Buddhist monuments were few compared to the Hindu temples that were still in worship.[3]

Despite the problems brought with purposeful damage by Muslim iconoclasts, tourists, and others, there are still many *stūpas* to be seen in Kashmir, especially small votive examples that must preserve in their form something of what larger versions were like. They are made primarily of metal, stone, and terra cotta. An especially fine metal example in the Peshawar Museum shows a circular base, then a square plinth with four steep stairways to the cardinal directions, then the hemispherical *aṇḍa* as a body of the *stūpa* with eight columns around its central mast so that, with curvilinear pediments above, they support a five-tiered *yaṣṭi* as honorific parasol. This *stūpa* is yet another kind of "pagoda" and its ties to Himalayan temple architecture are many. The question remains—along with the mystery of the exact appearance of the giant pagoda that was reportedly constructed by the Kushan Dynasty Emperor Kaniṣka in the second century A.D.—whether such an elaborate votive miniature had a counterpart in full-scale architecture. A similar design, on a terra cotta plaque from Harwan that is now in the Śrī Pratap Singh Museum in Srinigar, is stamped with a date belonging to the fourth century A.D. Fisher, who refers to these points, continues on to state that apart from Harwan, the only Buddhist remains of archaeological value in Kashmir are found at Ushkur and Parihasapura, both of which are sites associated with Lalitāditya in the eighth century. Only foundations are visible in these places, but enough remains to show that there was a new type of composite structure where the separate halls *(chaityas)* that were used for worship are found joined to monasteries *(vihāras)* as single compound structures. Such early buildings could be related to monastic compounds in later Nepal, to the assembly of halls at a place like Bhima Kālī temple in Himachal Pradesh, perhaps even to the development of *satra* compounds in Assam, and to other complex Himalayan monuments. None of these developed in isolation.

Kashmir provides one of the earliest beginnings of Himalayan cultural history. Records show that Ushkur was founded during the Kushan Dynasty (50–320 A.D.) and that this was the place where the Chinese pilgrim Hsüan-Tsang spent his first night in Kashmir in the seventh century. A great *vihāra* is reported to have been built there by Lalitāditya, along with a large *stūpa*. It is possible, according to Fisher, that Lalitāditva had the *stūpa* at Ushkur moved inside of the *vihāra* compound, thereby creating a composite structure.[4] It would echo the design of early Buddhist temple/monastery art in Gandhara, and enough survives in Ushkur to prove that the resultant monument was cruciform in plan, with stairs on all four sides, and that each side was nearly thirty-three meters wide. Such a plan is known at only one site in Gandhara, at Bhamala near Taxila. The elaborate type as found in the Himalaya proper may be related to other areas in the almost pan-Asian occurrence of *stūpa* art and—at least in terms of its four stairways, directional orientation, and presumably great height—it may prefigure the towers of wood and stone that this study has treated, especially those in Nepal and Himachal Pradesh.[5]

While early works of scholars like James Fergusson will not be directly quoted here, they relate to the recognition of early monuments that reveal the growing influence of Kashmir in mountain arts. Hindu stone temples are better preserved than Buddhist monuments here, as noted, but they are mostly still in ruinous condition. Unlike the Buddhist remains, Hindu temples in Kashmir belong very clearly to the category of pagoda arts of the Himalaya. This has long been recognized, but Percy Brown is especially precise as he states,

> The temples which appear to have an affinity to those of Kashmir, are produced in Kathiawar by an immigrant tribe known as the Mers, during the last half of the first millenium, and therefore contemporary with the Kashmir examples. Both the Mer and Kashmir temples are square in plan, with a central sanctuary, but the principal parallelism is in the formation of the roofs. In each type these are pyramidal in shape, and rise up into two tiers, the upper overhanging the lower, rather in the manner of the stories of a Chinese pagoda. Added to this in the Mer design, although the temples are Brahmanical, there are Buddhist chaitya arches in the form of dormer-windows projecting from the sloping portion, but these, in Kashmir structure, are in the shape of pediments and trefoil arches . . . In view of their wide geographical separation, any direct contact between the two countries is improbable; what is more likely is that some mutual pattern of thought-mould evolved, which accounts for this approximation of forms, rather than any interchange of technical experience.[6]

The Wangnath temple complex devoted to Śiva is walled with stone, one temple with front and rear chambers, one with a single entry, one with two doors, and at least one with four doors around its square body—all showing a kind of experimentation with Hindu design in the medieval period. Buniar Temple is more complete, the best preserved in Kashmir in fact. One notes its pyramidal roof, which would have been steeply pitched to harmonize with its substructure and the relief niches of elongated triangular pediments that are carved upon the walls. These elements relate to later developments in Himalayan pagoda architecture. The temple is made of granite rather than the usual limestone, and its rectangular court that

Trilobe arches at the temple of Martand, Kashmir (copyright Archaeological Survey of India).

Detail of Martand sun temple, Kashmir (copyright Archaeological Survey of India).

measures 44 meters by 36½ meters is surrounded by a colonnade of 53 cells. The entablature above the columns is a series of miniature trefoils while the small size of the cells and their elevated placement suggest that they once held images rather than monks. This would prove a link to Gandhara, especially Buddhist quadrangles around *stūpas,* as at Takht-i-Bahi.

The better-known temple complex of Martand, although more ruined than Buniar, supports the same conclusions, and its walls are rich with reliefs that present Hindu gods, including Sūrya, to whom the temple is dedicated, in frames of elongated pagoda-roof type. The best Kashmiri comparisons to freestanding pagodas as discussed in Nepal and Himachal Pradesh and, to some degree, Lahaul, are found in double-roof pagoda towers that are made of stone and raised on a high base at Payar while remaining partly submerged in water at Pandrenthan. The second of these buildings is puzzling in terms of its date, although Fisher suggests that a foundation as early as Lalitāditya's time is possible, even though local legends usually term it late. It is a concisely presented version of the towering Buniar Temple, being a tall building with perfectly square plan and alcoves directed to the cardinal points. Its lantern ceiling is the most elaborate and best preserved in Kashmir, suggesting comparison to the lantern ceilings of Lakṣanā Devī temple in Brahmor as well as to the temple of Chamuṇḍa Devī in Chamba town. There are flying *gandharvas* in its eight corners, the circle at its center is lotiform, and the outer two squares that come down to meet the walls are occupied by bracket figures that lean forward to offer support, as in Nepal and many other places on the plains and in the hills.

The stone temple of Pandrenthan near Srinigar in Kashmir. First half of the twelfth century. Copyright the American Academy of Benares, used with permission.

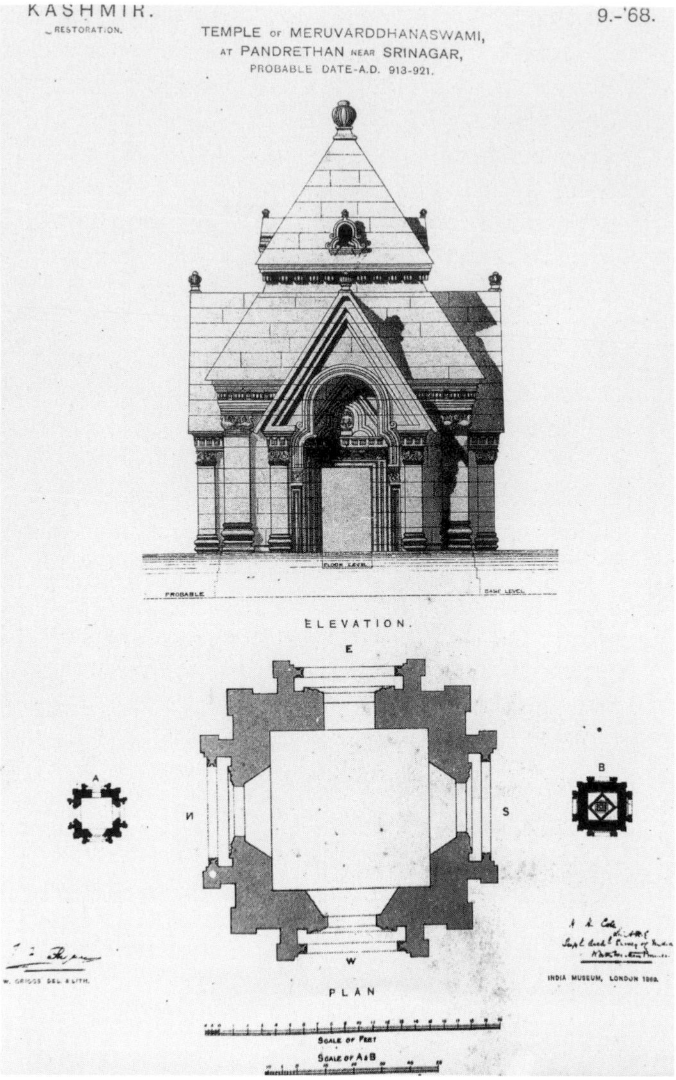

Pandrenthan temple in Srinigar, Kashmir (copyright Archaeological Survey of India).

The outside of the Pandrenthan structure has four steeply pointed pediments, each enclosing a trefoil arch as in Gandhara, and it is double-roofed. The upper and lower roofs are each "supported" by projecting beams like those found in cornice levels of Nepalese architecture, and there are small dormers on each side of the upper roof that suggest Hindu temples of Kerala and perhaps call for repetition of the fact that South Indian Brahmins are traditionally in charge of some Hindu centers in Nepal and the northwest. The roof is layered, almost as if in imitation of slate shingles. But the repeated use of architectural niches is the single most prominent feature. The uppermost stone of the pyramidal roof is, unfortunately, lost.

At Payar the crowning stone remains intact and the temple here, small and very well preserved, is impressive. It is six meters high, and Fisher points

Detail of lantern ceiling, Pandrenthan temple, Kashmir (copyright Archaeological Survey of India).

out that it was built of only ten stones. There are no records of its existence before Europeans came and wrote about it. It is an elevated shrine with openings on all four sides, like Gandharan prototypes or certain pagodas in Nepal, and there are flying figures at each corner of its ceiling that is, quite unexpectedly, a dome. Less than two and one-half meters in diameter, the dome was carved, not built, from a single piece of stone. Is this element, like the classical figures of Mediterranean type that appear to support it, more a memory of Greco-Roman beginnings than Himalayan modes? Pediments above each door hold images inside trefoil arches that are themselves held within a triangular surround. These images represent Lakulīśa on the east, Dancing Śiva on the west, a three-headed Śiva on the north, and Śiva as Bhairava with Devī on the south. The story, at least, is very Asian, and the towers are key examples of pagoda design that precede almost all other Himalayan monuments.

With Avantisvāmin Temple that was built by King Avantivārman, and other medieval remains in stone at Narannag and Pattan, medieval art of Kashmir provides an essential base from which local Islamic art and architecture grow. Even Islamic art is transformed by being transplanted to the Himalayan and Karakoram ranges. It is affected by contact with both Buddhist and Hindu precedents. Looking back upon the development of medieval architecture in Kashmir, one returns again and again to the intriguing character of King Lalitāditya, called "the first really indigenous ruler of note." In his classic nineteenth-century study, *Kashmir,* Sir Francis Younghusband wrote,

> Whether Lalitaditva was a pure Kashmiri it is impossible to discover . . . but his family had at any rate been settled in Kashmir for a couple of generations, and Kashmir was not at this time the mere appendage of a greater kingdom, but was a distinct and isolated kingdom in itself . . . it was from Kashmir that con-

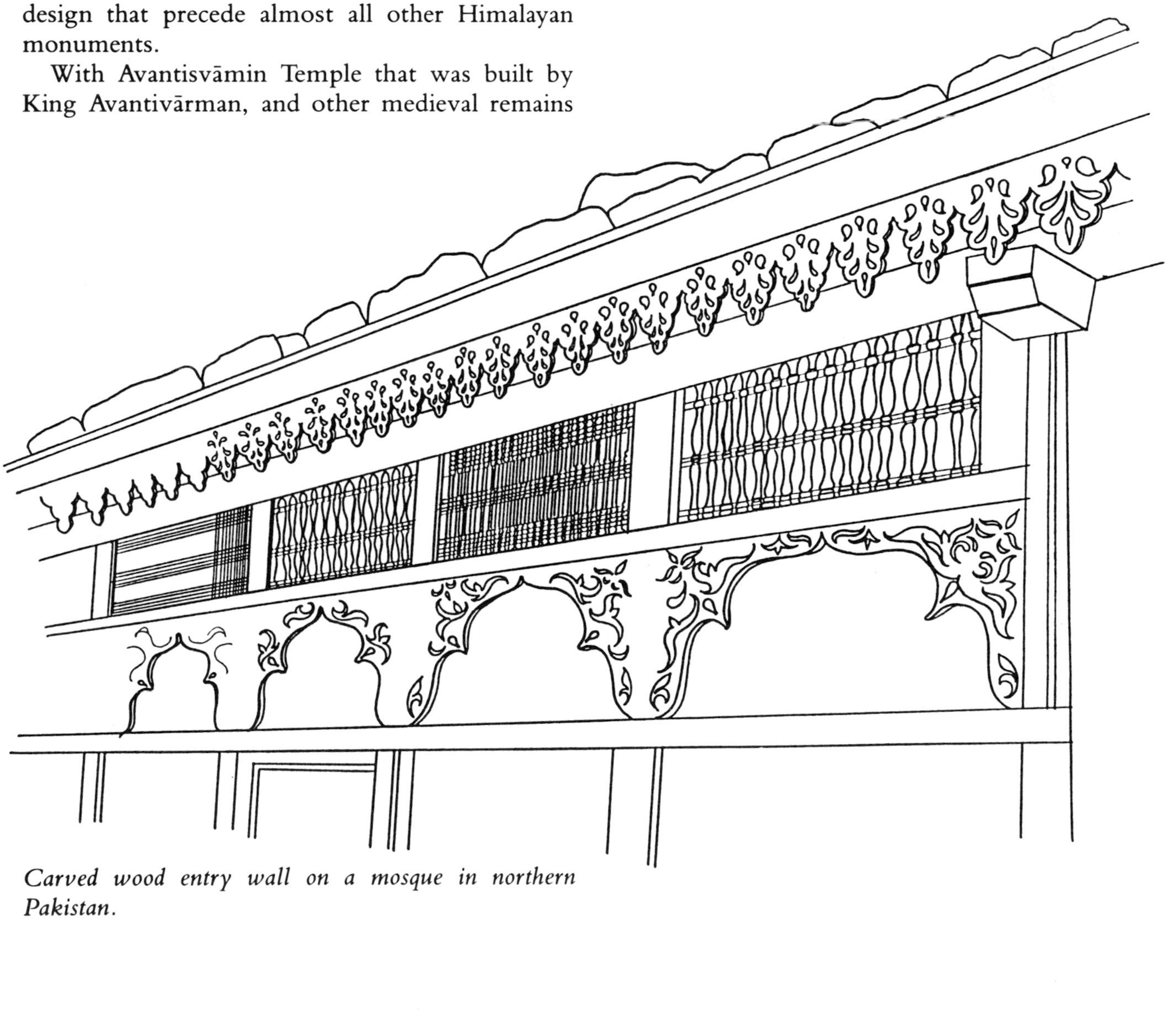

Carved wood entry wall on a mosque in northern Pakistan.

> querors were to go forth to extend their sway over neighboring districts in the Punjab . . . Lalitaditva's reign extended from about 699 to 736. He was therefore a contemporary of Charlemagne, and preceded our own King Alfred by more than a century. Mohamed was already dead a hundred years, but his religion had not yet spread to India.[7]

When Islam did arrive, its architectural requirements, while very different in function from those of sanctum-oriented temples and the monasteries and nunneries that had preceded them, were translated into the "language" of Himalayan art. Fountains and gardens and pleasure pavilions may sometimes appear to be virtual imports, but major constructions show the hand of mountain artisans. Four Islamic structures stand out for their integration with mountain styles and mountain techniques: Shah Hamadan Mosque in Srinigar, Jama Masjid or the Friday Mosque in Srinigar, the mosque in Char-i-Sharif (destroyed by fighting in 1995), and the mosque and saint's tomb in the village of Aishimuqam. Each of these uses wood in a trabeate way with stone or brick fill, making the monuments cousins to their Himalayan forebears. Selected elements at each of these late medieval structures that continue to be modified in "modern traditional" ways are noteworthy in themselves, and they help to build a Himalayan whole that embraces Islam within the broad architectural tradition that is simple in structural method, open in columned space, delicate in surface relief, and splendid in nonrepresentational art.

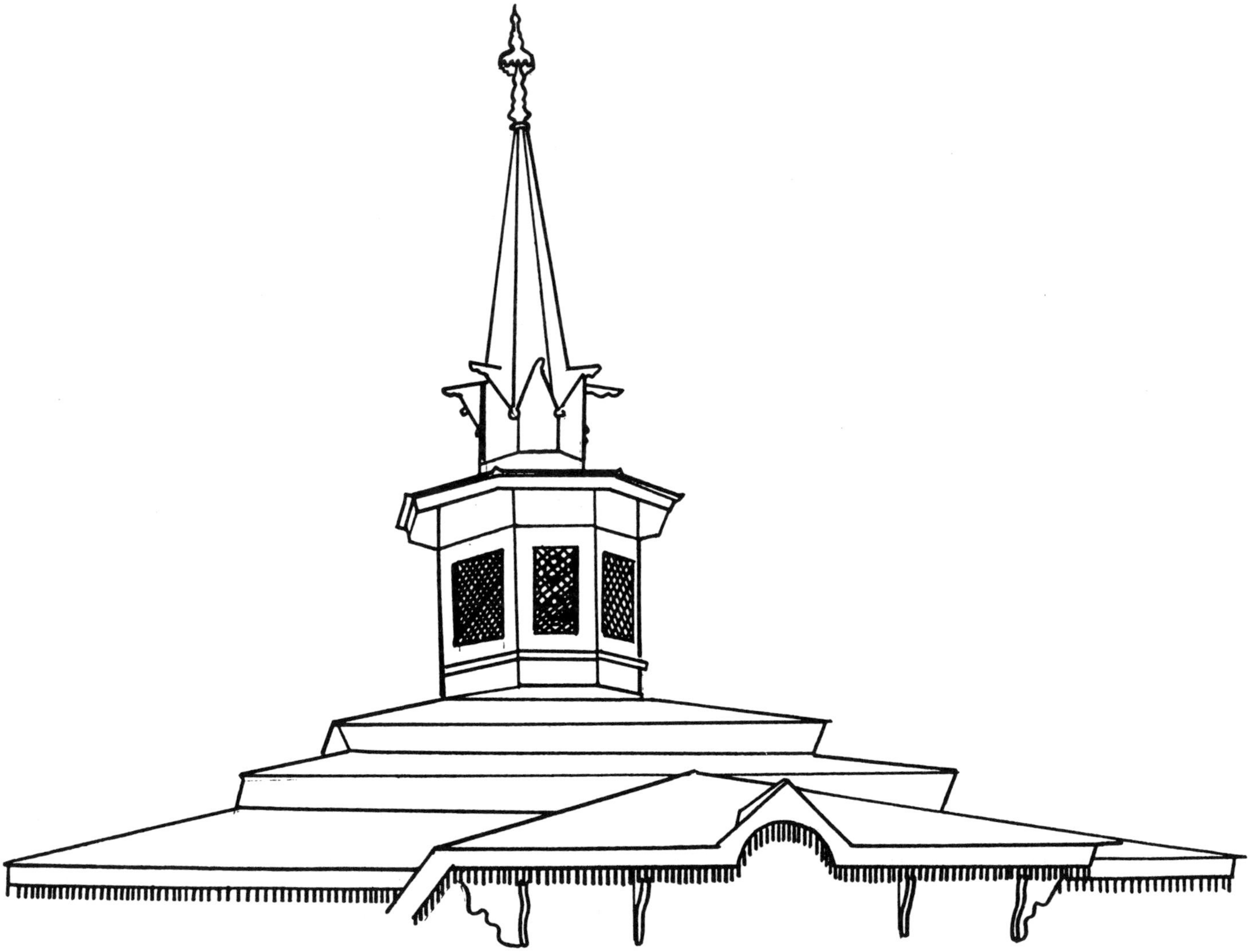

Qubbah *tower of Char-i-Sharif Islamic shrine in Kashmir. Now reportedly destroyed.*

Of them all, the mosque of Shah Hamadan is perhaps most outstanding. Painted Islamic green in its riverside setting in Srinigar, this enclosure of Islamic preaching and prayer glitters with additive bits of glass and floral painting. Geometric tracery of wood moves across its ceilings, and there are graceful curved arches in largely nonfunctional balconies that bring softness to the boldly angular form of the building as a whole. The *qubbah* or spearlike steeple above the mosque's bulk is a most dramatic climax for the wooden design, and it calls for precise comparison to similar forms at Gilgit and elsewhere in Pakistan. The history of *masjid* (mosque) design is like that of synagogue architecture in that the local building traditions of a given place are likely to be absorbed into the design of important and sacred structures, but there are few regional styles to equal the drama of Islamic art in Kashmir. At Char-i-Sharif, floral and geometric patterns sweep across exterior walls of wood with a delicacy that surpasses Himachal Pradesh. At the small village of Aishimuqam, three-dimensional woodcarving on window and *qubbah* equals the delicacy of wooden arts in Nepal. The great interior spaces of the Jama Masjid or Friday Mosque in Srinigar are filled with a forest of deodar pillars that are as high as the trees that surround the temple of Hiḍimba Devī in Manali. Islamic architecture in Kashmir makes itself at home.

9

Wooden Arts of Northern Pakistan

NORTHERN PAKISTAN BELONGS TO THE KARAkoram rather than Himalayan land mass, but it is clear that it is continuous with the areas already discussed in its development of elaborate and sturdy wooden architecture that, once again, is resistant to destruction in the unstable seismic zone of the mountains. As the following pages reveal, there is a sharing of mountain materials, mountain methods, and mountain ideals. With modernization the patterns of the hills are changing, however, and in some ways it is already rather late to survey the wooden accomplishments in Pakistan art. Fortunately the Folk Arts Museum, Lok Birsa, in Islamabad has gathered a valuable collection of arts in wood, and this may be added to the collections at the National Museum in Karachi and the fine museums in Lahore and Peshawar. One is aware of Islamic identity at every turn in Pakistan, and Hindu remains are hard to find although the earliest Buddhist sites are well protected. Still, tribal law remains in effect in some regions, and languages—such as Burushaki spoken in Hunza—define the many populations that coexist in this land that has accepted many migrations and cultural interchange.

The partition of India that has been mentioned in 1947–48 led to the movement of four million Indians from the new country, and today only about one and one-half million Hindus remain in Pakistan. Their temples are often destroyed or defaced, like a tower in Multan that still holds an abstracted *liṅga* of Śiva while the faces of Hindu gods shown in relief tiles have all been chopped away. Still, there is a program supported by non-Hindus, including architects, to preserve the ruins of the country's medieval monuments of Hindu orientation. It should be remembered that the great saint of the Sikh religion, Guru Nanak (1469–1538) was born near Lahore and that the Sikh brother-

A Kalash chest in the Peshawar Museum, Pakistan.

hood with its rejection of caste reached its height of development under Ranjit Singh in the nineteenth century. Shrines of great veneration remain open to Sikh pilgrims and protected by the central government, as in Lahore, although nearly all Sikhs left Pakistan for India at the time of partition. The Sikh monuments are not noted for art in wood and they are not part of this survey. It is only what was once West Pakistan that concerns this study, with East Pakistan having new identity as Bangladesh. On the other hand, Hindu and Buddhist arts do relate to the growth of Islamic architecture in the country. Among recent resources on Pakistan's architecture are *Islamic Architecture—The Wooden Style of Northern Pakistan* by Ahmad Hasan Dani (Islamabad, 1989) and Johannes Kalter, *The Arts and Crafts of the Swat Valley—Living Traditions of the Hindu Kush* (London, 1990).

The Northwest Frontier Agency is most fruitful for the investigator of traditional mountain architecture. Baltistan, with its main city of Skardu, and the district of Gilgit with its main town of Baltit are under direct control by the central government, while the part of Kashmir that belongs to Pakistan has already been referred to as Azad or "Free" Kashmir. There is a great mix of languages as indication of formerly separate existence of the mountain groups, as the Hunza and Nagar people speak their own languages, the Pathans speak an Afghanistan dialect, while the Ladakhis and people of Baltistan speak Tibetan dialects (the Balti are the only Tibetan group that is Muslim). The land feels the forces of the collision of the Eurasian and Indian geological plates of about sixty million years ago, and the areas of northernmost Kashmir, Azad Kashmir, and the Gilgit Agency join to form the largest connecting glacial area outside of the polar regions. The Karakoram range holds K-2 as the world's second highest mountain while Mt. Everest stands at 29,198 feet, Dhaulagiri at 26,400 feet, and Annapurna at 23,100 feet, all in Nepal.

When Kashmir did not become part of Pakistan in spite of having a seventy-seven percent Muslim population, an Islamic revolt rose in the Punjab even as Pathan forces invaded northwest Pakistan. Amid the chaos the Hindu *mahārāja* asked India for help and signed a treaty to unite Kashmir with India on 26 October 1947. The Pathan troops were forced back by Indian forces but Pakistani troops then attacked. United Nations troops brought that intervention to an end in 1948. The monarchy was abolished in Kashmir in 1952, and two-thirds of the land was formally annexed by the Indian union in 1957. A referendum to determine the final status of Kashmir was never held. War broke out in 1965 and again in 1977, with Azad Kashmir incorporated as the fifth province of the Pakistan Federal Union in 1974. In the midst of such political activities, time-honored patterns of living and building and carving continued.

Traditional materials and ways of building houses and other structures still survive, with only the substitution of metal roofing changing time-honored patterns here as in many Himalayan areas. The old towns of Karachi and especially both Lahore and Peshawar are filled with multistory houses and shops with living space above that have carved exteriors, especially balconies. Such structures are part of pan-South Asian taste for architectural decoration in wood, but they are also part of a fashion that died with the early twentieth century and introduction of more substantial building methods. Victorian tastes were a definite part of its appeal, and today wooden "gingerbread" may still be seen in hill stations like Muree in Pakistan or Simla, Darjeeling, and Naini Tal in the Himalayan foothills.

With its northwestern border marked by transition to Afghanistan at the head of the Khyber Pass, Pakistan has long been the high country that was closest to the Silk Road and contacts with the west. Alexander the Great knew that, and with his followers he made a profound mark upon this land and, through it, the rest of Asia. At Hund above the Attock Gorge, he crossed the Indus River on a bridge of boats with his army of 50,000 and their animals. The valley of Swat opened before them. Butkara Stūpa, possibly erected by Emperor Aśoka in the third century B.C. to hold ashes of Buddha, is a sign of the long history of Buddhism here, having been enlarged five times.

Buddhism spread widely in the hills of what is now Pakistan as part of the northwestern India campaign that was furthered by Emperor Kaniṣka of the second century A.D., and the Kushan Dynasty in general (50–320 A.D.). His model was Emperor Aśoka of the third century B.C. and his followers included the enlightened monarchs of the Gupta Dynasty (320–650 A.D.). Buddhism spread by land with the caravans that moved across

Petroglyph on the Karakoram Highway showing a stupa *with possible bracket supports for the superstructure in northern Pakistan.*

Central Asia and on to China, Korea, and Japan. It spread by sea from India's eastern coast to all of the countries of island and mainland Southeast Asia. Rock engravings near Chilas that show *stūpas* along with Buddha and Bodhisattva are attributed to the sixth and seventh centuries A.D. while rock carvings of oryx and other animals in the hills are prehistoric and related to other petroglyphic finds, including those in Kashmir. Architecture of almost half the world shares techniques and artistic forms that are rooted in the classical world of Alexander (356–323 B.C.) and in the Asian world of Buddha (563–483 B.C.).

The headwaters of the Indus River concern this study as the home of Ladakhis and their remarkable accomplishments in late Buddhist arts just as the headwaters of the Ganges are the spiritual home of all Hindus. But it must be remembered that the lower waters and the delta of the Indus, like the Nile and the Tigris-Euphrates, gave rise to one of the world's first true civilizations—the Indus Valley civilization of ca. 3000–1500 B.C. We note that the height of indigenous Dravidian accomplishments in northern India came to an end around 1500 B.C. as a new people moved in: the Aryans. So the languages of north India today are Indo-European. It is proposed here that the architecture is as well, and Pakistan's Karakoram Highway to China is just one more definition of the Silk Road.

Remains of the Indus Valley culture are frequent along the river and even far beyond it, while the hills of the Gandhara area yield surprisingly well-preserved remnants of a Buddhist age in Greco-Roman colonies and settlements of the early centuries A.D. In the generally dry climate of Pakistan some wood has even survived, showing continuity with furniture and woodcarving that remains from early times in Afghanistan, India, and Persia. Wood does not quickly decay if it is kept in a state of climatic constancy, like the deserts of Turkestan with early Buddha images carved of wood or the always swampy everglades of Florida with its almost naturalistic wood sculpture from the Glade Culture. What is most surprising, perhaps, is that terra cotta images of Buddha, made during the experimental period, which show him in physical form for the first time in the first or second century A.D. or even earlier, still stand as part of *stūpa* monuments in Pakistan. The trilobate frames or triangular surrounds of sculptures that are found today in Ladakh, Nepal, Kashmir, and Central Asia are also found in the ruins of Takht-i-Bahi, Taxila, and other Pakistani locations that were touched by Alexander and his followers.

Such art is only one link in the east-west net of exchange that has always been background to the information on these pages, but it is a very strong link indeed. There are even remains of Alexander's mud fort still visible at Sehwan in Sindh Province. The famous sculptures in schist of the Buddha fasting that may be seen in the Lahore Museum and the Peshawar Museum are grisly but important as an example of naturalism from the west joining religious story from the east in an accommodation that has not always been comfortable.

The complexity of early arts is to be expected in terms of Gandhara having been part of a province of Achaemenid Persia under Darius the Great in the sixth century B.C. and then part of Alexander's Empire in the fourth century B.C. The Mauryan Empire of India controlled what is now Pakistan during the Mauryan Dynasty of 322–185 B.C., and the northern area was subjected to invasions from Persia, Central Asia, and Afghanistan from the third century B.C. to the sixth century A.D. Bactrian Greeks as descendents of Alexander's soldiers in Bactria, now Balk in north-central Afghanistan, came in about 185 B.C. to build new cities at Taxila and Pushkalavati. They, in turn, were followed by Iranian nomads, Scythians (Śakas) and, in about 20 A.D., by the mighty Parthians who had already beaten the Roman armies in 53 B.C. By the second century A.D. the Parthians were driven out by the Kushans from Central Asia who extended their empire from China to eastern Iran and southward to the Ganges River. Their summer capital was north of Kabul in Afghanistan while their winter capital was in Peshawar in today's Pakistan. Sassanian, Gupta, White Hun (Hephthalite), and Turkish forces also made their mark on this land, and Hinduism spread and overshadowed Buddhism with Hun support. Many Buddhist monuments reportedly were destroyed by Hindus, and today even the Hindu remains are very few. One site that is an exception is Ketas in the Tahr Desert at the southern edge of Sind where a grouping of Hindu temples in stone still stands from the eighth to tenth centuries A.D.

The artistic wonders that Pakistan is best known for are Islamic, especially the glorious architecture of the Mughal Dynasty in Lahore and elsewhere

Domestic balcony of wood, Karachi, Pakistan.

during late medieval times. Islam reached Pakistan from both the north and the south, and in 711 A.D. an Arab naval force came to establish control over the Indus Valley as far north as Multan. In the eleventh century Turkish rulers of Afghanistan attacked India from the northwest, and raids by Mahmud of Ghazni (979–1030) from Afghanistan brought much of the north into the Ghaznavid Empire. Muhammad of Ghor captured Delhi in 1193, marking the beginning of the Sultanate period that lasted for three hundred years, and Turkish forces of Tamerlane sacked Delhi in 1398–99. All of these happenings affected the "sequestered" art of the hills and mountains.

The Mughal period beginning with Babur, a descendent of Tamerlane and Genghiz Khan, dates from the defeat of the last of the Delhi sultans in 1526 and lasted until the nineteenth century and rule by the British Raj. Thatta, about one hundred kilometers east of Karachi, is the place at which Alexander rested his troops before marching across the Makran Desert to Baluchistan, and today it is known for the beautiful Jami Mosque of 1647 that is sometimes called the Shah Jahan Mosque after its imperial builder who also built the Taj Mahal. In the usual pattern of Islam, the sacred arts are nonrepresentational while secular arts may be as naturalistic as any in Europe, and its architecture follows its own direction with emphasis upon true arches and domes that were never part of the Indian tradition. Tombs and mosques are most perfected, and *imambaras* as teaching centers are important support buildings. Especially in hill areas, any of these may be timberbonded and adorned with carvings.

Lahore survives as an essentially Mughal city in today's Pakistan with its spectacular tomb of Emperor Jahangir, the Shish Mahal, Badshahi Mosque, Wazir Khan's Mosque, Lahore Fort, and Shalimar Garden, while outlying areas have such outstanding monuments as the mausoleum of Ruknud-din Alam at Multan and the tomb of Bibi

Surviving colonial structures in Karachi, Pakistan.

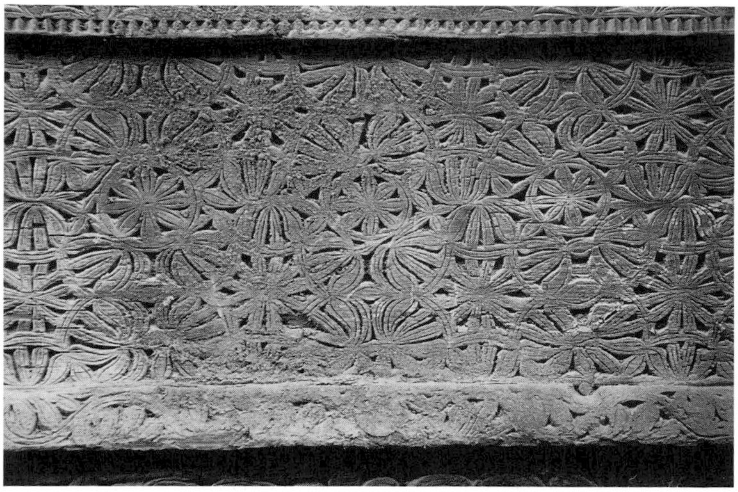

Shallow carved wall relief, northern Pakistan.

Jawindi in Uch, Punjab. Islamic architecture incorporates colored tiles and mirrors and even papier mache, but more relevant to the current study is its architectural relief. Akbar's city of Fatehpur Sikri near Agra in India, the capital of the Mughal Empire from 1570 to 1586, is by no means the only Islamic complex to show copying of wooden forms in stone, and earlier Indian efforts to do the same may be traced back at least as early as the time of Lomāś Ṛṣi Cave in the Barabar Hills that dates from the third century B.C. The Chaukhandi tombs located seventeen miles from Karachi present hundreds of fifteenth- through nineteenth-century tombs, the women's marked with flowers and jewelry while the men's have guns and horses with riders, in overall geometric patterning and piercing of balustrades to suggest wooden prototypes. An average tomb cenotaph measures seven to fourteen feet high and it may be covered with zig-zags, herringbone patterns, crosses, diamonds, triangles, *svastikas,* and squares. Rosettes are frequently carved, perhaps as signs of the flowers of heaven or perhaps as forgotten signs of pre-Islamic worship of the sun as still observed by Zoroastrians. Or could it be a memory of the Buddhist lotus? The relationship between wooden window or wall screens and the cut stone *jhali* screens of mosques, tombs, and other buildings is well known, on the other hand. Hindu incorporation

Sandstone carving of wood-chipping pattern at the Chaukhandi necropolis in Pakistan.

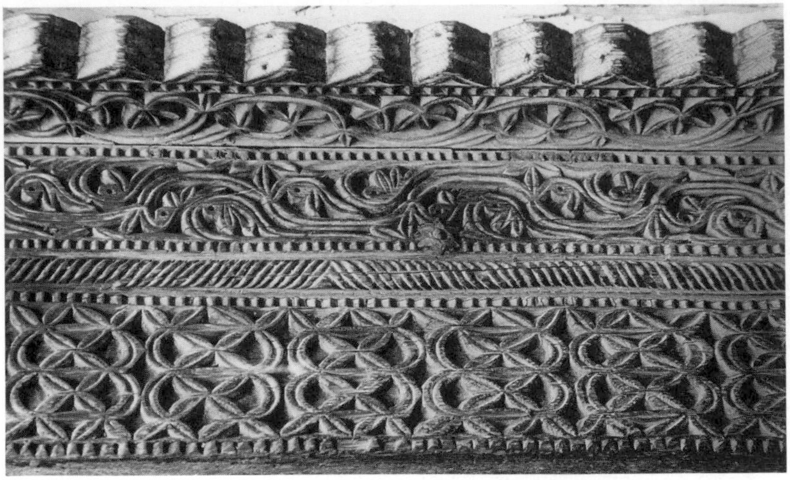

Detail of wood-chipped architecture, northern Pakistan.

of wood and stone screening in absolute combination is perhaps best illustrated by the city of Jaisalmer, just across the great Thar Desert from Pakistan.

Wooden windows and balconies in Lahore, Pakistan.

Wooden arts of Pakistan are, of course, the most important subject to this volume because preference for wood used in certain recognizable ways is one subject that has been shown to provide unity to mountain architecture. The buildings are flat-roofed and fairly simple in northern Pakistan, even royal buildings like the palace of the Mir of Hunza at Baltit, with its breathtaking view of the Rakaposhi range, or mosques like the Ismaili Mosque at Altit in Hunza Valley. A dilapidated but still occupied Rāja's palace in Khaplu, the largest kingdom in former Baltistan, recalls close contacts that were kept with the trading power at Gilgit.

The roof tops of houses are perfect places for drying fruit in the intense sun. Yet domestic structures are kin to the *bhandars, gompas,* pagodas, and *satras* that have been seen, for they follow timber-bonded structural methods and give pride of place to wood and woodcarving. In Chitral, an example from Rambur Valley will typically rest on a fairly loose foundation of piled rocks while walls show courses of wood separated by masses of roughly shaped stones. Wooden verandahs appear there as in the higher elevations. This, too, is an active seismic region. Altit houses are simpler, being mud-brick boxes with inset wooden windows and doors along with wooden frame supports, and the same is true of Skardu. Its ground-riding buildings with flexible joints and layering of timber and fill continue to reveal adaptability to earthquake. These small towns were on the caravan route that brought Hinduism, Buddhism, animism, Christianity, Islam, and many more religious systems into contact with one another. Again, the arts

Wooden balconies, Rawalpindi, Pakistan.

Streets of Rawalpindi, Pakistan.

Wooden windows with colored glass, Rawalpindi, Pakistan.

Mihrab and wooden pulpit, Lahore, Pakistan.

Lobate capital and column of mosque in northern Pakistan.

Mosque under repair, northern Pakistan.

show it. Traveling artists, so well defined by B. N. Goswamy of Punjab University in terms of their impact upon miniature painting in the Pahāri hills of northwest India, moved through all of the foothill areas, as did missionaries, conquerors, refugees, and, as always, traders.

Unlike Ladakh, Pakistan has only scattered evidence of woodcarving as living art, even though houses are still constructed in ways of the past. In making this statement the present author must confess to having had too little time in Pakistan to complete a full survey, however, Inayat-ur-Rahman of the Department of Archaeology in Peshawar writes that woodcarving is practiced extensively at various places in Pakistan, including Chiniot, Lahore, Sialkot, and Peshawar where,

> On the doors and windows of houses, the best efforts of the carvers are utilized in which the style of carvings in the panels of framed lattice is indeed marvelous . . . Walnut trees grow abundantly in Kashmir and carving on this soft and delicately toned wood is a specialty of the area. Here the doors and windows of the houses bear beautiful carvings, the Khatambandi style of ceiling is the lone monopoly of Kashmir and perhaps has not yet been imitated at any other place.

He goes on to say that,

> The columns, capitals and beams of mosques in Swat, specially at Bedara, Chamtalai, Durushkhaila, Madyan, Bahrain and Kalam, present the best examples of wooden architecture and thus admirably delight the viewers. The whole wooden structure as in the mosque of Bedera, Bahrain, and Kalam is so framed where the colonnade of massive columns and capitals are treated with pattern of scrolls and decorated with beautiful carvings. In the winter rooms of the mosques, the shafts of the columns are lavishly carved in floriated pattern. The stocky beam with supporting columns in the mosque at Kalam, and the admirably decorated beams in the mosque at Bedara, are the object of real wonder.[1]

There is much work to be done, including study of local publications like the fine *Journal of Central Asia* published in Islamabad through Quaid-i-Islam University, and seeking council with Pakistani authorities. Mosques of the northern areas are massively timbered with wooden columns and very heavy roof beams as well as very heavy doors and frames. The extended capitals at the top of the columns widen to meet the ceiling beams in the manner of Nepal but are much heavier in appearance. Carving is in the woodchipping category

Typical zapacitos-*type lobate capital and column, northern Pakistan.*

but, again, larger in scale and visual effect. These points hold true for houses and palaces as well as mosques and *imambaras,* from the dwellings in Gilgit to the large palace that the former Mir or king of Hunza occupied until 1960.

The palace is now being ruined by exposure to the elements but it still shows a kind of grandeur due to the long pillars that raise it above its stony foundation high on its hilltop setting and its open verandah with trellis-like openwork below the roof and a windowed half-circle as a sitting room. Baltit Fort of the sixteenth century in Hunza and Altit Fort near Karimabad and at the top of a 1,000-foot cliff above the Hunza River, also dating from the sixteenth century, are richer in terms of wood carving, all of which is decorative.

Baltit Fort has three levels, the lowest of which consists of a maze of storerooms and dungeons where prisoners were kept in total darkness and where the Mir of three generations ago murdered his two brothers in a struggle for succession. Above this are royal dwelling spaces and a throne to the east side, all with cantilevered wood ceilings. It will be useful to compare these features to architecture in the Kalash valleys and Chitral at a future time. The kitchen, lavatory, and bath are also on this floor, and the top level is open with a watchtower and some apartments for the ruler that

A wooden minaret in northern Pakistan.

A collapsing watchtower outside of Rawalpindi, Pakistan.

Carved and painted pavilion of today's Mir of Hunza, Pakistan.

Historical carved wooden door and window, Lahore Museum, Pakistan.

were added to the twentieth century. As reminder of much earlier centuries, a "Sacred Rock of Ganesh" beside the Karakoram Highway is covered with petroglyphs and inscriptions that are in five different scripts: Tibetan, Gupta, Sogdian, Brahmi, and Kharoshthi. A portrait of Gondophares, Kushan king in the first century A.D., is labelled with his name and date while another message gives the name of Chandrgupta II of the Gupta Dynasty in the early fifth century. There are ibex, some with human hunters, as Isobel Shaw provides the useful information that in more remote parts of Hunza people still perform ritual ibex dances at festivals while a local shaman *(bitan)* wears an ibex headdress when going into a trance to foretell the future.[2]

An unfortunate occurrence is that wooden architectural pieces are being sold off of the buildings in Pakistan for export, evidently without restriction, to many parts of the world. The finest carvings that were found by the present author were in an art gallery in Santa Fe, New Mexico, where they are evidently attractive to buyers because of their slight resemblance to Southwestern American carving under Spanish influence. A single godown (storage or warehouse space) in the Pakistani hills held more quality art in wood than the present author found in a month of travels. An exception is the three-level mosque at Shigar that was built by Kashmiri craftsmen several centuries ago, with a splendid superstructure that is angular and steep,

A richly carved doorway for sale through a northern Pakistani antique dealer.

almost exactly like the Gilgit tower that is described below.

On a brighter note than the reference to disappearing wooden arts, Gilgit is the next-to-last settlement to be considered in this brief glimpse of mountain art in Pakistan. Gilgit shows evidence of occupation for thousands of years, and from at least as early as the first century B.C. it was a post of importance on the Silk Road. In the classic work *Tribes of the Hindu Koosh,* John Biddulph recorded his impressions of Gilgit in the late nineteenth century:

> A glance at the map will show that Gilgit is situated in the centre of the most mountainous region in the Himalayas. Nowhere else in the world, probably, is there to be found so great a number of deep valleys and lofty mountains in so small a compass . . . Immediately above the bend of the river is the district of Chaprot, consisting of the fort and the village of that name and three other villages. This has always been a fruitful source of contention among the rulers of the three states of Hunza, Nagar, and Gilgit, between which it is situated, principally because of the fort, which, according to local ideas, is impregnable.

The witness goes on to another center as he notes,

> Above Hunza, the course of the river, which rises in the Hindoo Koosh, lies entirely in Hunza territory. The people of these two states, of whom so little is known, have been counted as mere robber tribes, who have brought themselves into notice by their depredations on the caravans between Yarkund and Leh. This is, however, scarcely a just estimation of them. They are of the same stock as the people of Yassin, Ponyal, and the majority of the people of Gilgit and the neighboring valleys. So far from being mere robber tribes, they are settled agricultural communities, living under rulers who boast of their long unbroken descent from princes of native blood.[3]

Gilgit was a Buddhist center from the third to eleventh centuries, as evidence by the Kargah Buddha of the seventh century that was carved to a height of ten feet in living rock six miles from the town. Four hundred meters upstream from this relief, a monastery and three *stūpas* were excavated in 1931, yielding manuscripts written in Sanskrit. During the Buddhist period, many foreign powers jostled for control, including Tibet, Kashmir, and Arabs. By the eleventh century Gilgit had grown to be the independent kingdom of Dardistan and then sometime later was converted to Islam. Today the Sunni, Shia, and Ismaili sects of Islam coexist there.

The most interesting architectural work in the Gilgit area is the old fort of Baltit, now very ruined but still a timber-bonded building that includes carved wood. Its flat roof that served as a watchtower is crowned by an unusual cupola or tower of wood that is striking in its steeple-like prominence. It stands a bit off-center in a large courtyard that is surrounded by the queens's room, winter and summer living rooms, storerooms, an extra bedroom, and a storeroom for food. Its base is roughly eight-sided and about six feet tall and supports an elongated tower or *qubbah* with four triangular gables around the main pointed roof that soars upward to support a decorative finial which has a *kalaśa*-like top and carved interlace at its base. Openwork boards form decorative borders for the four triangles and all around the angular base where its wooden windows alternate with wooden walls. From this spot the entire Hunza valley may be seen. The wooden superstructure as a whole is exactly the type that crowns the famous mosques in Indian Kashmir, and it is the clearest link of all between the architecture of Pakistan and the Himalaya.

Of special importance and in need of further research are the domestic and sacred architecture and woodcarving of the Kalash people in the area of Chitral. Sometimes called Kafir Kalash or "infidels" because of their animistic religion that pre-dates the coming of Islam and to which most people still remain faithful, the Kalash present a remarkable survival of past traditions.

Kalash villages cling to steep hillsides, and during the summer months the men take the herds of sheep and goats into the higher elevations for grazing. Women, who may make brief excusions into the pasture lands to visit their husbands, are responsible for limited agriculture at home and maintenance of the households. Besides grain the main crop is apricots, as in much of the northwestern hill region, and every house has a large grain storage structure that stands in front of the main dwelling. The houses are raised on high, timber-bonded foundations that provide shelter to animals during the winter, and the superstructures are made entirely of wood. Dwellings are quite dark inside with two or three rooms and furniture includes very low chairs and low beds.

As in so many of the hill houses, entrance is by a steep ladder to the upper-level living area. A

A Kalash woman in her house, Pakistan.

Kalash wooden furniture, National Museum, Karachi, Pakistan.

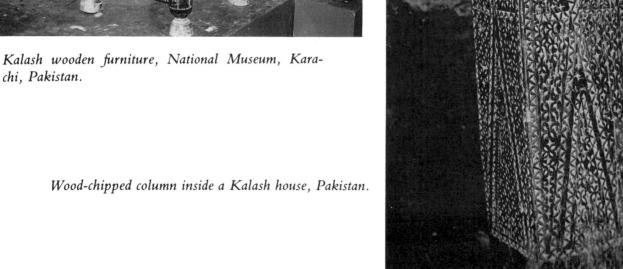

Wood-chipped column inside a Kalash house, Pakistan.

A Kalash woman, Pakistan.

Outdoor dance pavilion for men with four horseheads carved of wood by Kalash participants, Pakistan.

cooking fire is built inside of the kitchen, and the walls and ceilings are typically sooty. A hole in the floor may afford access to stored grain. There is a large veranda on the front side of every Kalash house, and this is where women work and children are attended during the daylight hours. One task that women excel in is the making of headdresses in black wool with the addition of cowrie shells, colored beads, metal buttons, and other sparkling materials. They compete with headpieces of Ladakh as the most flamboyant items of female costume in the mountains.

As in Nepal, there is a kind of invisible order to any Kalash village, and this becomes apparent at times of village dances, especially in late summer and harvest time. Dances are performed in a square that is kept open for such occasions, and there may be a special dance building as well. Women dance in circular formation. A dance structure may be marked at the front by the carved heads of animals while the interior columns are adorned by wood-chipped geometric patterns. The emphasis upon animals, especially goats as reminder of blood sacrifice, is also apparent in the carved wood additions to a courtyard-enclosing Kalash shrine.

A Kalash ancestor carving made of wood for mortuary use, Pakistan.

Female ancestor on throne, Peshawar Museum, Pakistan.

Male ancestor astride two horses, Peshawar Museum, Pakistan.

Ancestor figures of carved wood may be nearly life size, and fine examples are found in the Karachi and Lahore museums. They are considered profane by Muslims and many have been destroyed. A few rare examples still stand in graveyards as attendants to wooden coffins in which the dead are interred above ground. They are one more variety of the wooden arts of the South Asian subcontinent, and they are deserving of in-depth analysis while they still exist among a people who are not part of the mainstream of modern Pakistani culture. Change is coming, and so it is evident that investigations remain to be made now that survey work is complete for the architecture and associated arts of the mountain region, a place that is definable and whole even as it preserves remarkable variety of monuments, peoples, and ideals.

Epilogue

THE PRECEDING PAGES CONTAIN AN ATTEMPT TO define a cultural entity in terms of the architecture and allied arts that are produced by societies that relate to one another in terms of artistic tastes and traditional building methods, if not always philosophical orientations. The Himalaya has long been studied in pieces, with Nepal and Kashmir probably enjoying the most attention. This study proposes a kind of regional unity that is not often recognized.

The Himalayan/Karakoram range may be taken as an identifiable and spectacular area of world art. While cultural differences are many and local invention is always important, there was never complete isolation of peoples, one group from another. Pilgrims and teachers moved widely and trade was constant from at least as early as the second century A.D. Mountain cultures accepted the influences of Tibet to the north and the Indian plains to the south but they maintained their own preferences as well. Determining the identity of those cultures is a large but rewarding task. The study of their architectural traditions is one tool that helps do so. Physical works of art do decay, and sometimes even large architectural pieces are sold off to buyers, including foreigners, but the important task of recording their excellence remains. Perhaps this analysis of towers and windows and doors and beliefs will be a contribution.

Notes

Chapter 1. Himalaya at a Crossroads

1. Pradyumna P. Karan and William M. Jenkins, Jr.. *The Himalayan Kingdoms,* Princeton, 8.

Chapter 2. Assam and Nagaland in the Eastern Himalayan Foothills

1. Christoph von Fürer-Haimendorf, *Himalayan Barbary* (London, 1955), x.
2. Ibid., 236.
3. J. S. Lal, ed., *The Himalaya—Aspects of Change* (Delhi, 1981) 14.
4. Jawaharlal Nehru, quoted in *The Arts and Crafts of Nagaland.*
5. Ibid., 32.
6. A. L. Basham, *The Wonder That Was India* (London, 1967, 3rd revised edition) 2.
7. Lal, *The Himalaya,* 158.
8. The best comparative summary of Assamese monuments is found in Nishipada Deva Choudhury, *Historical Archaeology of Central Assam* (Delhi, 1985).
9. Details of the spread of Aryan civilization in Assam are given by R. D. Choudhury in *Archaeology of the Brahmaputra Valley of Assam (Pre-Ahom Period)* (Delhi, 1985).
10. *A Source Book of the Archaeology of Assam and Other States of North-eastern India,* 12.
11. Ibid., 16.
12. Basham, *Wonder,* 196.
13. Vincent A. Smith, *The Oxford History of India,* 3d ed. (Oxford, 1958), 196.
14. Percy Brown, *Indian Art and Architecture (Buddhist and Hindu),* Bombay, n.d., 101.

Chapter 3. Sikkim, Kalimpong, and Darjeeling: Tradition and Hill Stations

1. A. P. Agarwala, ed., *Hill Resorts of India, Nepal, and Bhutan* (New Delhi, 1982), 74.
2. Vincent Smith, *The Oxford History of India,* 3d ed. (Oxford, 1958), 238.
3. *Lama* is the Tibetan term for monk, and Tibetan Buddhism is often referred to as Lamaism.
4. Axis-orientation is a constant mark of two- and three-dimensional arts throughout the mountain region.
5. R. A. Stein, *Tibetan Civilization* (London, 1972), 283.
6. Ibid., 289.
7. John Blofeld, *The Tantric Mysticism of Tibet* (New York, 1970), 120–21.
8. The "vassal" status of Sikkim fluctuates throughout the history of the kingdom.
9. In his discussion of the cosmic symbolism of the *stūpa,* Adrian Snodgrass excels, as does his entire study of *The Symbolism of the Stupa* (Ithaca, 1985). It is useful to consider Giuseppe Tocci, Stupa—Art, Architectonics and Symbolism (1932; reprint, New Delhi, 1988); and *The Theory and Practice of the Mandala* (New York, 1973).
10. See Snodgrass for both the spatial significance of the levels and their cosmological significance, 233–45.
11. Among important tradegoods are salt and gold.
12. Syncretism of Buddhist and Hindu ideals is surprisingly frequent in the arts of Sikkim, Bhutan, and other northern areas while being the rule in Nepal.
13. Madanjeet Singh, *Himalayan Art* (New York, 1968), 243.
14. Alexandra David-Neel, *Magic and Mystery in Tibet* (Baltimore, 1971).
15. The complexity of structural parts is absolutely melded with the repeated symbols that are carved and painted upon the three-dimensional members.
16. Blofeld, *Tantric Mysticism,* 40–41.
17. Stein, *Tibetan Civilization,* 281.

Chapter 4. Palaces and Monasteries of Bhutan

1. Vincent A. Smith, *The Oxford History of India,* 3d ed. (Oxford, 1958), 75.
2. G. N. Mehra, *Bhutan—Land of the Peaceful Dragon* (New Delhi, 1974), 45.

3. Karan and Jenkins, *Himalayan Kingdoms,* 14.
4. Ibid., 17.
5. Ibid., 40.
6. R. A. Stein, *Tibetan Civilization* (London, 1972), 283.
7. Ibid., 289.
8. Ram Rahul, *Modern Bhutan* (New York, 1972), 18.
9. It is noteworthy that pieces of armor, including early types of chain mail, are sometimes kept in Himalayan monasteries as reminders of essentially medieval battles of the past.
10. Karan and Jenkins, *Himalayan Kingdoms,* 32.
11. Mehra, *Bhutan,* 39.
12. Françoise Pommaret-Imaeda and Yoshiro Imaeda, *Bhutan—A Kingdom of the Eastern Himalayas,* trans. Ian Nobel (Boston, 1989), 68.
13. The directional emphasis relates to the "all-seeing eyes" of Adi-Buddha that gaze toward the four cardinal directions on monuments that include the ancient Nepalese *stupas* at Bodhnath, Svayambhunath, and Cha Bahil as well as Chendebji *chorten* in Bhutan.
14. Nagendra Singh, *Bhutan—A Kingdom in the Himalayas* (New Delhi, 1978), 23.
15. Mehra, *Peaceful Dragon,* 78.
16. Pommaret-Imaeda and Imaeda, *Bhutan—A Kingdom,* 46.
17. Ibid., 47.
18. Rahul, *Modern Bhutan,* 119.
19. Pommaret-Imaeda and Imaeda, *Bhutan—A Kingdom,* 24.
20. Thubten Legshey Gyatsio, *Gateway to the Temple—Manual of Tibetan Monastic Customs, Art, Building and Celebrations* (Kathmandu, 1979) 30.
21. Ibid., 33.
22. Ibid., 35.

Chapter 5. Late and Early Arts of Nepal

1. Mary Shepherd, in *Nepal Mandala,* vol. 1 (Princeton: Princeton University Press, 1982), 15, provides an extraordinary blending of anthropology and the arts, as indicated by this short quotation.
2. Giuseppe Tucci, *Tibet—Land of Snows* (New York, 1967), 115.
3. Ibid., 111.
4. Ibid., 112.
5. David Snellgrove and Hugh Richardson, *A Cultural History of Tibet* (New York, 1968), 141.
6. Ibid.
7. Tucci, *Tibet—Land of Snows,* 121.
8. Ludwig F. Stiller, S.J., *The Rise of the House of Gorkha* (New Delhi, 1973), 60.
9. Ibid., 66.
10. Ibid., 75.
11. Prthvī Nārāyaṇa Śah, *Dibya Upadesh,* 95, as noted in the bibliography of Stiller, *House of Gorkha.*
12. Francis Hamilton, *An Account of the Kingdom of Nepal* 245.
13. Stiller, *House of Gorkha,* 99.
14. Shantaram Bhalchandra Deo, "Glimpses of Nepal Woodwork," Umakant P. Shah, ed.; *The Journal of the Indian Society of Oriental Art* 3 (1968–69): 14.
15. The reader is especially directed to Deo's photographs and accompanying drawings with labelled parts that define pillars, doorframes, bracket capitals, screens, and supportive struts.
16. Nelson I. Wu, *Chinese and Indian Architecture—The City of Man, the Mountain of God, and the Realm of the Immortals* New York, 1963, 21.
17. Andreas Volwahsen, *Living Architecture: Indian* (New York, 1969), 3.
18. John Blofeld, *The Tantric Mysticism of Tibet* (New York, 1970), 35.
19. Ibid.
20. George Michell, *The Hindu Temple—An Introduction to its Meaning and Forms* (New Delhi, 1977), 61–62.
21. Deo, "Glimpses," 17.
22. Ibid., 19.
23. Ulrich Weisner, *Nepalese Temple Architecture* (Leiden, 1978), 37.
24. Weisner, *Nepalese,* 4.
25. Mary Shepherd Slusser, *Nepal Mandala,* vol. 1 (Princeton, 1982), 311.
26. Ibid., 251.
27. Ibid., 252.
28. Ibid.
29. Ibid., 255.
30. Ibid., 254–55.
31. Jeffrey Lidke, "Vishvarupa Mandir—A Study of Changu Narayan, Nepal's Most Ancient Temple," p. 88.
32. Although the term *pagoda* is not Asian, but rather a European designation for multi-roof towers, it is used here rather than the general term *mandir* (temple) or the confusing terms "Newar style temple building" of "multi-stage temple tower."
33. Detailed examination of Napalese monastery organization is found in Slusser, *Nepal Mandala,* 1: 136–41.

Chapter 6. Building Arts of Himachal Pradesh

1. Major H. P. S. Ahluwalia and George Francis White, *Eternal Himalaya* (New Delhi, 1982), 29.
2. Other woods are detailed in Ronald M. Bernier, *Himalayan Towers* (New Delhi, 1989), 9.
3. Blanche C. Olschak, Augusto Gansser, and Evil M. Buhrer, *Himalayas—Growing Mountains, Living Myths, Migrating Peoples* (Lucerne, 1987), 26.
4. Ahluwalia, *Eternal,* 28.
5. M.S. Randhawa, *Travels in the Western Himalaya* 123.
6. For further detail, see J. C. French, *Himalayan Art* (London, 1931).
7. Penelope Chetwode, *Kulu—The End of the Habitable World* (New Delhi, 1980), 218.
8. James B. Fraser, *Journal of a Tour thru the Snowy Ranges of the Himalay Mountains and up to the source of the Rivers Jumna and Ganges* is an intriguing early source on this subject.
9. V. C. Ohri, *Arts of Himachal* 131.
10. Mian Goverdhan Singh, *Art and Architecture of Himachal Pradesh* (New Delhi, n.d.), plates 109 and 113.
11. Shanti Lal Nagar, *The Temples of Himachal Pradesh* (New Delhi, 1990), 31.
12. Ibid., 30–33.
13. Chandra L. Reedy, "Tibetan Art as an Expression of North Indian Buddhism," *Himalayas at a Crossroads: Portrait of a Changing World* 35–62.
14. See Thomas Metcalf, *An Imperial Vision—Indian Architecture and Britain's Raj* (
15. R. C. French, "Art in Chamba," *Art and Letters* 135–36.
16. J. Ph. Vogel, *Antiquities of Chamba State* (Calcutta, 1911), 100.

17. M. Postel, A. Neven, and K. Mankodi, *Antiquities of Himachal* (Bombay, 1985), 106.
18. Hermann Goetz, *Studies in the History and Art of Kashmir and the Indian Himalaya* (Weisbaden, 1967), 131.
19. Postel et al., *Antiquities,* 45.
20. Vogel, *Antiquities of Chamba,* 140.
21. The oddly sectioned temple, with a back roof that almost appears to be cut in half, is illustrated in Postel et al., *Antiquities of Himachal,* fig. 51.
22. Goetz, *Studies,* 139.
23. Postel, et al., *Antiquities of Himachal,* 44–45
24. A. H. Francke, *Antiquities of Indian Tibet* 2 vols. (New Delhi, 1972), 1:5.
25. Ibid., 1:8.

Chapter 7. Survival Arts of Ladakh

1. Blanche C. Olschak, *Ancient Bhutan—A Study on Early Buddhism in the Himalayas* (Zurich, 1979), 286.
2. Romi Khosla, *Buddhist Monasteries in the Western Himalaya* 93.
3. J. S. Lal, ed., *The Himalaya—Aspects of Change* (Delhi, 1981), 279.
4. Khosla, *Buddhist Monasteries,* 108–9.
5. Francke, *Antiquities of Indian Tibet,* 2 vols. (New Delhi, 1972), 76.
6. Khosla, *Buddhist Monasteries,* 123.
7. Ibid., 54.
8. Madanjeet Singh, *Himalayan Art* (New York, 1968), 67. Snellgrove and Scorupski are more cautious, however, stating that a twelfth-century date would not be impossible. They also add that the Lotsawa and Manjusri temples were probably early additions that may be dated to the twelfth century, while the Lhakhang Some ("New Temple") suggests, by its iconography, a date not later than the thirteenth century. They also see the fourteenth century as probably witnessing the end of painting in the Kashmiri Buddhist tradition. Kashmir fell to Muslim rule in 1337 A.D. (p. 79).
9. David Snellgrove and Tadevsz Scorupski, *The Cultural Heritage of Ladakh.* (New Delhi, 1977), 29.
10. Khosla, *Buddhist Monasteries,* 255.
11. Pratapaditya Pal, *A Buddhist Paradise: The Murals of Alchi, Western Himalayas* (New Delhi, 1982), 3.
12. Ibid., 20.
13. Snellgrove and Skorupski, *Cultural Heritage,* 45.
14. Ibid., 53.

Chapter 8. Heritage of Wooden Arts in Kashmir

1. Blanche C. Olschak, Augusto Gansser, Emil M. Buhler, *Himalayas—Growing Mountains, Living Myths, Migrating Peoples* (Lucerne, 1987), 286.
2. Robert F. Fisher, "Buddhist Architecture," in Pratapaditya Pal, ed., *Art and Architecture of Ancient Kashmir* (Bombay, 1989), 17.
3. Ibid., 25.
4. Ibid., 23.
5. For a much more complete analysis of *stūpa* traditions, see Adrian Snodgrass, *The Symbolism of the Stupa* (Ithaca, 1985).
6. Percy Brown, *Indian Architecture,* 2 vols. (Bombay, 1964), 1: 131.
7. Francis Younghusband, *Kashmir,* 142–43.

Chapter 9. Wooden Arts of Northern Pakistan

1. Inayat-ur-Rahman, "Wooden Mosques of Swat and Dir and List of Monuments," *Journal of Central Asia* 12, no. 1 (July 1989): 131–33.
2. Isobel Shaw, *An Illustrated Guide to Pakistan* 198.
3. John Biddulph, *Tribes of the Hindoo Koosh* 23.

Bibliography

Agarwala, A. P., ed. *Hill Resorts of India, Nepal, and Bhutan*. New Delhi, 1982.

Ahluwalia, H. P. S. *Eternal Himalaya*. New Delhi, 1982.

Anderson, Mary M. *The Festivals of Nepal*. Calcutta, 1975.

Aran, Lydia. *The Art of Nepal*. Kathmandu, 1979.

Aris, Michael. *Bhutan—The Early History of a Himalayan Kingdom*. Warminster (England), 1979.

———. *Views of Medieval Bhutan—The Diary and Drawings of Samuel Davis 1783*. London, 1982.

Aryan, K. C. *Rural Art of the Western Himalaya*. New Delhi, 1985.

Asher, Frederick M. *The Art of Eastern India 300–800*. Minneapolis, 1980.

Banerjee, N. R. *Nepalese Architecture*. Delhi, 1980.

Barrett, Douglas. "Bronzes from Northwest India and Western Pakistan." *Lalit Kala*, no. 11 (April 1962): 35–44.

Basilov, Vladimir N., ed. *Nomads of Eurasia*. Los Angeles, 1989.

Basham, A. L. *The Wonder That Was India*, London, 1967.

Bell, Charles. *The Religion of Tibet*. Oxford, 1970.

Bernbaum, Edwin, *The Way to Shambala*. Garden City, NY, 1980.

Bernier, Ronald M. *Himalayan Towers*. New Delhi, 1989.

———. "Himalayan Woodcarving: A Search for Origins." In *Himalayas at a Crossroads: Portrait of a Changing World*, Deepak Shimkhada, ed. Pasadena, CA, 1987.

———. *The Nepalese Pagoda—Origins and Style*. New Delhi, 1979.

———. "Notes on Chusya-bahal in Kathmandu." *Bulletin of the Assam State Museum*, no. 3 (1978): 69–75.

———. *Temples of Nepal—An Introductory Survey*. New Delhi, 1979.

———. "Tradition and Invention in the Himachal Pradesh Temple Arts." *Artibus Asiae* (Ascona, Switzerland) 44, no. 1 (1983): 65–91.

Berreman, Gerald D. *Hindus of the Himalaya—Ethnography and Change*. Berkeley, 1972.

Blofeld, John. *The Tantric Mysticism of Tibet*. New York, 1970.

Brown, Percy. *Indian Architecture*, 2 vols. Bombay, 1964.

Charak, Sukhdev Singh. *History and Culture of Himalayan States*, 2 vols. New Delhi, 1979.

Chetwode, Penelope. *Kulu—The End of the Habitable World*. New Delhi, 1980.

Choudhury, Nishipada Deva. *Historical Archaeology of Central Assam*. Delhi, 1985.

Choudhury, R. D. *Archaeology of the Brahmaputra Valley of Assam*. Delhi, 1985.

Das, Sarat Chandra. *Journey to Lhasa and Central Tibet*. New Delhi, 1970.

David-Neel, Alexandra. *Magic and Mystery in Tibet*. Baltimore, 1971.

Deo, Shantaram Bhalchandra. "Glimpses of Nepal Woodwork. *The Journal of the Indian Society of Oriental Art*, n.s., 3 (1968–69).

Douie, James. *The Panjab, North-west Frontier Province and Kashmir.* Delhi, 1974.

Elwin, Verrier. *Nagaland.* Shillong, 1961.

Evans-Wentz, W. Y., ed. *The Tibetan Book of the Dead.* London, 1960.

———. *The Tibetan Book of Great Liberation,* London, 1968.

———. *Tibetan Yoga and Secret Doctrines.* London, 1958.

Fisher, James F. *Sherpas—Reflections on Change in Himalayan Nepal.* Berkeley, 1990.

Fisher, Welthy Honsinger. *The Top of the World.* New York, 1926.

Francke, A. H. *Antiquities of Indian Tibet,* 2 vols. New Delhi, 1972.

French, J. C. *Himalayan Art.* London, 1931.

Fürer-Haimendorf, Christoph von. *Himalayan Barbary.* London, 1955.

Gajja, Irene N. *Ancient Indian Art and the West.* Bombay, 1971.

Goetz, Hermann. *Early Wooden Temples of Chamba.* Leiden, 1955.

———. *Studies in the History and Art of Kashmir and the Indian Himalaya.* Weisbaden, 1967.

Gole, Susan. *Indian Maps and Plans—From Earliest Times to the Advent of European Surveys.* New Delhi, 1989.

Gordon, Antoinette K. *The Iconography of Tibetan Lamaism.* New Delhi, 1978.

Gutschow, Niels, and Bernhard Kolver. *Ordered Space Concepts and Functions in a Town of Nepal* (Bhaktapur). Wiesbaden/Brd, 1975.

Gyatso, Thubten Legshay. *Gateway to the Temple—Manual of Tibetan Monastic Customs, Art, Building and Celebrations.* Kathmandu, 1979.

Hagin, Toni, G. O. Dyhrenfurth, Ch. von Fürer-Haimendorf, and Erwin Schneider. *Mount Everest—Formation, Population and Exploration of the Everest Region.* London, 1963.

Hamilton, Francis Buchanan. *An Account of the Kingdom of Nepal.* New Delhi, 1986.

Harcourt, A. F. P. *The Himalayan Districts of Kooloo, Lahoul and Spiti.* 1871; reprint, Delhi, 1972.

His Majesty's Government of Nepal. *The Physical Development Plan for the Kathmandu Valley.* Kathmandu, 1969.

Hassnain, F. M. *Hindu Kashmir.* New Delhi, 1977.

Hassrat, Bikrama Jit, ed. *History of Nepal.* Hoshiarpur, Punjab, India, 1970.

Ions, Veronica. *Indian Mythology.* London, 1967.

Jackson, David P., and Janice A. Jackson. *Tibetan Thangka Painting—Methods and Materials.* London, 1984.

Jacobs, Julian. *The Nagas—Society, Culture and Colonial Encounter.* London, 1990.

Jettmar, Karl, ed. *Cultures of the Hindu Kush.* Wiesbaden, 1974.

Joshi, Maheshwar P., Allen C. Fanger, Charles W. Brown, eds. *Himalaya: Past and Present.* Almorah, 1990.

Kamrupa Anusandhana Samiti. *Readings in the History and Culture of Assam.* Guwahati, 1984.

———. *A Source Book of the Archaeology of Assam and Other States of North-eastern India.* Guwahati, 1984.

Karan, Pradyumna P., and William Jenkins, Jr. *The Himalayan Kingdoms—Bhutan, Sikkim, and Nepal.* Princeton, 1963.

Kaul, Manohar. *Kashmir—Hindu, Buddhist, and Muslim Architecture.* New Delhi, 1971.

Khosla, Romi. *Buddhist Monasteries in the Western Himalaya.* Kathmandu, 1979.

Kirkpatrick, William. *An Account of the Kingdom of Nepaul.* 1811. Reprint, New Delhi, 1969.

Korn, Wolfgang. *The Traditional Architecture of the Kathmandu Valley.* Kathmandu, 1977.

Lal, J. S., ed. *The Himalaya—Aspects of Change.* Delhi, 1981.

Landon, Perceval. *Nepal.* 1928. Reprint, Kathmandu, 1976.

Lauf, Detlef Ingo. *Tibetan Sacred Art—The Heritage of Tantra.* Berkeley, 1976.

Maitra, Kiranshankar. *Himalayan Dreamland—Journey to Kinnarlok.* Delhi, 1989.

Majumdar, R. C., H. C. Raychaudhuri, and Datta Kalikinkar. *An Advanced History of India.* New York, 1967.

Majupuria, Trilok Chandra, and Indra Majupuria. *Glimpses of Nepal.* Kathmandu, 1979.

Maxwell, T. "Lakhamandal and Triloknath: The Transformed Functions of Hindu Architecture in Two Cross-Cultural Zones of the Western Himalaya." *Art International.* 34, no. 1.(September–October, 1981): 9–74.

Mehra, G. N. *Bhutan—Land of the Peaceful Dragon*. New Delhi, 1974.

Michell, George. *The Hindu Temple—An Introduction to its Meaning and Forms*. New Delhi, 1977.

Mittal, Jagdish. "Mural Painting in Chamba." *Journal of the Indian Society of Oriental Art* 19 (1952–53): 11–18.

Nagar, S. L. *The Temples of Himachal Pradesh*. New Delhi, 1990.

Nepali, Gopal Singh. *The Newars*. Bombay, 1965.

Olschak, Blanche C. *Ancient Bhutan—A Study on Early Buddhism in the Himalayas*. Zurich, 1979.

———, Augusto Gansser, Emil M. Buhler. *Himalayas—Growing Mountains, Living Myths, Migrating Peoples*. Lucerne, 1987.

Pal, Pratapaditya. *Art and Architecture of Ancient Kashmir*. Bombay, 1989.

———. *Art of Nepal*. Berkeley, 1985.

———. *A Buddhist Paradise—The Murals of Alchi Western Himalayas*. New Delhi, 1982.

Peissel, Michel. *Mustang—A Lost Tibetan Kingdom*. London, 1968.

———. *Zanskar—The Hidden Kingdom*. London, 1979.

Petech, Luciano. *Mediaeval History of Nepal (ca. 750–1482)*. Rome, 1984.

Pieper, Jan, ed. *Ritual Space in India: Studies in Architectural Anthropology. aarp* 17. London, 1980.

Pommaret-Imaeda, Francoise, and Yoshiro Imaeda. *Bhutan—A Kingdom of the Eastern Himalayas*. Boston, 1989.

Postel, M., A. Neven, and K. Mankodi. *Antiquities of Himachal*. Bombay, 1985.

Randhawa, M. S. *Travels in the Western Himalaya*. Delhi, 1974.

Rahul, Ram. *The Himalaya as a Frontier*. New Delhi, 1978.

———. *Modern Bhutan*. New York, 1972.

Rawson, Philip. *The Art of Tantra*. Greenwich, Conn., 1973.

Sierksma, F. *Tibet's Terrifying Deities*. Rutland, Vt., 1966.

Singh, Madanjeet. *Himalayan Art*. New York, 1968.

Singh, Mistri Goverdhan. *Art and Architecture of Himachal Pradesh*. New Delhi, n.d.

Slusser, Mary Shepherd. *Nepal Mandala*, 2 vols. Princeton, 1982.

Smith, Vincent. *The Oxford History of India*, 3d ed. Oxford, 1958.

Snellgrove, David. *Himalayan Pilgrimage*. Oxford, 1961.

———, and Hugh Richardson. *A Cultural History of Tibet*. New York, 1968.

———, and Tadeusz Skorupski. *The Cultural Heritage of Ladakh*. New Delhi, 1977.

Snodgrass, Adrian. *The Symbolism of the Stupa*. Ithaca, 1985.

Stein, R. A. *Tibetan Civilization*. London, 1972.

Stiller, Ludwig F. *The Rise of the House of Gorkha*. New Delhi, 1973.

Thapar, Romila. *A History of India*, vol. 1. Harmondsworth, Middlesex, England, 1966.

Thaye, Pema Namdol. *Concise Tibetan Art Book*. Kalimpong, 1987.

Tsering, Nawang. *Buddhism in Ladakh*. New Delhi, 1979.

Tucci, Giuseppe. *Stupa—Art, Architectonics and Symbolism*. 1932. Reprint, Delhi, 1988.

———. *The Theory and Practice of the Mandala*. New York, 1973.

———. *Tibet—Land of Snows*. New York, 1967.

———. *TransHimalaya, Archaeologia Mundi*. Delhi, 1973.

University Art Museum, The University of Texas. *Himalaya—An Exhibition of the Arts and Crafts of Tibet and Nepal*. Austin, 1964.

Vatsyayan, Kapila. *The Square and the Circle of the Indian Arts*. New Delhi, 1983.

Vogel, J. Ph. *Antiquities of Chamba State—Part I, Inscriptions of the pre-Muhammadan period*. Calcutta, 1911.

Volwahsen, Andreas. *Living Architecture: Indian*. New York, 1969.

Waddell, Austine. *Buddhism and Lamaism of Tibet*. 1895. Reprint, New Delhi, 1974.

Wiesner, Ulrich. *Nepalese Temple Architecture*. Leiden, 1978.

Wojkowitz, Rene de Nebesky. *Oracles and Demons of Tibet*. The Hague, 1956.

Wright, Daniel. *History of Nepal*. 1877. Reprint, Kathmandu, 1972.

Wu, Nelson I. *Chinese and Indian Architecture—The City of Man, the Mountain of God, and the Realm of the Immortals*, New York, 1963.

Index